Environmental Governance

CENTER
for **PUBLIC**
SERVICE

The Brookings Institution established the Center for Public Service in 1999 to improve the odds that America's most talented citizens will choose careers in the public service. Toward that goal, the center is committed to rigorous research and practical recommendations for making public service more attractive, be it in traditional government settings, nonprofit agencies, or the growing number of private firms that provide services once delivered inside government. As the center's logo suggests, the single-sectored, government-centered public service of the 1970s has been replaced by the multisectored, highly mobile public service of today. The center was created to track the rise of this new public service, while making sure that both government and the nonprofit sector can compete for their fair share of talent in an ever-tightening labor market.

As part of this effort, the Center for Public Service is committed to publishing timely reports on the state of the public service. These reports, which vary in length from short reports to books, attempt to lay the foundation for long-needed policy reforms. Because these reports are designed to move quickly into publication, some will not be verified to the same level of detail as other Brookings publications. As with all Brookings publications, the judgments, conclusions, and recommendations presented in any individual study are solely those of the author or authors and should not be attributed to the trustees, officers, or other staff members of the institution.

DONALD F. KETTL
Editor

Environmental Governance

A REPORT ON THE NEXT GENERATION OF ENVIRONMENTAL POLICY

BROOKINGS INSTITUTION PRESS
Washington, D.C.

Copyright © 2002
THE BROOKINGS INSTITUTION

1775 Massachusetts Avenue, N.W., Washington, D.C. 20036
www.brookings.edu

Library of Congress Cataloging-in-Publication data

Environmental governance : a report on the next generation of environmental policy / Donald F. Kettl, editor
   p.   cm.
Includes bibliographical references and index.
ISBN 0-8157-0255-8 (pbk. : alk. paper)
1. Environmental policy—United States.   I. Kettl, Donald F.

JGE180 .E54 2002
363.7'056'0973—dc21   2001005927

9 8 7 6 5 4 3 2 1

The paper used in this publication meets minimum requirements of the American National Standard for Information Sciences—Permanence of Paper for Printed Library Materials: ANSI Z39.48-1992.

Typeset in Sabon

Composition by Betsy Kulamer
Washington, DC

Printed by
R. R. Donnelley and Sons
Harrisonburg, Virginia

Foreword

Few areas of American public policy have proved more contentious during the past three decades than environmental politics. Business groups complained that government regulations were pushing up costs out of proportion to the benefits produced. Environmentalists charged that businesses were trying to escape responsibility for the pollution they created and that government was not pursuing environmental protection vigorously enough. Environmental policy since the early 1970s unquestionably has produced a far cleaner environment, but as the gains have mounted, so too has the political conflict. In fact, environmental policy is at a crossroads. Continued pursuit of existing regulations is producing less environmental improvement, and existing policy is sharpening political conflict.

This book builds on an effort to gauge that conflict and explore the potential for moving environmental policy onto new terrain. With the assistance of a generous grant from the Joyce Foundation and another from Pacific Gas & Electric Corporation, a research team led by Donald F. Kettl conducted four forums to explore these issues. Two were held at the University of Wisconsin-Madison and brought together grassroots perspectives. Two were held at the Brookings Institution and gathered participants with a national viewpoint.

Research teams, corporate leaders, government officials, and academics pursued answers to questions for a new generation. Is it possible to build a new, productive dialogue among the many parties in environmental policy? And could that dialogue lead to improving environmental policy?

The forums produced a frank and open interchange, demonstrating that genuine communication is indeed possible. And they culminated in important new ideas for framing a new generation of environmental policy. The chapters that follow develop those ideas.

The authors would like to acknowledge the invaluable research and logistical help of William Fanaras and Jennifer Lieb in supporting the forums and assisting with the preparation of this volume. Theresa Walker edited the manuscript, Tanjam Jacobson proofread it, and Scott Smiley prepared the index.

The views expressed in this book are those of the authors and should not be ascribed to any of the institutions acknowledged above or to the trustees, officers, or other staff members of the Brookings Institution.

MICHAEL H. ARMACOST
President

Washington, D.C.
October 2001

Contents

Environmental Governance

CHAPTER ONE

Introduction

DONALD F. KETTL

By any conceivable measure, the United States made great progress in producing a cleaner environment during the last third of the twentieth century. Air pollution dropped substantially even as the nation's population, automobile miles driven, and industrial production grew. More rivers became swimmable, and the leaching of toxic chemicals from landfills slowed dramatically.

In the wake of this clear success, new questions arise. Can the twentieth-century strategy produce continued progress in the twenty-first century? Or are there better ways of getting the job done? Will the twentieth-century strategy simply prove unworkable for current environmental and political problems? Is it time for a new generation of environmental policy?

Lessons from the First Generation

The first generation of environmental policy resulted in several things.

—The regulations unquestionably produced dramatic environmental improvements. Many dirty waters became swimmable, fishable, and drinkable again. Boston Harbor, Galveston Bay, and the Connecticut River are all far cleaner. Even Cleveland's Cuyahoga River, famous for its oily film and obnoxious smell—and for catching fire in 1969—now sports tourist cruise ships and only occasional residue. The war on air pollution has reduced smog, even in places like Los Angeles. Some waste dumps have been reclaimed, while others have been safely contained.

—Despite the wins, the first generation left major economic and political problems. Companies persistently complain about the high cost of compliance. Estimates of these costs vary widely. The Office of Management and Budget, for example, calculated that the cost of complying with environmental regulations for 1997 was $144 billion, compared with benefits of $162 billion.[1] Some estimates have been far higher, while other have argued that economic analysts frequently have overestimated the costs of compliance because market competition promotes innovation, which reduces the costs of compliance.[2] Clearly, the costs cause political conflict. Businesses complain that new rules will achieve only marginal environmental improvement at a high cost, cause jobs to be lost, and make American businesses less competitive with companies abroad.

—Environmental regulations have become so contentious that most important regulations regularly end up in court. The litigiousness of the process increases the costs and complexity of the system. It makes the EPA hypercautious in drafting regulations, companies hyperconcerned about potential impacts, and environmental groups hypersensitive about the risk to environmental quality of a process hard to predict, let alone manage. The constant battling and bickering adds enormously to everyone's costs, often without producing significant environmental gains.

—The debate about environmental policy has become more politically polarized. In 1995 Republicans used environmental regulations as a key example in their campaign to reduce the cost of federal rules. In 1995 Republican House whip Tom DeLay (Tex.) claimed that the EPA had transformed itself into "the Gestapo of government," and he led a campaign to force the EPA away from its cleanup and regulatory responsibilities.[3] Democrats capitalized on the Republican campaign by portraying themselves as protectors of clean soil, water, and air. When the dust cleared, the EPA's conservative opponents had retreated.

—The EPA has increasingly found itself squeezed between a status quo too complex to defend and environmental problems that existing policies can not solve. The EPA will undoubtedly survive the attacks against it. The real questions are the form in which it can survive, whether it can protect the environment without finding itself under constant attack from all sides, and whether new policy strategies can enhance environmental performance. As a National Academy of Public Administration study concluded in 2000, "The nation's current environmental protection system cannot deliver the healthy and sustaining world that Americans want." Moreover, "The regulatory programs in place in this country simply cannot address those problems at a price America can afford. A different kind of program can, however."[4] Can the EPA be more protective and practical? Or will it evolve with even more layers of regulatory expectations, provoking increasing criticism?

Challenges for the Next Generation

Although the EPA has fought off political challenges, it faces new problems that it cannot easily attack with its current tools. While the first generation of environmental policy focused on reducing the kinds of pollution for which sources could be readily identified, the next generation must tackle a dual problem. First, some pollution sources were left relatively untouched by the first generation. Second, the first generation of rules had great difficulty identifying and regulating more dispersed sources of pollution, often referred to as nonpoint sources. The next generation thus faces the tough challenge of devising effective and politically viable strategies for controlling pollution problems from these dispersed sources.[5]

The great advances in the first generation of environmental policy came in addressing pollution from large sources, whether directly from factory smokestacks or from the products, such as automobiles. Regulators could establish a direct link between the source and its impact. They could establish regulations that encouraged large firms to invest and develop pollution-reducing technologies. The auto manufacturers, for example, developed special canisters and new engine designs that dramatically reduced pollution from automobile exhaust. Scrubbers have removed particles from factory smokestacks, while new sewage treatment technologies have made rivers cleaner.

Reducing automobile and manufacturing pollution has often proved much easier than lessening contamination from large poultry ranches, fertilizer runoff from farms, and the growing environmental risks from homeowners dousing their lawns with pesticides. Such nonpoint source pollutants pose an important challenge to the campaign to clean the environment. Fertilizer runoff into rivers, for example, threatens the balance of life downstream (fish die if water becomes too nitrogen rich) and the long-run sustainability of agriculture (short-term overuse of fertilizers can disrupt the long-run productivity of the land). It has been difficult politically to adopt traditional command-and-control regulations (supported by fines and litigation), as they work poorly against nonpoint source pollution problems. No one wants to force individual homeowners to get wastewater permits, and farmers have long resisted efforts to regulate their runoff.

To complicate the problem, such nonpoint sources are almost universal. They extend from large commercial operations to individual families, from large turkey farms to sprayed-on insecticides for lawn care. Reducing pollution from these sources requires more than first-generation solutions, such as installing new technology like smokestack scrubbers or catalytic converters. Widespread sources of pollution create a new breed of complex collective-action problems. No strategy can be successful without developing creative new technologies *and* creating new ways of encouraging behavioral changes by almost everyone.

Complicating the problem is the growing recognition of pollution problems, such as global warming, that know no national boundaries. The collective-action problem is not limited to local communities or even national policies. Reducing nonpoint source pollution problems, especially greenhouse gases, requires policy strategies that encompass the world. The next generation thus requires a fresh, boundary-spanning approach: across technologies, geographic boundaries, environmental media, and socioeconomic groups.

In the first generation of environmental policy, the EPA focused on its media-based approach, which was organized by air, water, and soil. Companies have long complained that this approach brought a constant parade of EPA inspectors, each representing a different medium, into their facilities. That multiplied the EPA's costs and complicated industrial operations. Moreover, such a fragmented approach reduced the effectiveness of environmental regulations. After all, the regulations focused on the company's operations, not the different media. Reformers have argued for an approach that is more place than media based: one set of environmental standards to cover an entire facility; one integrated set of permits to regulate the standards; and one inspector to oversee compliance. For an agency that has long been Washington based and media centered, such a geographical focus poses enormous challenges. Air inspectors might unwittingly suggest solutions to an air problem that caused water problems. Perhaps more significant, an air inspector might walk past a major, environmentally damaging water problem and not see it, cite it, or compel its correction.

First-generation problems remain unresolved as these new next-generation issues arise. Hundreds of Superfund toxic waste dumps remain untreated. Fifty years of nuclear weapons production and military facilities dispersed across the nation have left a cold war mortgage that will take perhaps a century to pay. For example, in Hanford, Washington, toxic and radioactive sludge—in many cases the exact composition and potential risks are unknown—are seeping from buried underground tanks toward the Columbia River. Lead from bullets buried in military test ranges is leaking into underground aquifers, which feed the water supply for many communities. Dangerous gases are building in other tanks and threaten to explode. For both Superfund and radioactive waste, the cleanup will require hundreds of billions of dollars, scores of years, and new technologies. The savings-and-loan bailout of the 1980s pales in comparison.

Moreover, the next generation of environmental policy must cope with the same political cross-pressures that plagued the first generation, as analysts Pietro Nivola and Jon Shields point out. The government must ensure consistency, fairness, and flexibility to promote innovation and allow adaptation to local differences. Another concern is the conflict between the pressure to control costs by focusing resources on the biggest problems and the pressure to protect all those being harmed. A third challenge is excessive adversarialism: despite pledges to create stronger partnerships, the EPA usually addresses issues in response to past lawsuits or anticipation of future ones. In fact, Nivola and Shields argue, EPA's prescriptions "seem partly intended to hedge against subsequent legal uncertainty."[6] The point, they say, is not that the government needs to retreat from strict enforcement of environmental standards. Rather, they contend, it is the government's responsibility to ensure that public environmental policy focuses first on the problems that need to be solved first, and that the government encourages solutions that produce the most performance bang for the environmental buck. Otherwise, the public and private sectors risk spending more money than is needed to produce environmental results—or not producing as clean an environment as would be possible with the given investment.

Karl Hausker reports that a wide range of thinkers suggest that the environmental system should become a "more performance-based, information-rich, technology-spurring, flexible, accountable regulatory system." There should be "a broader array of policy tools that promote continuous environmental improvement," along with "stronger private sector management systems" that make private companies strong partners in the search for stronger performance.[7]

These next-generation problems stretch the EPA far beyond its traditional ways of doing business into complex new partnerships—with other nations, state and local governments, private companies, and citizens. They pose daunting technological—and political—challenges. Most important, they focus as much on governance as management. They require the EPA to chart new relationships with those who share responsibility for environmental quality. Increasingly, that means building partnerships with everyone involved.

Next-Generation Environmental Strategies

The central problem for twenty-first-century environmental policy is how to develop new strategies for attacking new environmental problems, how to develop better strategies for solving the old ones, and how to do both in ways that are more efficient, less taxing, and engender less political opposition. The most promising strategies move from a front-end approach—designing and enforcing regulatory systems—to a back-end focus—setting goals and allowing participants to determine how best to meet them. If the first generation of environmental strategies was concerned with compliance, the next generation promises to focus on performance. The EPA is pursuing two strategies: market-based approaches designed to use competition to increase efficiency; and federalism forces designed to build new state-federal partnerships.

One market-based approach with which the EPA is experimenting is emissions trading. Coal-fired and oil-fired power plants and industrial boilers, for example, produce sulfur dioxide, which rises into the atmosphere and later falls as acid rain. Under the EPA's guidance, states establish ceilings on allowable sulfur dioxide emissions. Some companies have found it cheaper than others to reduce emissions; they get credits, which they can sell to other companies that find the job more expensive. Traditional regulation would have mandated all operations to reduce pollution to the same level, regardless of cost. Emissions trading uses the competitive market to define who can best reduce pollution and how. Through it, the EPA was able to reduce sulfur dioxide emissions by 30 percent and reduce compliance costs for boiler operators to less than command-and-control regulations would have permitted. Satisfied with its success, the EPA is planning an expansion of emissions trading to other pollutants, including nitrogen dioxide, a chief component of smog.

For all its merits, however, emissions trading has sharp limitations. It works only for pollutants for which markets can be established. This requires the ability to measure the pollutant and clearly identify its origin, which makes the practice difficult to apply to nonpoint source pollution. Trading requires agreement on allowable levels of pollution, which makes it difficult to apply to high-risk carcinogens and nucleotides, cases in which even minimal exposure can prove dangerous. Such judgment calls also make it difficult to apply to pollutants with high political visibility (and, therefore, political risk). Emissions trading requires the ability to isolate the pollutant and its effects, which makes this approach a difficult fit for companies with complex cross-media pollution problems. Finally, it requires the ability to create and sustain a workable market, which limits the technique to large-scale operations with the capacity to cost out their alternatives (reduce pollution below the ceiling and sell the credits—or buy credits from other operations because it costs less than meeting the standards). Small companies are likely to find it difficult to play such a complex game. These problems leave emissions trading an important, useful, but in the end limited twenty-first-century strategy.

For other problems not readily reducible to pollution markets, the EPA has been quietly exploring new performance-based partnerships with the states. Although the EPA has long devolved operating responsibility for environmental regulations to the states, new experiments give states far greater responsibility for designing and maintaining environmental management systems in exchange for reports on their performance. During the past twenty-five years the states have become the EPA's front-line managers for many regulatory programs. The process has often proved just as burdensome on the states as the regulations have been for private companies. The states, not surprisingly, have become just as fed up as the private sector with the high costs of the current system and have led the charge for performance-based partnerships.

The transformation of environmental devolution from enforcement to performance has proved widely attractive. Making it work, however, requires solving two tough problems. The first is building the partnerships and holding them together. The partnerships depend on building trust by measuring performance, but this technology is now rudimentary at best. The strategy, therefore, requires constructing new measurement methodologies. The second problem is building the confidence of everyone—companies, environmental groups, neighborhood associations, state regulators, the EPA, and elected officials at all levels—in the process and its decisions. Because performance-based systems tend also to be community-based systems, success depends on getting the groups who often warred in the past to work together. That in turn requires building trust among the participants in the performance-based process and confidence in the results it produces.

Underlying all of these issues is the public interest puzzle: while the battles over environmental regulation often become enmeshed in hyper-technical *how* questions, they typically boil down to critical *who* problems. Who will shape environmental policy? Whose values will prevail? How will the decision process be structured, and whose voices will be heard? Many environmental groups frankly assert that they view perfor-mance-based regulation as a tactic to turn more decisions over to private industry and to state environmental agencies that industry has captured. Performance measurement, some people fear, is simply an effort to reduce government's commitment to a clean environment. Thus, along with the big questions of the cost of regulations for all players comes the problem of devising a structure for resolving those questions. Who speaks for citizens, and how should their voice be heard?

The policymaking process is not only about reducing the costs of environmental regulation while improving environmental quality but also about reconstituting the process of environmental debate and defin-ing which values prevail. On one level, then, environmental perfor-mance is the problem. On a broader level, the question is how reshaped intergovernmental partnerships will affect how America is governed.

Environmental Policy for the New Millennium

The challenge of environmental policy for the new millennium is to do everything that the first generation of environmental policy did—but to do it better—*and* to devise a next generation of environmental policy to solve problems that the first generation did not or could not solve. At the core of the next generation is a shift from managing inputs and out-puts for their own sake (including inspections and rulemakings) to man-aging outcomes (most notably performance), with inputs and outputs treated as tools supporting the achievement of outcomes. It seeks to improve the cost effectiveness of the current system, lower the political heat, and improve results. The puzzle is how best to produce construc-tive change—a cleaner, safer environment at a price the nation can afford—in a highly politicized system—one that struggles to cope with risk and cost, is highly litigious, and produces great conflict over almost any significant environmental policy decision.

The next generation of environmental policy revolves around fundamental and richly layered questions of governance:

—*Policy.* How much are we willing to pay, for how much environmental improvement? Who should pay? In the end, of course, consumers pay the costs. In politics and economics, however, it makes a great deal of difference on whom government's requirements fix the price tag: producers, users, a general population, or a narrow set of consumers.

—*EPA management.* Since the next generation requires new management technologies, how can the EPA effectively develop and prove these new technologies? And since many of these technologies are experimental, the EPA will have to maintain first-generation regulations while perfecting next-generation strategies. What problems will the EPA face in simultaneously pursuing such different regulatory approaches?

—*Devolution.* The next-generation strategies mean substantial devolution to private markets and state governments. How can the EPA construct the trustworthy performance systems required to make the market- and federalism-based systems work effectively?

—*Participation.* The next-generation strategies heighten the importance of reaching beyond traditional boundaries. How will these boundaries be overcome, and who will reach beyond them? As next-generation environmental policy problems evolve, everyone—governments, companies, and citizens in the United States and around the world—must come more closely into partnership. How will these partnerships be created and sustained?

The next generation of environmental policy promises to create the most advanced of all devolution projects, whose implications will be even greater than welfare reform. The political and administrative relationships applicable to environmental policy are, if anything, more complex than those of welfare reform. Yet the state of knowledge is far less developed than in welfare reform.

Environmental policymaking is a world of massive experimentation, uncertain results, complex relationships, and an inescapable mandate for improvement. Neither the EPA nor the states can stay where they are. They must learn to go where no one has gone before. Market incentives are part of the mix, but they fail to attack many of the hardest problems. Those problems are being left to the states, with the states held accountable to national policy through performance measurement. While many states have eagerly seized the flexibility that environmental partnerships offer, many of them so far have used the tool primarily to smooth the paperwork processes. Preventing pollution, improving environmental performance, and integrating approaches across media have lagged behind. The performance-based process, therefore, is more an embryonic idea than a proven practice.

The states will be wending their way through the intricate interrelationships of companies, interest groups, cross-media pollution problems, and technical uncertainties. This devolution requires solving tough political problems—most notably building a consensus that is trustworthy. It also requires increasing management capacity—especially to produce the environmental performance measures on which the system depends.

Within the environmental community, powerful forces are betting that the states will fail; they are ready to call for a retreat to first-generation command-and-control regulations. Among opponents of environmental regulation, powerful forces are ready to renew the call for rolling back the rules. Finding a route between these regressive reactions will require skillful navigation. The EPA will be in the wheelhouse to steer the effort. But the states will be manning the oars.

This book charts the politics of the next generation of environmental policy: how citizens will sort competing goals and responsibilities, how conflict and collaboration will shape the policy options, and how the nation's political institutions will respond.

Barry G. Rabe helps us understand the challenges and perils of making change in a political world. His analysis of reform in the states, especially in the process that grants permits, has built on initiatives from the regulated community, whose members have sought a friendlier and more certain regulatory system. In all but one state, he shows us, efforts at permit reform were designed to deal with the problems that the regulated had identified. Only one state also tried to reform the permit system to improve the quality of the environment. This helps explain the legitimacy of the environmental community's suspicion of environmental reform efforts. When regulatory changes grow from the initiative of the regulated, environmentalists worry that the next steps in environmental quality might be sacrificed to the demands of businesses. It also helps us understand the difficulty of achieving sustained progress in reform instead of swinging back and forth between regulatory episodes of stringency and relief. Rabe shows us the difficulty of maintaining reform without an adequate legislative foundation. Government officials face strong incentives to create their own brand of "reform." Without the competitive pressures that shape private sector action, government can find itself without adequate incentives to assess and improve or to ensure that initiatives designed to improve the market meet market-based tests.

Shelley H. Metzenbaum presents a strategy for making changes that embraces, rather than ignores, the political forces. She suggests it is possible to build trust and agreement if officials focus on environmental outcomes, rather than on the bureaucratic status quo. Her case examines how officials engaged and enlisted constituencies, on all sides, in a debate about environmental goals and information. She contends that a win-win negotiation strategy is possible by redefining the size and shape of the policy debate to bring environmental outcomes explicitly into the discussion. To the surprise of many reformers, some interests worked to keep the debate over outcomes off the negotiating table. Indeed, although everyone agrees that the system's results matter most, many combatants have discovered subtle ways of pursuing their own advantage through the existing process. A focus on results short circuits those underlying political tactics and thus dramatically transforms the process.

Graham K. Wilson gives us a glimpse of how these issues play out overseas. His chapter outlines the potential and the limits of experiments tried there. Even more important, his comparison with American environmental strategies helps identify clearly the fundamental political battles that undergird the enduring debates over environmental policy wherever they occur. Many environmental issues facing American regulators, from global warming to requirements for manufacturing processes, spill across national borders. Moreover, Wilson ironically poses the possibility that global economic competition and multinational regulation together may threaten the public-private and compact-partnership strategies Europe has used, and America admires. Europe may thus find itself drawn into the more legalistic, adversarial American way. The United States might become the model for Europe, rather than the other way around.

Finally, Christopher H. Foreman Jr. reminds us that these political struggles have real impact on communities. Moreover, government and corporate strategies sometimes affect different citizens in these communities very differently. Environmental policy is not simply a matter of government's relationships with business. Those relationships have distributive implications for citizens, in economic, political, and social terms. No assessment of environmental policy and of policy reforms can be complete without a careful look at how those policies affect individuals, especially minority groups.

Environmental policy has been at the center of policy reform for more than a generation. Change will continue to rocket through the system, in the United States, and around the world. But it is hard to escape the fact that policymakers face a new and challenging generation of issues. Those issues, moreover, raise tough political problems that define which options are viable and how different options will reshape politics. These puzzles require a next generation of analysis and fresh understanding of the politics that support them. The chapters that follow outline a path to fresh perspectives on the critical problems that must be addressed.

Notes

1. Office of Management and Budget, *Report to Congress on the Costs and Benefits of Regulation* (www.whitehouse.gov/omb/inforeg/chap2.html [January 19, 2001]).

2. Eban Goodstein and Hart Hodges, "Polluted Data: Environmental Costs," *American Prospect*, no. 35 (November–December 1997), pp. 64–69.

3. Ken Miller, "GOP Moderates Flex Environmental Muscle; House Rebuffs Effort to Curb EPA Powers," *Chicago Sun-Times*, July 30, 1995, p. 24.

4. National Academy of Public Administration, *environment.gov: Transforming Environmental Protection for the 21st Century* (Washington, 2000), p. 11.

5. See, for example, Mary Graham, *The Morning after Earth Day* (Brookings, 1999).

6. Pietro Nivola and Jon Shields, "Coping with the Jolly Green Giant: Local Rigors of U.S. Environmental Regulation," Working Paper (Brookings, 2000), esp. p. 12.

7. Karl Hausker, "The Convergence of Ideas on Improving the Environmental Protection System" (Washington: Center for Strategic and Environmental Studies, 1999), p. 4. For support of this argument, see National Academy of Public Administration, *Setting Priorities, Getting Results: A New Direction for EPA* (Washington, 1995), *Resolving the Paradox: EPA and the States Focus on Results* (Washington, 1997), and *environment.gov*. See also Enterprise for the Environment, *The Environmental Protection System in Transition: Toward a*

More Desirable Future (Washington: Center for Strategic and International Studies, 1998) (www.csis.org/e4e/e4ereport.pdf [February 13, 2001]); Aspen Institute, *The Alternative Path: A Cleaner, Cheaper Way to Protect and Enhance the Environment* (Washington, 1996); and Shelley H. Metzenbaum, *Making Measurement Matter: The Challenge and Promise of Building a Performance-Focused Environmental Protection System* (Brookings, 1998).

CHAPTER TWO

Permitting, Prevention, and Integration: Lessons from the States

BARRY G. RABE

A growing chorus of respected studies of the recent performance of American environmental policy laments the failures of the existing pollution control system and endorses broad reforms. In the past half-decade alone, distinguished organizations such as the National Academy of Public Administration, the President's Commission on Sustainable Development, Resources for the Future, Yale University's Center for Environmental Law and Policy, and the National Environmental Policy Institute, as well as broad-based projects such as Enterprise for the Environment (E4E), have addressed these issues. Their analyses offer sobering testimony that reveal serious limitations to conventional approaches to environmental protection, often concluding with an appeal to accelerate the "next generation" or "new epoch" of environmental protection efforts.

The proposed reforms vary from report to report and also tend to lack specificity. But they largely concur in one principal respect. They note the desirability of a more unified and integrated approach, one that emphasizes preventing rather than controlling pollution; ending the shell game of pollutant transfer across the media of air, land, and water; and concentrating resources on the most serious environmental threats. The anticipated political impediments to this more organic approach are regularly noted in these reports, but little guidance is offered on how to surmount them.

If there is a silver bullet to drive desired reforms, reflected in many of

these reports and in the increasingly conventional wisdom in the bur-
geoning literature on intergovernmental relations, it is the hope that regulatory decentralization might cure much if not all of what ails the
American environmental protection system. This remedy is touted
because of the consistent failure of the federal government in recent
decades to reauthorize existing environmental legislation, much less
address fundamental shortcomings produced by the pollution control
regime. At the same time, the maturation of state governments in all
areas of domestic policy, including environmental protection, is widely
heralded and clearly one of the more heartening developments in American governance of the past quarter-century. Many people assume that
state policy systems are best equipped to manage any transition from a
medium-based system to one that approaches individual places and
firms in an integrative manner.

In turn themes such as "civic environmentalism" and "place-based
environmental protection" are becoming part of the American environmental policy vernacular. Proponents contend that profound commitment
to environmental protection at the state and local levels is growing and
that decentralization of traditional regulatory authority could unleash a
dynamic era of innovation. By preventing pollutant generation at its
source through localized approaches tailored to particular communities
and industries, states are deemed well qualified to eliminate releases that
would otherwise cross medium and jurisdictional boundaries.

The promise of decentralization is appealing, but it remains unclear
how far diverse states and regions have advanced during the past decade
in confronting some of these fundamental problems in the existing system. There has been no legislative devolution of federal government
authority to rival the far-reaching experience of social welfare policy.
But both the first Bush and the Clinton administrations experimented
with methods that would facilitate considerable devolution while
remaining within the context of established legislation. The current
Bush administration has indicated strong interest in building on these
experiments, most notably in the area of enforcement. Most state environmental agencies have already obtained federal delegation for implementing key provisions of water pollution, hazardous and solid waste,
and pesticide laws.[1] States have been given tremendous latitude to negotiate solutions to thorny cross-boundary problems such as ozone transfer and low-level radioactive waste management. Perhaps most significant, approximately four-fifths of the states have entered into the

National Environmental Performance Partnership System (NEPPS).[2] Under this system, participating states have been offered substantial flexibility and opportunity for innovation in program implementation and in the allocation of federal grant dollars.

When combined with the growth of state resources devoted to environmental protection efforts and their heralded maturation and capacity for innovation, these recent efforts to shift some authority from Washington, D.C., to state capitals provide a rich context for examining how states have begun to take concrete steps in the directions endorsed in so much of the recent analysis of environmental policy. This chapter offers an examination of current practice, drawing on comparative case studies of four diverse states (Colorado, New Jersey, Oklahoma, and Pennsylvania).[3] The cases focus on the evolution of permitting as a regulatory tool central to many major environmental protection programs. Have states used their expanded capacity and latitude to transform permitting from its medium-based pollution control traditions into more dynamic instruments designed to minimize cross-media transfer and to foster pollution prevention? Have they devised methods to make permitting more efficient, making decisions more rapidly and consistently than in earlier decades? Have they found ways to make permitting a tool of performance-based environmental management, focused on environmental quality outcomes rather than the traditional bean counting of the numbers of permits issued? Have states found the federal government a willing partner in experimentation or an impediment to innovation?

This small sample of intensive case studies offers a snapshot of current practice that produces a very mixed picture. All of the states in this analysis have significantly improved permit efficiency, demonstrated in several methods to systematize permit issuance and create clearer expectations for regulated parties. At the same time, one indeed begins to envision what the "next generation" of environmental policy might entail in those select instances, most notably evident in New Jersey, that show a systematic effort to transform broad reform goals into concrete policy initiatives. The early years of experience with the New Jersey Facility-Wide Permit (FWP) program demonstrate the limitations of the traditional regulatory system. The program also indicates the potential for development of an alternative that confronts cross-media transfers, pushes pollution prevention into every facet of the regulatory review process, and creates a method that moves the idea of environmental performance assessment well beyond mere conceptualization. In this case and more modest examples from other states, intra-agency entrepreneurship has facilitated new working relationships across traditional state and intergovernmental boundaries.

At the same time, recent experience from New Jersey and other states also underscores the enduring limitations of these types of initiatives and the rather primitive status of their development in other states. In two cases, Colorado and Oklahoma, permit innovation has become synonymous with accelerated decisionmaking, with little if any link to the development of a process to secure better environmental outcomes through institutional tinkering. Not only has the New Jersey innovation failed to diffuse elsewhere, despite some initial exploration in Pennsylvania and other states, but it has encountered a set of intrastate political difficulties that has severely undermined its effectiveness and left its future uncertain.

What thus emerges from this analysis is a decidedly mixed picture. Recent reform proponents have clearly highlighted a series of significant shortcomings in the current practice of environmental policy. However, the translation of the broad goals that emanate from those assessments into new policy instruments is analytically challenging and politically uncertain. Further devolution of authority may be a desirable goal and may indeed foster more innovation. But the ultimate architects of any such strategy will need to consider the wide range of state-level capacity for pursuing such steps rather than blithely assume that the mere delegation of authority from federal to state hands will usher in the next generation of environmental policy so widely desired.

Permitting across Environmental Media

Permitting is a core regulatory function common in the environmental policy systems of the United States and most other Western democracies. Permits in most instances are legally binding documents that formally constrain emission or pollutant releases to individual media and are developed to fulfill technical requirements set forth in medium-specific legislation. Environmental permits are notoriously fragmented in their design and management by separate agency units. In the United States, water permits tend to concentrate on discharges from an entire industrial facility and are governed by the Clean Water Act. Air permits focus on each individual piece of equipment that releases specified types and amounts of emissions, under the auspices of the Clean Air Act. Permits for hazardous waste management, authorized under still another piece of legislation, the Resource Conservation and Recovery Act, are based on engineering design or operating standards. Additional permits under separate legislation can come into play in certain instances. Consequently, such a system has made it difficult, if not impossible, to compare information on air releases with information on water releases even when the same chemical is analyzed within a single industrial facility.

Moreover, different officials from different units of state environmental and natural resource agencies tend to administer individual permit programs, and the total number of permits required can soar into the hundreds for large industrial facilities. As a result, the mere compilation of a unified environmental profile for an individual facility remains a herculean task in many states. At the same time, experience abroad suggests that permitting need not solely be viewed as a one-way path toward regulatory fragmentation. In Norway and Sweden, for example, the development of a permit system that formally incorporates multimedia considerations into data collection and permit review is widely thought to be a cornerstone of those nations' relatively successful efforts in promoting a more integrated approach to environmental protection.[4]

Each of the four states included in this study has received authority from the U.S. Environmental Protection Agency (EPA) to administer most of the core programs involving environmental permits. But the states differ greatly in the per capita resources they allocate to environmental protection, comparative ranking in regulatory capacity and rigor, and general commitment demonstrated in pursuit of the goals of regulatory innovation.[5] All of these distinctions were considered during the site selection process to maximize diversity. In addition, each state is located in a different EPA region. Despite the small sample size, these four states possess sufficient diversity to offer insight into the current status of state approaches to permitting and integration.

Permit Streamlining: Efficiency and Customer Service

The willingness and capacity of states to pursue environmental policy innovation is perhaps best illustrated in the ongoing quest in almost every state environmental agency to find methods that facilitate more rapid decisions on permit issuance and develop more collaborative and collegial relations with regulated parties. This effort, evident in all four states included in this analysis and reflected across the nation, is not a new one. During the 1980s and early 1990s, many states experimented with methods such as designating a permit coordinator to work directly with firms in order to try to coordinate and expedite decisions on permits. At times, this entailed creation of a one-stop permitting office or permit assistance center and also included experimentation with new technology to attempt to provide more systematic information on permit processes to applicants.[6]

Most states have moved well beyond these initial efforts in more recent years with a variety of permit streamlining mechanisms, some reliant on expanded use of technology and others emphasizing administrative reforms. In some instances, state initiative has been actively encouraged by federal support, including the EPA's Permits Integration Team, which was formed after the Clinton administration designated permit innovation a "high priority action" in 1995 under its reinventing government initiative.[7] For the most part, however, these state efforts are homegrown activities, and their breadth illustrates the many opportunities open to states under the current intergovernmental system.

Perhaps no state has moved as boldly into this area as Oklahoma. Enactment of the 1994 Oklahoma Uniform Permitting Act ushered in a set of fundamental reforms of the way in which the state Department of Environmental Quality (DEQ) and related units would address permit implementation. These reforms have had several key elements, all of which have shown signs of diffusing to other states and becoming a national model. They are bundled under the heading of the Simplified Uniform Process for Environmental Regulation initiative, known by the acronym of SUPER. This initiative began with an effort to sort all major types of permit decisions into three separate categories or tiers. For those decisions thought to pose relatively little risk, such as a proposed alteration of a discharge permit, tier 1 status allows for a streamlined review to proceed with no formal mechanism for public input and a review by a DEQ technical supervisor. For those decisions thought to entail moderate risk, such as a new wastewater treatment permit, tier 2 status is applied and somewhat more complex review procedures are used. These include publication of the application notice in an area newspaper, an opportunity for citizens to request a public meeting on the proposal, and a final decision by the appropriate DEQ division director. Finally, those decisions entailing the highest levels of risk, such as a new hazardous waste management facility, require a more extensive review and allow the public to request a meeting early in the review process or a formal administrative hearing on a proposed final permit. Tier 3 cases also require more frequent agency monitoring of a facility and more frequent compliance reporting to the agency. In these cases, final approval is determined by the DEQ executive director.[8]

This effort to reclassify permits into broad categories coincided with the creation of a Customer Services Division (CSD), which joined four existing divisions (such as Air Quality and Waste Management) and is headed by an official who reports directly to the DEQ executive director. Numerous additional streamlining activities have been launched under the auspices of the CSD, including development of a permit tracking system designed to pinpoint areas in which decisions are delayed and ultimately move the agency toward its goal of processing all permit requests within ninety days of application. The centrality of these types of efforts to the DEQ is evident from the frequent coverage they have received in all recent annual reports issued by the departments as well as the fact that further permit streamlining is a central focal point in *FOCUS* 2000, the DEQ strategic plan used to secure EPA approval of an NEPPS agreement. The ubiquity of references to streamlined permitting in the *FOCUS* reports is illustrated by the following "task" outlined for future DEQ implementation: "Conduct tracking of permits by extracting information from air, water, and waste data bases and compiling weekly permit status reports. Each Friday prepare summaries and charts for weekly reports which identify applications that have been in-house longer than target timelines and reflect trends in permit review."[9]

The SUPER strategy has also led the CSD to actively support permit applicants with extensive "customer assistance" programs that offer technical support and the promise of putting pressure on other DEQ divisions if permit decisions are delayed. Involvement is extensive when a firm is considering locating a new facility somewhere in Oklahoma. In these cases, the CSD works closely with the Oklahoma Department of Commerce in establishing an Economic Development Permit Assistance Team. The team is designed to bring together representatives of each permit program that may come into consideration in the proposed facility to meet with representatives of the firm. The CSD, according to DEQ documents, "works with the applicant and within the Agency to assure that agreed upon time frames are met for submittal of permit applications and that permit review is performed in an expeditious manner. Action is taken, if necessary, to prioritize reviews."[10]

Permit streamlining is thus seen in Oklahoma as a central tool to facilitate economic development. "Business recruitment is a big issue in Oklahoma," noted one senior state official, "and our Department of Commerce likes to advertise the fact that we have a simpler permit process than any other state." As a 1997 DEQ report noted, the agency "does not want to be placed in the position of halting or slowing a project that will bring jobs to the state."[11] State officials express some concern that their comparative edge in this area may be weakened as other states begin to pursue similar strategies. In fact, several states have modeled recent permit streamlining efforts on parts of the Oklahoma experience and one, Arkansas, has essentially adopted the entire approach.

Oklahoma officials are attempting to stay ahead of neighboring states through developing ever more exact measures of permit performance. The DEQ annual reports are unique in the detail with which they attempt to provide quantitative measures of permit implementation. This information includes regular reports on numbers of permits issued and denied by division, averages and ranges of time needed to process various permits, and numbers of public complaints, protests, and protest hearings. Officials and departments vie to claim credit for efficiency and customer satisfaction, particularly when neither a single permit is denied nor a public hearing required in a given year. The DEQ has attempted to supplement these measures with regular distribution and analysis of "permit satisfaction surveys." Each permit completed by the DEQ is sent to the regulated party along with a questionnaire to evaluate agency performance. These data have produced formal satisfaction rates that can be compared among years and agency units and also led to the claim in a 1999 DEQ report that "98% of respondents rated the Agency's overall performance as good or excellent."[12]

Pennsylvania has not developed as extensive a set of permit streamlining innovations as Oklahoma but offers its own unique approach. Alongside a set of traditional methods, such as a comprehensive guidebook to permitting and designation of one official as a permit coordinator for complex cases, Pennsylvania launched a new initiative in 1995 designed to accelerate permit decisions by offering a full refund of all permit fees if formal deadlines for permit completion are not met. The so-called Pennsylvania Money-Back Guarantee Program borrowed heavily from prior experience in Massachusetts and was created through an executive order issued by Governor Tom Ridge in 1995. This initiative emanated from Ridge's 1994 campaign promises to make state envi-

ronmental officials more responsive to regulated parties and was an element in a broader strategy to reorganize the Department of Environmental Protection (DEP) and related entities.

The Money-Back Program establishes fixed timetables for the DEP to
complete its review of various permit proposals, ranging from 30 days
for a backyard waste composting application to 230 days for a major
National Pollutant Discharge Elimination System (NPDES) permit
renewal under the Clean Water Act. These time periods are designed to
allow for submission of all necessary documents and completion of each
stage of technical review. Failure to meet these deadlines results in a full
refund of all permit fees, which can range from $500 for a five-year
NPDES permit to $36,000 for a new commercial storage facility for
hazardous waste generated off-site. However, the DEP is not required to
approve any permit automatically if deadlines are missed, and any applicant failure to provide needed information or address proposal deficien-
cies stops the refund clock. As in Oklahoma, this approach creates
incentives for state permit officials to move expeditiously and also
allows for the development of quantitative measures of certain aspects
of performance. For example, the state can calculate the percentage of
permit applications that complete the review process under deadlines
and also provide a broad indicator of performance by reporting annual
permit fees that must be returned each year.

Colorado and New Jersey have devised their own variations on permit streamlining, consistent with the general thrust of Oklahoma and
Pennsylvania, if not as far reaching. The Colorado Department of Public
Health and Environment completed a systematic review of five other
states' practices and concluded that it could best foster streamlining
through compilation of a guidebook offering a detailed description of
each possible permit that an applicant might need to acquire. The 1997
publication of "Permitting Made Easy" incorporated this information
and has since been available on the agency website. In New Jersey,
recent permit streamlining efforts have focused on technical assistance
for small businesses and a one-stop process to review all requirements
for prospective applicants.

These permit streamlining efficiencies all offer considerable promise
for making permit decisions more rapidly and thereby reducing traditional tensions between state environmental agencies and regulated parties. And in Oklahoma, the creation of a tiered system to concentrate
resources on those cases perceived to pose the greater environmental

and public health risk is consistent with proposals to prioritize environmental threats and reallocate resources accordingly. However, all of these initiatives are exceedingly limited in their linkage to any effort to promote more integrated environmental management. Interviews in all four states suggest little if any consideration of ways to link streamlining with attempts to reduce cross-media transfers or promote pollution prevention. Instead, the emphasis is on making traditional permit decisions as quickly as possible. As one state official noted, "This whole emphasis on streamlining is essentially making the same bad decisions as before but taking less time in making them."

Even in Oklahoma, where the wide range of initiatives could conceivably be linked to integration and prevention, there is little indication that these connections are occurring. All recent agency reports and the FOCUS activity leading to NEPPS designation placed almost exclusive emphasis on decisionmaking speed and achieving high satisfaction rates among regulated customers. State officials have difficulty identifying any instances in which this range of initiatives has contributed to greater consideration of cross-media concerns or pollution prevention opportunities in permit decisions. "There is nothing concrete on cross-media that I can think of in this program," noted one senior state official, "and we're not really sure how to do it. We're waiting for EPA to tell us things we don't have to do any longer before we're prepared to go forward with that sort of thing." Officials involved with permit streamlining in other states offered similar evaluations. "It is really hard to speed up permits and try at the same time to encourage thinking about pollution prevention," explained a senior official in the Pennsylvania Department of Environmental Protection. "We really have found some ways to standardize permit steps and eliminate the backlog," added a colleague. "But this hasn't done anything in terms of pushing prevention or integration into the process."

Officials involved in permit streamlining in the other selected states offer similar assessments. One-stop approaches in Colorado and New Jersey and money-back guarantees in Pennsylvania may thus have some very salutary qualities in accelerating permit decisionmaking. But they appear unlikely to have any significant impact on environmental quality or advance the sorts of remedies so commonly cited by proponents of environmental policy reform. Permit streamlining, however, is not the only approach that states can take in thinking about the next steps of permitting reform.

Steps toward Integration and Prevention

None of the states included in this analysis has gone so far as to fully incorporate the concepts of integration and prevention into such core environmental regulatory functions as permitting. But in three of the four cases, most notably New Jersey but also Pennsylvania and Oklahoma, one can begin to discern what a "next generation" of policy might entail. These case reviews underscore the great potential for state innovation in these areas and offer some common design features that may warrant emulation in other jurisdictions or formal embrace by the federal government. But they also underscore the political and managerial fragility of innovation, particularly when it runs counter to agency norms and the prevailing tone of federal and state environmental legislation.

Each case features important distinctions, suggesting that there is no obvious "one best system" for promoting integration and prevention. However, all followed relatively similar processes of policy formation, which may be instructive in considering the possible diffusion of these initiatives in the future. First, much of the impetus for each state's effort emanated from the middle to upper-middle ranks of state environmental agencies. There was relatively little pressure from environmental advocacy groups or industry for these innovations, although advocates and industry often became central participants in implementation. Moreover, this type of innovation runs counter to the traditional process of environmental policy formation in which elected officials attempt to cobble together policy in response to some environmental calamity.[13] Instead, these initiatives moved forward in a relatively quiet manner, with intra-agency "policy entrepreneurs" both developing key concepts and gradually winning support, whether from top agency officials or eventually, in some instances, governors and key legislators.

This pattern of policy formation is consistent with a growing body of literature that indicates that agency officials may have far greater latitude to pursue innovation than is acknowledged in traditional models that emphasize more hierarchical, principal-agent relationships. As political scientists John Brehm and Scott Gates have noted, "Despite significant efforts to constrain bureaucratic choices, bureaucrats possess [a] significant degree of discretion."[14] Indeed, recent studies of subnational policy innovation move beyond elected officials and agency heads to indicate a much more expansive role for agency officials below the top levels than widely assumed.[15] Even in policy areas with generally high saliency, intra-agency policy entrepreneurship may be an essential component of policy innovation.[16]

These cases that demonstrate the potential linkage between integration and prevention with core environmental regulatory tools such as permitting also illustrate the potential for effective collaboration on intergovernmental boundaries. Recent research on patterns of federal-state relations in environmental policy indicates enormous variation by issue area and may allow for creative patterns of cooperation to emerge in some instances.[17] Despite the prevailing intergovernmental tensions surrounding such issues as unfunded—or underfunded—mandates, these state cases of permit innovation suggest mechanisms whereby federal resources and willingness to experiment can help facilitate new state approaches. All of this collaboration occurred independently of the new NEPPS agreements in place in three of the four states (Pennsylvania opted not to participate in that program), although further implementation of NEPPS could indeed reinforce these patterns.

Finally, these cases also underscore the fragility of single-state innovation. Many of the most exciting examples of state environmental policy innovation have demonstrated, in the words of Robert Hersh of Resources for the Future, a "high decay function."[18] Many receive only tentative resource support and little publicity, and they are often vulnerable to changes in state political or agency leadership. Consequently, all of the innovations discussed in the following sections lack a firm institutional footing and could indeed disappear without much public notice or establishment of precedent.

Facility-Wide Permitting in New Jersey

New Jersey is commonly recognized as a national leader in attempting to link core regulatory tools, including permitting, with pollution prevention and reduction of cross-media pollutant transfers. One of the primary methods the state has developed is a Facility-Wide Permit (FWP) program that builds directly on the 1991 New Jersey Pollution Prevention Act. This program has issued fourteen facility-wide permits to a diverse set of New Jersey industrial firms between 1994 and 2001, with each permit designed to incorporate every specific permit into a single document that examines the environmental impact of each industrial facility in a comprehensive fashion. All relevant officials of regulatory agencies and regulated firms are expected to review every area of the facility in a unified fashion, searching for previously undisclosed emissions, cross-media transfers, and pollution prevention opportunities. This is directly contrary to conventional point-source-by-point-source permit review that characteristically depends on different agency and industry officials at each step of the process. It also constitutes a novel experiment in attempting to implement a place-based approach to environmental protection, moving beyond medium-based divides.

New Jersey's venture into facility-wide permitting hinged on the development of a series of information disclosure and pollution prevention tools by the federal and state governments in the late 1980s and early 1990s. The federal Toxics Release Inventory (TRI), enacted in 1986 and based in large part on earlier experiments in New Jersey and Maryland, provides an annual report on the release of hundreds of chemicals to all media by nearly 900 New Jersey firms. Unlike the more cautious approach of many other states, New Jersey chose to make immediate and extensive use of this new database through its 1991 pollution prevention legislation. The law required all TRI reportees to submit pollution prevention plans to the state Department of Environmental Protection (DEP) every five years, along with annual progress reports.[19] This mandatory planning activity included development of a "materials accounting" process, designed to assess the flow of each hazardous substance through an entire production process and thereby track the input, loss, and final destination of each substance. A pivotal component of this process was the measurement of so-called nonproduct output, which includes any hazardous substance that does not leave the facility in the form of a product with commercial value or gain value when further utilized elsewhere. The concept of nonproduct output was first developed in the 1980s by the former congressional Office of Technology Assessment, most notably in its 1986 report "Serious Reduction of Hazardous Waste." Nonproduct output measures have become the common denominator for assessing pollution prevention trends under the New Jersey planning requirement. The rate of nonproduct output "per unit of product" is intended to provide a consistent, comparable annual measure of environmental performance.[20]

The FWP program was endorsed in the 1991 pollution prevention legislation as a way to explore potential links between these broad pollution prevention planning efforts and core tools of the conventional regulatory process. Three firms volunteered to participate in a pilot project, which was later expanded to include fifteen additional volunteers.

As of October 2001, fourteen facility-wide permits had been issued, several of which received subsequent revisions, two additional permits were pending, and two original participants had withdrawn from the program. Facilities were selected from a larger set of volunteers, with consideration given to maximize diversity across industrial sectors and various geographic regions of New Jersey. Permit recipients include facilities that manufacture pharmaceutical products, polypropylene, air conditioners and dehumidifiers, laminated foil and paper, adhesive products, vinyl chloride, and specialty organic chemicals, as well as those that provide chemical repackaging and distribution services. All of the participants had dozens, and in some cases hundreds, of separate permits, including specialized permits for air, water, hazardous waste, and solid waste, before their involvement in the program.

Policy Entrepreneurship and Managerial Innovation

Facility-wide permitting in New Jersey developed largely through the entrepreneurial efforts of DEP officials, advancing new ideas and building key partnerships with senior agency officials and ultimately elected allies. Discussions of such a permitting initiative between agency staff and industry representatives began well in advance of the 1991 pollution prevention legislation, and agency officials played a central role in every stage of program development. The implementation of the New Jersey program suggests that it is possible for such entrepreneurs to not only secure needed support and resources but also assemble a team of diverse specialists within an agency and work in a creative and constructive fashion with industry participants on cross-media and pollution prevention issues. Agency and industry participants alike indicate that while the development of facility-wide permits is wrought with uncertainties, they found the experience stimulating and worthwhile, contrary to the conventional characterization of permitting as a tedious, perfunctory exercise. All observers concur that a key component in this process was the leadership of Jeanne Herb, who was hired by then-commissioner Christopher Daggett in 1989 as the director of the Office of Pollution Prevention during the administration of Republican governor Thomas Kean. Herb participated in all of the preliminary discussions of pollution prevention policy and permitting options with legislators and stakeholders, and she secured support for innovation from diverse quarters. Herb was also authorized through the state's 1991 pollution prevention legislation to report directly to the DEP commissioner, thereby gaining far more visibility and access to the top channels of the agency than pollution prevention leaders in almost all other states.

Herb also took the lead in recruiting a staff qualified to address the complex technical and policy issues likely to emerge under a facility-wide permitting experiment affecting all media and related programs. "My upper management gave me a lot of latitude," Herb recalled. "We followed civil service rules but got to hire who we wanted."[21] Recruitment required considerable persuasion, as there were no added monetary incentives for anyone contemplating a transfer and some potential career risks in the event the program failed. Nonetheless, those staff selected to participate demonstrated strong commitment and routinely speak of their experience as among the highlights of their professional careers. "It was all very positive and very successful," noted Steven Anderson, former project manager of the FWP program. "There was a lot going for us. We were high profile, and we were able to recruit very good people who really wanted to be part of this. And Jeanne was just a tremendous buffer between politics and the permits, allowing the staff to do what it needed to do."[22] Not all staff recruits were comfortable with the complexity and uncertainty prevalent. In fact, one permit writer, who only had prior experience in air quality regulations, left after six months. "He was so used to existing policies, having the piles of paper on his desk with certain ways of doing things, he wanted to go back to the air program," recalled one FWP staff member. "This was new and different, involving blank pieces of paper with nothing fixed in advance." However, this adverse reaction was exceptional, and each position vacancy triggered an unusually large number of applications from officials elsewhere in the DEP.

What emerged from this recruitment process was a team that shared responsibility for each FWP throughout all stages of its development. However, one individual was usually singled out as the lead person for each facility. Unlike traditional permitting duties, where individual officials usually focus on a single concern or type of point source, all staff members active in a review were expected to get to know the entire facility. "Everybody in the program knows each of these facilities through and through," explained an FWP staff member. "That really was obvious when Schering [the first facility to receive its permit, a pharmaceutical firm located in Kenilworth] invited EPA down to give them a tour. They said that Mike [DeGiore, a permit writer] could give the tour as well as Schering staff, because he knew so much about the plant." In turn, industry officials concur that this type of process, though exhausting at times, leads to an entirely different dynamic from conventional agency-industry reviews. According to Frank Gorski, manager of environmental and industrial health at Huntsman Chemical's West Deptford polypropylene plant, facility-wide permitting allows state officials to get their first true sense of what occurs inside an industrial facility and, in turn, enables industry officials to begin to more fully understand what the various facets of permitting are intended to accomplish. Gorski explained, in a published interview, that under facility-wide permitting, "the state permit writer knows when a single molecule of propylene comes into the plant, and he can trace that molecule all the way through until it leaves as polypropane. This has never happened before. In the old days when we were permitting a pump or compressor, the guy would know about this compressor or that pump, but would have no idea how it interacts with the entire process."[23]

Securing State Political Support

The New Jersey program also indicates that such a complex initiative as facility-wide permitting can also secure a broad and fairly enduring base of high-level political support. A succession of governors (Republican Kean, Democrat James Florio, and Republican Christine Whitman) and their respective DEP commissioners all attempted to embrace the program as their own brainchild, contending it was illustrative of their innovative approaches to environmental matters. Program staff worked hard to cultivate their relationships and provide elected officials, including legislators, opportunities for claiming credit. For example, both Florio and Whitman took the unprecedented steps of elevating formal permit issuance into a public ceremony in which they played a starring role. These governors regularly attended permit approvals held during their respective terms of office, touring the permitted plant, touting the virtues of the approach in public remarks, and usually garnering favorable publicity in the immediate area and statewide.

For Kean, the launching of the experimental program was one of a large series of environmental policy initiatives introduced during his governorship, many of which attempted to cut across traditional regulatory boundaries and establish New Jersey as a national leader in environmental policy. Florio sought to modify his image as extremely adversarial with the private sector on environmental issues. "This is the kind of public-private partnership that will allow us to take a smarter approach to protecting the environment," he said.[24] He characterized facility-wide permitting as "a 'win-win' proposition for everyone" that would be a hallmark of his future environmental policy initiatives. For Whitman, subsequent permit agreements concluded during her term were used to counter frequent allegations by environmental groups and journalists that she was indifferent to environmental protection, committed to weaken the capacity of the DEP through budget cuts, and overly absorbed with economic development goals. Whitman and top aides made repeated efforts to suggest that the program was her idea and that she systematically supported it, even as it encountered a variety of funding and managerial problems in more recent years. She gave special attention to the FWP program in her 1995 State of the State Address, describing it as "a welcome sign that New Jerseyans are connecting greenways and golden opportunities."[25]

Intra-Agency and Intergovernmental Cooperation

Broad, integrative efforts to promote greater environmental policy integration have often succumbed to a lack of intra-agency or intergovernmental ability to work toward a common cause.[26] In contrast, the New Jersey FWP program experienced reasonable success in working cooperatively with various DEP units, at least in its earlier years of operation, and maintained constructive working relations with key officials in regional and national offices of the U.S. EPA. Supportive decisions from other DEP and EPA units with jurisdiction for air quality regulations proved instrumental in completing many of the initial permits. In turn, federal grants supported program efforts and provided financial incentives to secure cooperation from medium-based units within the DEP.

Perhaps the most significant intra-agency action involved the August 1993 adoption by the DEP Air Quality Regulatory program of a significant modification in conventional regulatory operations. This shift enabled facilities participating in the integrated program to make changes in their operational processes without securing DEP "pre-approval," as long as these changes meant no increase in the rate of concentration of nonproduct output or multimedia emissions.[27] Under conventional practice in New Jersey and most other states, securing formal "alterations" in existing permits can be extremely time consuming and costly and is often a fundamental concern for facilities that must make regular changes in their product line. Industry leaders have long decried this process as a huge disincentive to product innovation. "We found that industry is constantly carping about disincentives to pollution prevention, but this pre-approval issue was the main concern they raised when we asked them to get specific," recalled Herb.[28] This very alteration was a crucial component in at least half of the firms that have received a facility-wide permit to date. "It was a strong sign to facilities that there was some real change coming through this program," explained Anderson.[29]

DEP officials connected with the facility-wide program used it to test the possible flexibility that might be feasible under various federal regulations, including the controversial Title V air quality permits that are being developed across the nation in conjunction with the 1990 Clean Air Act Amendments. In some states, the complexity and uncertainty surrounding Title V permits have slowed down any consideration of permit or related policy experiments. But New Jersey officials actively attempted to engage their EPA counterparts, using the facility-wide permit program to explore basic issues concerning Title V compliance and the possible links between it and other permits. This did not result in a uniform method for incorporating Title V into every facility-wide permit but gave New Jersey an edge over other states in finding ways to work cooperatively and creatively with EPA on implementation. "Our plan all along has been to work with EPA on Title V," noted an FWP staff member. "We feel that our facility-wide permit offers such better environmental results that it should be more than adequate" to satisfy federal standards.

More generally, the DEP has not found the EPA a stumbling block in its integrative efforts. Aside from the Title V issue, no existing federal regulation has emerged as a significant challenge for facility-wide permit development. New Jersey had acquired formal authority over most federal environmental programs before the passage of its 1991 pollution prevention legislation, and the DEP completed a series of Memoranda of Understanding with region 2 of EPA and industry participants early in the development of the permitting program. Subsequently, DEP interaction with EPA officials has been fairly limited. "Overall, relations with EPA have been fine," noted one FWP staff member. According to a senior DEP official, "What we haven't done is go outside the scope of federal rules, which would put us into conflict with EPA. Should the time come where we want to go outside the box, our relationship with EPA is strong enough that we might be able to do it."

So far, the federal government's action has been most meaningful in the provision of federal grant support. The EPA underwrote many of the costs of state pollution prevention experimentation during the 1990s, and this clearly has been evident in New Jersey. [30] For example, the DEP received $240,000 from the EPA between fiscal years 1993 and 1996 under the Pollution Prevention Incentives for States program to cover the costs incurred when staff from medium-based programs were needed to participate in various facility-wide permit reviews. This not only ensured input from outside the permit team but also reduced potential frictions with medium-specific programs, since they received financial compensation for lost staff time. Additional opportunity for the DEP to shift resources into pollution prevention and regulatory integration has arisen since the completion of its Performance Partnership Agreement with the EPA in 1997.

Environmental Ramifications

The fourteen facility-wide permits issued to date not only look fundamentally different from conventional permits but also seem to be making superior environmental outcomes possible. These permits divide each participating facility into separate processes and examine each process in an integrated fashion, contrary to traditional approaches that review each major point source in isolation from all others. In the case of the 1996 permit issued to the Frigidaire Company of Edison, for example, the facility was divided into sixteen distinct processes, including injection molding, copper tubing, metal press, paint spray booth, and touch-up stations. Each process is described in the permit, with particular attention to major environmental concerns at each level and key administrative and technical issues that must be addressed to comply with the permit agreement. Rather than dozens or hundreds of separate documents that are often filed with separate agencies and sections of a facility, each facility-wide permit reads like a unified volume. Not only is the overall paperwork reduced markedly in most cases, but the permit yields a comprehensive overview of the facility and its environmental impacts. Such portraits are simply not available under traditional approaches to permitting in New Jersey and other states. They provide a unique basis for assessing the overall environmental performance of the facility and targeting areas of concern.

That unusually wide vantage point has translated into significant discoveries about the limitations of the current permitting system and opportunities to pursue significant improvements in environmental protection. "We discovered that three people [in the DEP] will develop three permits in three different ways," noted one member of the FWP team. "There are just huge inconsistencies in existing laws, rules, and permits." For facilities whose only prior experience in permitting had involved responding to specialized requirements for distinct programs, the facility-wide review offered an unprecedented opportunity to examine their facility in a more holistic fashion. At the Fabricolor Manufacturing Corporation in Patterson, for example, officials developed a comprehensive spreadsheet based on all products and equipment in use, integrating an overview of everything they use and manufacture into one document. "Now, if they are out of compliance, they can figure out why," explained the FWP staff member. "They even know how many batches they can make before their permit runs out, whereas before they were operating by guesswork."

Fugitive Emissions

Perhaps the most significant discovery from the cases completed under the FWP program is the extent of previously undetected emissions discovered at each participating facility. None of these facilities was new; most had long-standing histories and solid regulatory compliance records. New Jersey became known throughout the 1980s and 1990s as one of the more vigorous states in regulatory monitoring, inspection, and overall enforcement. Consequently, these participating facilities were initially thought to be among those least likely to have a major problem with so-called fugitive emissions.

Nonetheless, the materials accounting process and comprehensive permit reviews discovered numerous emission sources that no prior permit or planning process had even identified, much less attempted to reduce or eliminate. For example, the Frigidaire Company permitting process discovered fifty-seven separate emission sources that had never been regulated in any manner. These included injection molding machines, plastic grinders, aluminum presses, metal processes, and other processes, many of which had been operating and presumably releasing fugitive emissions for a decade or more. In one instance, a 750-gallon degreaser using the toxic substance TCE as a solvent had been in operation since 1969. A materials accounting assessment conducted as part of the FWP process discovered that an annual average of thirty-five tons of TCE was disappearing from the facility, which triggered a review that revealed the degreaser as the source. The ultimate FWP issued to

Frigidaire addressed this violation in detail, establishing provisions to discontinue use of TCE and "go beyond rule compliance" with plans to remove the degreaser from the facility. The DEP will conduct monthly materials accounting for TCE until these steps are completed and has reserved the right to take legal action for past and future TCE emission violations by Frigidaire. In concert with other pollution prevention steps mandated through its FWP, Frigidaire's total use of TCE at its Edison facility is scheduled to drop from 720,000 pounds per year to approximately 90,000 pounds per year in the near term. It will be eliminated over several years. At other facilities participating in the integrative program, undisclosed emissions have been discovered from a dizzying array of diverse sources never previously detected by medium-specific permitting, monitoring, and enforcement programs or pollution prevention planning requirements.

The magnitude of these sorts of discoveries becomes evident when each FWP outlines total facility release limits in tabular form. As typified by the facility summary table included in the Frigidaire permit, existing levels of permitting releases often bear no relationship to actual levels discovered through the more integrative FWP process (table 2-1). "This was a total shock, probably the most unexpected discovery of the program," recalled one member of the permit team. "It meant we often had to start from scratch with a facility because the existing numbers just don't mean very much. This took a lot of extra time but gave us a chance to concentrate on some serious problems." Under the FWP process, newly established emission levels included a reconciliation of actual versus reported practice, as discerned through materials accounting, review of pollution prevention opportunities, and consideration of future activity likely to take place at the facility. "It was just a huge surprise to realize that so many significant releases had never been reported under the existing system," explained Herb. "You develop all of the data for each company and then fall off your chair when you realize all the stuff that they or the agency never thought about. Then, of course, you have to decide what to do about it."[31]

A somewhat related form of fugitive emission is a cross-media transfer, which has also been a focal point of the FWP program. In some of the integrative permits completed to date, the DEP has found instances when existing regulations foster pollutant transfer across medium boundaries. In the FWP issued in 1996 to Fisher Scientific of Somerville, for example, a major concern stemmed from the discovery of significant

Table 2-1. *Total Facility Release Limits under Facility-wide Permit (FWP) for the Frigidaire Company, Edison, New Jersey*
Tons per year

Contaminant	Existing facility permit limits	Actual facility emissions, 1994	FWP facility emission limits
VOC (Total)	9.73	113.7[a]	59.5
NO$_x$	88.068	10.7	11.5
CO	8.8646	2.6	2.8
SO$_x$	64.2487	0.35	0.307
TSP (total)	8.5866	0.42	2.82
PM10 (total)	0	n.a.	1.8
Pb	0	0	0.0001
HAPs (total)	2.0966	43.945[b]	1.9
TCE	0.914	43.9[b]	0[c]
Other	0.019	0	0.11

Source: New Jersey Department of Environmental Protection, 1996.
n.a. Not available
a. Includes the fugitive TCE and unpermitted VOC emissions.
b. Includes fugitive emissions.
c. The FWP contains a compliance date for the elimination of all TCE sources.

releases to air of volatile organic compounds (VOCs) through a process established to ensure permitted wastewater discharge to a public treatment facility. The wastewater was discharged along a 100-foot conveyance into a catch-basin before transfer to the facility. But through the FWP review, permit officials recognized an unexpectedly high loss of VOCs, and they traced this loss to volatilization to air en route to wastewater treatment. "We got their air and water people together to discuss this, and they said, 'This sort of thing happens a lot; we should do this more,'" recalled a member of the FWP team working on this case. The permit team presented a series of options to Fisher officials, who in the end chose to eliminate the wastewater discharge and thereby end the VOC volatilization.

Pollution Prevention

The discovery of undetected pollutant releases and transfers has been integrated into pollution prevention decisions in each FWP signed to date. In many instances, these previously undetected releases forced participating firms to revamp their existing pollution prevention plans and base future prevention decisions on a more comprehensive—and accurate—picture of the facility. It remains uncertain whether these types of problems would eventually have been identified as prevention planning matured, but most observers concur that the FWP process discerned many problems that would have likely escaped detection under traditional regulation and the new prevention planning process. In each of the first twelve FWPs, specific discussions of pollution prevention strategies and reduction commitments are outlined in the introductory section. Each of these is later revisited and explained in much greater detail in the individual process sections of each permit. Consequently, these permits read very differently from conventional permits issued in Colorado, Oklahoma, Pennsylvania, or other states, including those issued under the sorts of permit streamlining programs just noted. Indeed, traditional permitting involves no specific reference to pollution prevention options, much less the relationship between a single point source and either related sources or the entire facility.

Each of the completed FWPs incorporates a wide range of pollution prevention initiatives, resulting in a recalculation of total facility releases projected for future years. In the case of Huntsman Polypropylene, for example, pollution prevention commitments included improved housekeeping procedures, product transfer upgrades, equipment replacements, chemical substitutions, elimination of further use of seven chemicals, installation of an in-process recycling system for propylene, and a reduction in the frequency of plant start-ups and shutdowns. Through the FWP review process, Huntsman and DEP officials were able to reconstruct a far more accurate picture of historic releases and thereby more effectively target facility problem areas and the most promising pollution prevention opportunities. As in other cases, FWP staff outlined prevention options and then allowed Huntsman officials to make the most economically sensible selection that would attain the desired goal. The overall process not only promises to achieve substantial reductions in releases to air, land, and water, as well as volumes of hazardous waste generated, but has also triggered a Huntsman commitment to reinvest about $20 million in a plant modernization program that will allow the aging facility to continue operation at its present site. Before the process, the firm had seriously considered relocating the plant.

In some cases, much of the pollution prevention review focused on specific and serious problems, many of which emerged through the discovery of fugitive emissions at a given site. In the instance of the 1997 FWP issued to Geon Company, vinyl chloride releases proved a central concern for this firm, which is active in all phases of polyvinyl chloride manufacturing. "We looked at every source of vinyl chloride at the facility and found total releases unacceptable, well above current reporting levels," noted an FWP staff member active in this case. The Geon FWP specified numerous mechanisms intended to achieve release reductions of 50 percent within one year, with a key component in this transformation a "self-designed closed loop system." This review process required Geon to examine, for the first time, all aspects of its vinyl chloride use and release and think systematically about how much of the substance was being used to manufacture each product at the facility. "Historically, one common way to deal with this sort of problem was to increase stack height," noted the DEP official. Indeed, average industrial stack height in the United States climbed from 243 feet in 1960 to 730 feet in 1980, largely to ease state and local compliance with federal air quality regulations.[32] "This approach is very different," explained the official. "We use existing authority but require them to look at options and deal with the problems."

Each FWP case followed this general pattern, and collectively they offer a tutorial on the range of pollution prevention options that may arise in individual circumstances. In the Schering case, an entirely new method for manufacturing labels was developed to eliminate significant—and previously undetected—releases of a highly toxic chemical into the air. Through the 1999 FWP issued to Chevron USA, in Perth Amboy, the facility was able to reverse its order of operations and recycle vapors, leading to major reductions in the annual release of benzene and cyclohexane, as well as develop an in-process recycling system to eliminate release of naphtha in its wharf loading and unloading operations. In the case of the 1998 FWP issued to Degussa Corporation of South Plainfield, pollution prevention initiatives included the capture of a fugitive source of methanol from a wastewater treatment system and discovery of a substitute for the hazardous chemical hydrazine.

Impediments to Expanded FWP Development

The initial experience from the New Jersey FWP case suggests great potential for linkage of permitting with long-desired goals of integration and prevention. However, its track record to date is tempered by serious problems. Ironically, for a program that has provided a fair amount of notoriety for elected Republican and Democratic officials and been generally well received by industry and environmental groups, the future of this program is very much in doubt. Moreover, its prospects for continuation beyond the initial set of participants remain uncertain. Thus far, the primary stumbling blocks have been managerial and political issues rather than technical feasibility.

Resource Intensity

One of the biggest criticisms raised of the FWP program has been its intensive use of agency and industry resources in permit development. The DEP staffing levels devoted to the program have shifted over time, but clearly the start-up costs of these new, comprehensive permits have consumed substantial agency resources. These costs have been far greater on a "per permit" basis than through traditional approaches to permit approval. Robert Shinn, DEP commissioner through much of the 1990s, has generally been a public supporter of the program, at times discussing it as a model for a vastly expanded future initiative in regulatory reform. However, he has noted, "If you looked at how many hours we've spent on the permits that we've issued and you said we're going to do facility-wide [permits] statewide, it's too intensive."[33] Representatives of industries that have participated in the program offer similar assessments of their own involvement. They are generally supportive of the program but note that no two firms are identical, and some may have complex compliance issues that will necessitate major adjustments under the facility-wide framework. "It's a very painstaking procedure" to develop an FWP, noted the regulatory compliance officer of one program participant. "Schering [the first permit recipient] has more points of emission, but we have a much broader product mix. Assessing our emissions is a much more complex process."[34]

Agency and industry participants emphasize that, in their view, the overall benefits exceed immediate managerial costs. They also concur that FWP costs would probably level out if the program were to move beyond its pilot phase and be implemented over time for a growing number of facilities. Permit-signing ceremonies have consistently afforded photo opportunities for facility officials to be pictured with the blizzards of paperwork previously required for compliance. In a typical example, Huntsman's earlier experience of maintaining eighty separate permits in eleven looseleaf binders was compressed into a single permit of seventy-five pages. Every completed permit recipient can point to large future reductions in operational costs. In turn, a few of the firms, such as Frigidaire and Huntsman, contend that the FWP process was instrumental in the continued operation of their facility, as the more flexible process allowed for facility reinvestment rather than abandonment of existing property. Program participants have also experienced great success in securing adjustments to their permits as their operating conditions changed, with the integrated permit proving easier to revise than dozens or hundreds of separate permit files. Moreover, all participants point to enormous long-term "transfer" benefits, whereby industry and agency officials could apply lessons from the early cases to other facilities, including those not formally involved in the FWP program.

But, at least in the short run, the FWP program has proved very expensive to manage, despite financial support from the federal government. Participating firms must be willing to generate and release information that their competitors need not develop and be amenable to active exploration of potentially far-reaching prevention and integration steps through extensive negotiations with DEP officials. They may also face embarrassing disclosures of fugitive emissions and cross-media transfers that would probably continue to fall through the cracks under conventional permitting. All the while they must comply with existing, medium-specific permit requirements until an FWP is approved. At the same time, the state must be prepared to devote extra fiscal resources and offer political support for the venture. Staffing conflicts and, in the cases thus far, delays that extend the review well beyond initial timelines before final permit approval is secured will be inevitable. All the while, all other agency functions must be pursued. Given the short-term time horizons of many governors, legislators, and agency heads, the sorts of long-term resource commitments that must be made and implementation delays that must be endured before benefits can be claimed in programs like FWP may indeed defer their development and expansion in New Jersey and elsewhere.

A further managerial impediment is the possible reluctance of other agency officials and units to cooperate with an FWP-type program. Although the program assembled a staff with diverse talents, it continually relied on other DEP units for input and approval. Many officials of other programs, including traditional medium-oriented entities, clearly resented the distinctive status accorded the FWP program, with its initial location on the elite seventh floor of the DEP offices and direct reporting line from the program director to the department commissioner. In many instances, the FWP staff struggled to secure timely and cooperative responses from program officials. As one industry representative, quoted in a report published by the Tellus Institute, noted, "A typical air inspector wants to see 'the pink form' and does not understand why there is no pink form. He may leave miffed."[35] It is difficult to calculate the costs added when other agency units shirk their responsibility to cooperate, but this lack of cooperation clearly exacerbated the problems of resource intensity needed for FWP programs.

Political Vicissitudes

Most environmental permitting occurs well below the political radar screens of elected officials, agenda heads, the media, or the general public. Usually only fundamental breakdowns in the existing system—most commonly, egregious pollutant releases at a facility or horrific backlogs in permit approval—ever receive much attention. In contrast, the New Jersey FWP program and related pollution prevention legislation have been extremely high-profile initiatives, spanning a series of partisan shifts in the executive and legislative branches of New Jersey government. Actions launched by these respective branches in recent years have further undermined the viability of the FWP program.

The 1991 New Jersey Pollution Prevention Act provides a cornerstone on which all FWP activities are based. During 1994 and 1995, a prime time in the life of the program as it began to move beyond pilot status to work with a larger and more diverse set of cases, a series of legislative challenges weakened confidence in the future of the FWP program. Amendments to the act introduced in both the state assembly and the senate did not address FWP directly but proposed fundamental changes in the pollution prevention planning process pivotal to FWP operation. These amendments would have eliminated the existing DEP definition of nonproduct output, allowed facilities submitting pollution prevention plans to treat many recycling activities as tantamount to prevention and reduction, established an earlier year as a baseline for comparisons of pollution prevention progress, and reduced reporting requirements on toxic chemical use.[36] These amendments were approved in the assembly in January 1995 but perished in the senate before the November 1995 statewide election. They received statewide media attention and were aggressively attacked by leading environmental groups such as the New

Jersey Environmental Federation. Groups representing major industries, such as the Chemical Industry Council, contended that reporting requirements reflected an overly expansive interpretation of the 1991 legislation by DEP officials and threatened the economic competitiveness of many New Jersey firms. Assemblyman Paul DiGaetano, cosponsor of the amendments, noted the international preeminence of such New Jersey industries as pharmaceuticals and argued, "If the amendment isn't approved, pharmaceutical manufacturers will stop producing, produce less or, worse, produce it somewhere else."[37]

Throughout the battles over the amendments, the FWP program never emerged as a target of criticism. It frequently was singled out for praise by elected officials and important stakeholders during the period. But while not directly implicated, the viability of the permitting program and the completion of the initial permits hinged on clear definitions of such matters as nonproduct output and what did—and did not—constitute pollution prevention. This legislative uncertainty followed several years of unsuccessful chemical industry challenges through the courts to the state's pollution prevention program. Next, a series of related New Jersey regulatory reform proposals, including the easing of a number of specific regulatory provisions, were signed into law during the mid-1990s, bringing into uncertainty some programs with direct relevance to the FWP program effort.[38] Consequently, the legislation underpinning the FWP initiative was on fragile political and legal footing through many important years of FWP implementation.

Executive Branch Changes: Cutting Staff

The pollution prevention legislation remained intact ultimately, but the agency and office charged with implementation did not. The Whitman administration's commitment to major reductions in state spending resulted in a decline of total DEP staff from 3,707 in January 1994 to 3,147 by October 1996.[39] The pollution prevention and FWP program staff were not targeted, although the various waves of cutbacks unleashed administrative bumping between personnel that wreaked havoc on the permitting program. Project Manager Steven Anderson, a pivotal figure in all stages of the program's development and implementation, was bumped to risk assessment duties in the Superfund program. He was replaced by a senior staff person from the pesticide laboratory, an individual lacking any experience in permitting. Anderson was eventually shifted back to FWP but finally left the agency in frustration. He has become a nationally recognized leader in consulting on pollution prevention issues. "We faced significant cuts for three straight years and it really dug into the program and the agency," he recalled. "People would get shifted, then returned, then shifted back again. There was constant uncertainty, the staff got demoralized, and facilities were very upset with all of the uncertainty."[40] The FWP team shifted after each round of budget cuts and the inevitable pattern of personnel shuffling throughout the DEP. According to Catherine Cowan, DEP assistant commissioner for environmental regulation, in 1996: "Most of [the facility-wide permit staff] have been there as a team for the past several years. Some of these people were there from the beginning and there will be a long learning curve for the people who come in."[41]

The DEP staffing cuts and their impact on programs like FWP have become an ongoing topic of debate in New Jersey since the mid-1990s. The Whitman administration contended that it promoted regulatory innovation and that any adverse policy impacts attributable to budget cuts stemmed from "a rigid system of bumping rights" that state employee unions were unwilling to alter.[42] It also insisted that it made a great effort to maintain, and in some instances expand, staff in innovative program areas. For example, DEP Chief of Staff Mark Smith wrote that the "total staff complement" of the Office of Pollution Prevention increased during the Whitman years, "a reflection of the Department's increasing emphasis on pollution prevention and facilitywide approaches to environmental management."[43]

In response, environmental groups and other critics of the cuts contend that the Whitman administration had a devastating impact on many important functions within the DEP. Groups such as the Stockton Alliance, formed in 1996 to represent a coalition of New Jersey corporate and environmental group leaders, and many state legislators, including several Republicans otherwise loyal to Whitman, offered outspoken criticism of the administration on environmental funding cuts.[44] "You can massage the numbers, I suppose, but it is awfully hard to argue that staffing for prevention and [facility-wide] permitting have somehow increased," noted one senior Republican legislator. "The DEP has just been decimated by these cuts, with the average person in the department totally demoralized. People getting bounced around the department had no idea what they were supposed to do, even at the clerical level."

Reorganizing the Office of Pollution Prevention

Confusion over staffing changes was compounded by a massive reorganization of the DEP Office of Pollution Prevention during 1996 and 1997. Under the reorganization, several other functions were brought together in the newly named Office of Pollution Prevention and Permit Coordination. Most notably, computer support for all regulatory programs and the programs designed to accelerate permit decisions through preapplication conferences and "fast-tracking" efforts were now housed within the same office as other pollution prevention initiatives.[45] The ethos of this office is much more oriented to the kind of permit streamlining efforts in states such as Oklahoma and Colorado, as earlier emphases on integration and prevention have become more peripheral.

Jeanne Herb remained in charge of the FWP program after the reorganization but no longer headed the office or reported directly to the commissioner. In September 1997, she announced a one-year leave of absence from the DEP to work at the Boston-based Tellus Institute for Resource and Environmental Strategies. One year later, she resigned from the DEP to take a permanent position with Tellus. The loss of Herb, coupled with the departure of Anderson, was a devastating setback for the program. Herb was widely acknowledged as the agency entrepreneur behind the program, respected for her capacity to build coalitions and move the program forward; Anderson had a unique grasp of the diverse technical elements necessary to complete an FWP process. Other talented staff remained, although subject to periodic bumping and budget cuts, but many observers contend the program suffered an enormous loss of leadership and capability through these two departures.

Some observers view the reorganization of the program and downgrading of Herb's status as a political payback, since her husband, Jeff Scott, worked for state environmental groups and a union that represented many DEP employees. Scott was an outspoken critic of Whitman administration budget cuts, placing Herb in a precarious political position, particularly as the 1997 election cycle began. Before her departure from the DEP, she was not allowed to speak with reporters or researchers unless a political appointee of the Whitman administration was present. "I have never seen anything like it," noted the head of a neighboring state's pollution prevention program. "It was as if Jeanne had to have a chaperone everywhere she went. Here was this national expert on pollution prevention and she had to have a political monitor at state expense during a budget crisis."

Media Scrutiny

Like other experimental programs that offer firms the possibility of increased flexibility in compliance, the New Jersey FWP has served as a lightning rod in receiving both favorable and negative media attention, contrary to the general pattern of media indifference to permitting except when outright malfeasance or extreme backlogs in permit issuance occur.[46] Alongside the positive coverage at permit signing ceremonies, the FWP took some significant political hits from journalists who contended that the program constituted a sell-out to major New Jersey firms. As part of a series of articles and editorials condemning almost every aspect of the Whitman administration's environmental record, for example, the *Bergen Record* attacked integrated permitting efforts in dramatic exposé style in 1996.[47] The newspaper examined some of the initial FWPs and contended that, in certain cases, some facility emissions had increased over a given year or period of time. Moreover, it noted that at least two of the early permit recipients had been cited for some prior violations of New Jersey environmental laws and therefore argued that they should not have been allowed to participate in the FWP program. On the whole, the accounts did not dismiss the concept of facility-wide permitting but alleged that the New Jersey program reflected a general pattern of capture of state regulatory authorities by regulated parties under the Whitman administration. Officials of the DEP, environmental groups, and industry concur that this type of visible assault did damage the image of the program, especially after the authors received an award for their coverage from a national environmental group.

The media coverage highlighted one potential political problem such a program may face. Under traditional permitting approaches, it is practically impossible to construct an overall profile of facility emissions and compare these over time, making any comprehensive assessment of facility environmental impact exceedingly difficult. But under the FWP approach, comprehensive emissions tables give a straightforward account of total facility activities as they relate to the environment. So, if previously undiscovered emissions are calculated into permits or certain chemical substitutions are made within a plant, some facility-wide emissions as registered on paper will increase from prior allowances. These can easily be seized on to allege environmental irresponsibility.

Moreover, manufacturing expansion or change in product lines may indeed result in an increase in some emissions; this will show up clearly in the facility-wide permit but will be virtually impossible to tease out of conventional permits. In the case of the Schering permit, for example, some increases in certain emissions were allowed for development of a new product, manufacture of the popular antiallergy drug Claritin. The *Bergen Record* authors seized on these sorts of changes as environmental outrages and focused on those chemical uses most likely to increase under the terms of the permit. In their view, any increase in any emission at any time, regardless of manufacturing process changes or chemical substitutions to foster pollution prevention, constituted an abuse of regulatory flexibility. "If the reporters had looked at product lines they would see huge efficiency gains and come away with a very different picture," explained a veteran FWP staff member. "Plus, they completely ignored the fact that they could not begin to generate comparable numbers or scores for other facilities [in New Jersey or elsewhere] because most other facilities don't know what they release or don't know what they have to report." Nonetheless, the kind of flexibility and extensive data disclosures incorporated into programs such as FWP in New Jersey leave them vulnerable to such attack, contrary to the continued capacity of traditional programs to preclude construction of a comprehensive picture of environmental impacts. Indeed, such political problems have emerged in some other states that have begun to experiment with other kinds of regulatory alternatives, including Arizona, Minnesota, and Oregon.

Prospects for Continuation and Diffusion

Despite the managerial and political challenges facing the program, the FWP program is still expected to issue its final two permits and revise existing ones, as authorized under legislation. However, it remains uncertain whether this program will be a one-time experiment or a model for future permitting in New Jersey and other states. The questions over intensive use of resources to complete an FWP, the absence of the legislatively mandated evaluation of the program, and the revolving door of program leadership have clouded the future of this approach and its prospects for expanded use in New Jersey and other states. A pair of proposals has been made to build on the FWP experience in recent years, although the future of the suggestions remains uncertain. First, legislation was introduced into the New Jersey Senate in the late 1990s to expand the initial program and provide a more secure funding base through a per pound fee on the use of hazardous substances by designated industries. However, these proposals never received extended consideration. Second, the DEP's most recent strategic planning efforts have utilized elements of the general approach advanced under FWP as part of a broader initiative to promote regulatory innovation.[48] The DEP is exploring methods that might allow the state to designate different regulatory status—or "tracks"—for regulated parties, depending on their overall environmental management record and future commitment to go "beyond compliance." Under this system, the most innovative and promising firms would be accorded distinctive status (labeled the "Gold Track" in one version) that would allow them to participate in specialized programs designed to couple flexibility with outstanding environmental performance. Among the key elements of this approach, some variation on the facility-wide permit theme would be included, possibly with other aspects of the regulatory process. "There would clearly be some key ingredients from facility-wide permitting put into this, even if it is called something else," explained a senior DEP official. However, this transition remains in early stages despite several years of deliberation, leaving the FWP legacy in limbo in New Jersey.

Beyond New Jersey, the state's FWP program has begun to be scrutinized closely by many other environmental agency and industry officials. New Jersey officials have spent much time briefing counterparts from Delaware, Massachusetts, Pennsylvania, and Vermont, among other states, as well as regional and national EPA officials, congressional staff, and government representatives from Canada and Germany. None of these interactions, however, has resulted in any formal adoption of the FWP approach in another jurisdiction.

The mid-1990s discussions between Pennsylvania and New Jersey officials on FWP are instructive, demonstrating the interest in the concept and the difficulty of translating that interest into practice. "New Jersey people went to Pennsylvania; Pennsylvania people went to New Jersey," recalled a senior official of the Pennsylvania DEP. Out of these broad deliberations, one regional office director of the Pennsylvania DEP took the lead and began to work with Sun Oil Company, located near Philadelphia, to explore the feasibility of a pilot FWP. There was no statutory foundation for this experiment, but great interest from both parties and early guidelines established through study of the New Jersey experience. This attempt quickly failed, however. The Pennsylvania DEP underwent a major reorganization, and new staff leaders responsible for pollution prevention were far less interested in exploring ways to use permitting to promote prevention. The FWP supporters within the agency encountered substantial resistance from officials in medium-specific programs whose cooperation was essential. "A number of us thought that this was the way to go, to try to develop a pilot or two and take advantage of what New Jersey had already learned about looking holistically at a facility," explained the DEP official. "But the majority of staff said that there was nothing to be gained from it and the lack of support from the top of the agency and the lack of a statute just killed it."

This pattern is typical of other states that have examined more far-reaching permit initiatives but generally backed away because of intra-agency problems and lack of state political support. However, Pennsylvania has not abandoned the idea to move beyond its permit streamlining efforts with initiatives designed to link permitting with integration and pollution prevention. The 1998 *Report of the Pennsylvania 21st Century Environment Commission* strongly endorses this linkage.[49] In addition, recent initiatives have emphasized improving the quality of information generated through permits and other regulatory tools and making them more publicly accessible.

These efforts have been gathered under the Foundation for Information eXchange (FIX) Project, headed by a team of Pennsylvania DEP officials with funding support from general departmental revenues and a special EPA grant of $950,000. This project has attempted to gather a series of important compliance indicators, including performance on permit implementation, for regulated facilities in Pennsylvania. "We have been trying to integrate data across programs so that you can begin to look at all programs for a single site or facility," explained a DEP official. "Once we integrate that data, it can become the core or hub of the permit system. In fact, we're trying to build the history of permits into the system and also bring in compliance actions, like violations for each facility."

One added dimension of this effort has been the attempt not only to gather this information in a unified fashion but to make it widely available to the general public through the Internet.[50] Officials in the DEP are hopeful that this approach will give the public a better idea of what is occurring within individual facilities, as well as enable the agency to consider more integrative approaches and target serious problems that might otherwise have gone undetected. "We can find out where violations are occurring, which we never really could before," noted the official. "Plus, it is there for the world to see." The long-term future of this initiative remains uncertain, both because of resistance from medium-based program officials, who "see this as an encroachment on their power base," and because of the lack of assured funding to implement and expand the program.

Neither Colorado nor Oklahoma has demonstrated this willingness to experiment, focusing instead on the sorts of permit streamlining efforts discussed above. There has, however, been a single-case experiment completed in Oklahoma, involving a cooperative effort between the EPA and state DEP, that has resulted in the issuance of an air permit designed to promote pollution prevention in exchange for greater regulatory flexibility. This Oklahoma case involves the Imation Corporation facility in Weatherford, a manufacturer of computer diskettes, operating under the auspices of the EPA's experimental Pollution Prevention in Permitting Program (P4). This program was launched in the mid-1990s, largely through the entrepreneurial efforts of staff in EPA region 10, based in Seattle. The Imation permit is one of a set of eight cases in which the EPA has attempted, with extensive input from state agency officials, to broker an air permit that would satisfy all Title V provisions at a specific facility and offer compliance flexibility in the event that certain pollution prevention commitments were made.

This P4 permit, consistent with others issued to date, offers Imation a set of provisions designed to provide far more latitude for making changes in the use of various raw materials. It also establishes "pre-approved classes of modifications" that would normally lead to minor New Source Review processes for criteria pollutants and toxics. These classes include, for example, "modification, installation, construction, and reconstruction of specified emission units."[51] In exchange for these benefits, Imation and other participants in the P4 program must incorporate into the permit an outline of a facility pollution prevention program, including provisions for a prevention "leadership review," creation of facility pollution prevention goals, and mechanisms for reporting and documenting pollution prevention activities. The development of the pollution prevention portion of the permit is characterized as "voluntary," but the regulatory flexibility provisions are directly linked to its incorporation.

The P4 approach offers some of the types of trade-offs evident in the New Jersey FWP cases. However, P4 remains confined to air quality issues, thereby limiting its overall scope. Moreover, the pollution prevention provisions included in the Imation permit are very general, far less detailed or expansive than in any of the FWPs issued thus far in New Jersey. Furthermore, these provisions are not enforceable, and it remains unclear how closely the allowances for flexibility will be linked to the implementation of the pollution prevention provisions. And, perhaps even more than in the case of the New Jersey FWP program, the long-term status of P4 is very uncertain within the EPA and its state participants. There is no federal statutory foundation for the P4 program, no commitment by the Bush administration to sustain it, and no indication that Oklahoma has any plan to build on the Imation experience as a broader model for the state. Instead, this experience remains an isolated exception to Oklahoma's emphasis on streamlining.

Conclusions

More than thirty years ago, the executive order that led to the creation of the U.S. Environmental Protection Agency set forth a compelling rationale for development of an integrative and prevention-oriented regulatory system. The statement lamented the tradition of medium-based programs and emphasized the need to bring about a new approach that brought together various programs and administrative units in an integrative manner. It emphasized that "a far more effective approach to pollution control would: identify pollutants; trace them through the entire ecological chain, observing and recording changes in form as they occur; determine the total exposure of man and his environment; examine interactions among forms of pollution; and identify where in the ecological chain interdiction would be most appropriate."[52]

The common theme linking the blizzard of reports and books analyzing the current state of American environmental policy reiterates, in essence, that 1970 message signed by President Richard Nixon. After the expenditures of tens of billions of dollars and passage of hundreds of environmental statutes at the federal and state levels, many of the problems in environmental policy highlighted around the time of the first

Earth Day persist. This is not to suggest that recent decades of policy have been wholly ineffective. Indeed, compelling analyses show significant instances of environmental improvement, often in the face of expansion of industrial activity, population, and usage of automobiles.[53] Nonetheless, the fundamental critique remains as persuasive today as in 1970; the basic fault lines of environmental regulatory programs and institutions leave gaping holes that limit the overall effectiveness of American environmental policy.

This chapter underscores the severity of those problems but also suggests that thinking about integration and prevention need not be some rhetorical exercise. Recent experience from select states, most notably that of the New Jersey FWP program, suggests that it is possible to construct policy that systematically moves toward significant reduction of fugitive emissions, captures previously undetected cross-media transfers, and seizes missed opportunities to register important gains in pollution prevention. These are significant accomplishments when weighed against the rather ethereal nature of many discussions of environmental policy reform, even though they are tempered by the managerial and political problems that this program has encountered in recent years. At the same time, lessons from those states that have emphasized permit streamlining suggest that it may be possible to clarify and routinize basic elements of the regulatory process that at present waste scarce public and private resources. The Oklahoma experience in particular shows that the opportunity exists within current statutory requirements to establish a hierarchy that devotes differing degrees of resources to permits on the basis of perceived risk. This comparative case study of the current status of permitting and innovation suggests the following broad guidelines for the future.

Finding the Most Appropriate Federal Role

It has been common to associate much that is wrong in American environmental policy with the federal government and to characterize states as powerhouses of creativity waiting to be unleashed. That depiction has merit, but this analysis suggests that the intergovernmental realities of integration and prevention are much more complex. Some states, such as New Jersey, have indeed demonstrated a capacity to innovate that targets directly some of the major system shortcomings regularly lamented by critics. Nonetheless, New Jersey has found it very difficult to sustain these efforts. And other states do not approach this capacity, as they focus almost exclusively on the laudable but limited goal of improving "customer satisfaction" with the regulatory process. Full-blown decentralization of regulatory authority, on the order of the current experiment in welfare policy, would shift authority to states with very different levels of competence and commitment.[54] Concerns over interstate "races to the bottom" in the event of devolution are probably exaggerated, but many states do appear unprepared to step up to the formidable challenges of integration and prevention.

These cases also suggest that it is inappropriate to characterize the federal government exclusively as a rigid defender of archaic rules that deter a more effective system of environmental management. In each of the most promising areas of innovation outlined in this chapter—the New Jersey FWP program, the information integration efforts in Pennsylvania, and the P4 permit in Oklahoma—the federal government has actively facilitated change. Washington has provided needed funding support and demonstrated a willingness to work cooperatively, most notably through the role of regional offices of the federal agency. Even in hugely complex regulatory matters, such as interpretation of Title V permit guidelines under the 1990 Clean Air Act Amendments, federal and state officials have attempted to work collaboratively and use these permits to foster greater integration than traditional point-source-by-point-source review.[55] "Everybody points to Title V as a big problem and EPA can be a real stickler on the details," noted one veteran of the New Jersey FWP program. "But you can also look to it as an opportunity, as we did. Title V does bring a lot of things together on one piece of paper and states can do creative things with it and other regulations if they want to. We're at a point where, on a lot of issues, if a state wants to come forward and try some larger, integrated things, they can get support for that from the feds."

All of this is not to suggest that the federal government has somehow transformed itself and an era of cooperative federalism is about to emerge. But during the 1990s the federal government offered an array of initiatives to encourage states to try new things. These ranged from pilot programs, such as P4, to regional support for state initiatives, such as FWP, to the more recent NEPPS experiments that offer greater flexibility in exchange for demonstrated willingness to innovate. Relatively little systematic analysis of these initiatives has been completed, and it is indeed possible that they could disappear now that national political leadership has changed, just as some of the more promising regulatory experiments of the earlier Bush administration were de-emphasized or gutted during the Clinton administration. Using these experiences to discern what does and does not work in fostering integration and prevention is essential in recrafting the federal role in environmental policy in the decade ahead. More generally, they offer an opportunity to move beyond conventional debates over the respective virtues of centralized versus decentralized approaches toward a more nuanced understanding based on empirical findings of federal and state performance.

Overcoming Fragility

One of the most common features of efforts to promote integration and prevention is their political fragility. Just as a change of political leadership may obliterate recent initiatives at the federal level, the same tendency is evident in state capitals. This vulnerability is heightened by the fact that many of the most promising new steps taken by states or at the federal level have lacked any statutory foundation. Instead, they often represent intra-agency initiatives that reflect a temporary coalition and are easily terminated given the rapid turnover rate of agency and elected leadership. The arrival of term limitations for legislators in nearly half of the states may only accelerate these trends in upcoming years.[56]

The New Jersey FWP program remains unique among permit integration innovation because of its scope and unique statutory base. The 1991 New Jersey Pollution Prevention Act provided formal support for the program and authorized an expansion from its initial pilot project. This created an unusually solid footing for implementation, despite later managerial and political problems that emerged. "We really wanted to get to the point where New Jersey was and spent a lot of time talking about facility-wide permitting," recalled one Pennsylvania DEP official. "But they had a specific statute and we didn't. Without one, it is hard to get very far." Almost all of the other state and federal innovations discussed in this chapter lack such a legislative foundation. This places them in a precarious state, facing an enormous challenge of securing cooperation from potentially reluctant agency, industry, and environmental group participants, especially when the presidency or governorships change hands.

Firm legislative steps to encourage and facilitate the next generation of environmental management would provide a far more solid basis to learn from and build on rather than just continuing to experiment on an ad hoc basis. One illustration of a state statute that offers formal and ongoing support for such initiatives is the Minnesota Environmental Regulatory Innovations Act. Passed unanimously by both legislative chambers and signed into law by then-governor Arne Carlson in April 1996, this legislation concluded that "environmental protection could be further enhanced by authorizing innovative advances in environmental regulatory methods"[57] The legislation built on the prior decades of regulatory experimentation in Minnesota, including a range of integration and prevention initiatives that place it alongside New Jersey and a few other states as the most active in these areas in the nation. It also responded to a strong state desire to participate fully in various experimental federal programs, including some of the ones discussed earlier, and provided a strong charge to the Minnesota Pollution Control Agency (MPCA) to explore intrastate or intergovernmental innovation opportunities.

The federal government might begin to establish a more promising footing for more expansive development and testing of regulatory alternatives through passage of legislation that actively encourages state-level experimentation and supports institutionalization of those initiatives that demonstrate measurable environmental improvement. A new administration searching for environmental policy achievements might use such a base to launch a constructive period of experimentation. Such legislation could prove useful in sorting out the respective successes and failures of the states through better definition of the goals sought by experimental programs and development of criteria for evaluating their performance.

Integrated permitting would be a logical place to begin legislatively authorized innovation, perhaps drawing directly on the New Jersey experience. New legislation could encourage the EPA to give a designated number of states formal authority to negotiate facility-wide permits with select industries or sectors deemed most capable of adapting to such a system and likely to reduce releases significantly through such an initiative. Federal Performance Partnership Grants, and the NEPPS process more generally, might be linked more systematically with these kinds of specific steps, rewarding the most promising state initiatives with greater funding and regulatory latitude.

Such steps might also yield thinking about how existing statutes might be rewritten to better encourage core integration and prevention goals. After a decade in which relatively little new environmental legislation has been enacted, established medium-based and related programs are due to be reexamined by Congress. Even the 1990 Clean Air Act Amendments, among the "newest" pieces of federal environmental legislation, will warrant a legislative revisit in the coming years. Perhaps the current search for areas where bipartisan initiatives could be launched might eschew piecemeal reauthorization. It might be supplemented with a big picture approach that contemplates a design of environmental legislation that begins to approach the integrative goals set forth by President Nixon at the time that the EPA was created.

All of this could lead to far more fundamental reforms than attempted by any recent presidency. Indeed, a Bush administration proposal for a unifying environmental statute would be particularly daring, given its early stumbles in environmental policy and the reluctance of previous Republican and Democratic administrations to take such bold steps. Such legislation could give substantial regulatory latitude to those states that demonstrated significant capacity to move "beyond compliance" with creative prevention and integration initiatives that delivered superior environmental protection. This legislation would, in all likelihood, create a two-tiered system of regulatory federalism, retaining traditional federal oversight of less effective states but accelerating devolution for their more active counterparts. It would be more far reaching than the NEPPS approach, possess a statutory foundation, and utilize incentives to allow states to think more seriously about their commitment to forging the next generation of environmental policy. If states could demonstrate their capacity to deliver superior environmental performance, they would be entitled to the regulatory latitude and added federal resources that they have long craved. If they cannot demonstrate such capacity, regulatory business-as-usual may still be in order.

Notes to Chapter 2

1. Mary Graham, *The Morning After Earth Day* (Brookings, 1999), p. 108.

2. See, especially, chapter 3 by Shelley H. Metzenbaum in this volume.

3. These case studies draw heavily on semistructured interviews with more than forty state, federal, and private sector environmental managers between 1999 and 2001. Most of these interviews were conducted with the understanding that their remarks would not be directly attributed. Permission was secured to make direct attribution in a few instances where it proved extremely difficult to veil source identity.

4. J. Clarence Davies and Jan Mazurek, *Pollution Control in the United States: Evaluating the System* (Washington: Resources for the Future,1998), p. 222.

5. Council of State Governments, *Resource Guide to State Environmental Management*, 5th ed. (Lexington, Ky.: Council of State Governments, 1999); James P. Lester, "A New Federalism? Environmental Policy in the States," in Norman J. Vig and Michael E. Kraft, eds., *Environmental Policy in the 1990s* (Washington: Congressional Quarterly, 1994), pp. 51–68; and Jeffrey L. Brudney, F. Ted Hebert, and Deil S. Wright, "Reinventing Government in the American States: Measuring and Explaining Administrative Reform," *Public Administration Review*, vol. 59 (January–February 1999), pp. 19–30.

6. U.S. Office of Technology Assessment, *Environmental Policy Tools: A User's Guide* (Washington, 1995); Deborah Hitchcock Jessup, *Guide to State Environmental Programs*, 2d ed. (Washington: Bureau of National Affairs, 1990); Barry G. Rabe, *Fragmentation and Integration in State Environmental Management* (Washington: Conservation Foundation, 1986).

7. U.S. Environmental Protection Agency, *Multimedia Pollution Prevention Permitting Project* (Washington, 1997).

8. David Clarke, "Oklahoma Permit Streamlining Initiative Called Reform Model," *State Environmental Monitor*, May 6, 1996, p. 15; Oklahoma Department of Environmental Quality, *FY98 Annual Report* (Oklahoma City, 1999), pp. 46–47.

9. Oklahoma Department of Environmental Quality, *FOCUS* (Oklahoma City, 1998), p. 10.

10. Oklahoma Department of Environmental Quality, *FY98 Annual Report*, p. 48.

11. Oklahoma Department of Environmental Quality, *Environmental Management for Oklahoma and the Nation: FY96 Annual Report* (Oklahoma City, 1997).

12. Oklahoma Department of Environmental Quality, *FY98 Annual Report*, p. 28.

13. Thomas Birkland, *After Disaster: Agenda Setting, Public Policy, and Focusing Events* (Georgetown University Press, 1998); and Frank Baumgartner and Bryan Jones, *Agendas and Instability in American Politics* (University of Chicago Press, 1993).

14. John Brehm and Scott Gates, *Working, Shirking, and Sabotage: Bureaucratic Response to a Democratic Public* (University of Michigan Press, 1997), p. 3.

15. Sandford Borins, *Integrating with Integrity* (Georgetown University Press, 1998), pp. 50–51.

16. Michael Mintrom, *Policy Entrepreneurs and School Choice* (Georgetown University Press, 2000).

17. Denise Scheberle, *Trust and the Politics of Implementation: Federalism and Environmental Policy* (Georgetown University Press, 1998).

18. Telephone conversation with Robert Hersh, July 6, 1999.

19. Susan W. Schuler, "New Jersey's Pollution Prevention Act of 1991: A Regulation That Even the Regulated Can Enjoy," *Seton Hall Legislative Journal*, vol. 16 (1992), pp. 814–42.

20. Barry G. Rabe, "Integrated Environmental Permitting: Experience and Innovation at the State Level," *State and Local Government Review*, vol. 27 (Summer 1995), pp. 209–20.

21. Interview with Jeanne Herb, Trenton, N. J., 1999.

22. Interview with Steven Anderson, Trenton, N. J., 1999.

23. Quoted in Peter Fairley, "TRI: Growing Pains," *Chemical Week*, June 12, 1996, pp. 18–20.

24. Office of the Governor, News Release, March 21, 1991, Trenton, N. J.

25. Peter Page, "Praised by Whitman, DEP Program Gutted by Cuts," *Gloucester Times*, June 12, 1996, p. 3.

26. Barry G. Rabe, "Federalism and Entrepreneurship: Explaining American and Canadian Innovation in Pollution Prevention and Regulatory Integration," *Policy Studies Journal*, vol. 27, no. 2 (1999), pp. 288–306.

27. *New Jersey Register*, September 7, 1993, pp. 4075–79.

28. Interview with Herb, 1999.

29. Interview with Anderson, 1999.

30. Barry G. Rabe, "Power to the States: The Promise and Pitfalls of Decentralization," in Norman J. Vig and Michael E. Kraft, eds., *Environmental Policy: New Directions for the Twenty-First Century* (Washington: Congressional Quarterly Press, 2000), p. 42.

31. Interview with Herb, 1999.

32. William Lowry, *The Dimensions of Federalism: State Governments and Pollution Control Policies* (Duke University Press, 1992).

33. Quoted in Kelly Richmond and Dunstan McNichol, "Lost in the Process: Vow to Cut Pollution," *Bergen Record*, June 23, 1996, pp. A1, A9–A11.

34. Quoted in Tom Barron, "N.J. a Test Bed for Multimedia Permits," *Environment Today*, vol. 5 (November 1994), p. 1.

35. Tellus Institute, *The Potential and Pitfalls of Innovative Permits: Lessons from New Jersey's Facility-Wide Permit Program* (Boston, 1999), p. 58.

36. Gordon Bishop, "Industry Sees a Plan Gone Astray in Jersey's Bid to Curb Pollution," *Sunday Star-Ledger*, February 20, 1994, p. 1; and Joseph F. Sullivan, "Assembly Backs a Revision of Law on Toxic Chemicals," *New York Times*, January 24, 1995, p. B2.

37. Sullivan, "Assembly Backs a Revision of Law on Toxic Chemicals," p. B2.

38. Alan Rosenthal, *The Decline of Representative Democracy: Process, Participation, and Power in the State Legislatures* (Washington: Congressional Quarterly Press, 1998), p. 212.

39. Amy Collings, Telefacsimile transmission from press office, New Jersey Department of Environmental Protection, Trenton, November 20, 1996.

40. Interview with Anderson, 1999.

41. Quoted in Page, "Praised by Whitman," p. 3.

42. News release from the Office of the Governor, Trenton, 1996.

43. Mark O. Smith, Letter to Lawrence O'Reilly, assistant attorney general, State of New Jersey, April 21, 1997.

44. "Business, Environmental Alliance Opposes New Jersey DEP Budget Cuts," *State Environmental Monitor*, vol. 1 (May 6, 1996), pp. 7–8.

45. New Jersey Department of Environmental Protection, *Performance Partnerships for the Next Generation: Annual Report 1996* (Trenton, 1997).

46. John Fialka, "U.S. Falling Behind in Pollution Fight; Texas Leads Nation in Expired Permits," *Wall Street Journal*, March 14, 2000, p. A32.

47. Kelly Richmond and Dunstan McNichol, "Lack of Funding May Hinder New Success Stories," *Bergen Record* June 23, 1996, p. A-11.

48. New Jersey Department of Environmental Protection, *NJDEP Strategic Plan 1998–2001* (Trenton, 1999).

49. Pennsylvania 21st Century Environment Commission, *Report of the Pennyslvania 21st Century Environment Commission* (Harrisburg, 1998).

50. Shelley H. Metzenbaum, *Making Measurement Matter* (Brookings, 1998), p. 67; and Tom Arrandale, "Tracking Polluters with a Mouse," *Governing*, vol. 11, no. 4 (April 1998), p. 56.

51. Ross & Associates Environmental Consulting Ltd., *P4 Benefits Assessment* (Seattle, 1999), p. 12.

52. Richard M. Nixon, "Message of the President Relative to Reorganization Plans 3 and 4 of 1970," in *Environmental Quality: The First Annual Report of the Council on Environmental Quality* (Government Printing Office, 1970), p. 295.

53. J. Clarence Davies and Jan Mazurek, *Pollution Control in the United States: Evaluating the System* (Washington: Resources for the Future, 1998).

54. R. Kent Weaver, *Ending Welfare as We Know It* (Brookings, 2000).

55. For further discussion of Title V implementation problems and alternative approaches to compliance under consideration by the EPA, see John J. Fialka, "EPA Is Considering Increased Flexibility in Issuing Industry Air-Pollution Permits," *Wall Street Journal*, June 5, 2000, p. A3.

56. John M. Carey, Richard G. Niemi, and Lynda W. Powell, *Term Limits in the State Legislature*, (University of Michigan Press, 2000).

57. Minnesota Statute 114C.01 (1996).

CHAPTER THREE

Measurement That Matters: Cleaning Up the Charles River

SHELLEY H. METZENBAUM

*O*n October 22, 1995, the regional administrator of the U.S. Environmental Protection Agency's (EPA's) New England office, John DeVillars, proclaimed to the press and all who would listen that the long-contaminated Lower Charles River—running between Cambridge and Boston out to the Boston Harbor—would be clean enough for swimming by 2005. Hooray, river advocates cheered, daring to dream for what had so long seemed impossible. Outrageous, skeptics cried. The sources of contamination to the river were not even known. How could the river be clean enough to swim in within ten years?

Five years after the initial announcement, as this chapter is being written, DeVillars's promise is becoming reality. By April 2000, the

I am grateful to the members of the Executive Session on Public Sector Performance Management, Harvard University, Kennedy School of Government, and the members of the Environmental Compliance Consortium, University of Maryland School of Public Affairs. The participants in these projects have helped me understand and articulate the ideas presented in this chapter much more vividly than would have been possible otherwise. Ken Jones, Jason Morrison, and those who attended several roundtable Brookings discussions on environmental management convened between 1988 and 2000 also contributed many valuable suggestions to improve this chapter. Many of the people interviewed, notably Ken Moraff, Bill Walsh-Rogalski, and John De Villars, not only helped me learn about the Clean Charles initiative but also graciously reviewed and commented on the accuracy of this chapter.

*Lower Charles River was clean enough for boating 90 percent of the
time, up from 39 percent in 1995. It was safe for swimming 65 percent
of the time, compared with 19 percent of the time five years earlier.*[1]

Where is the story here? An environmental agency leader announces
an environmental goal. Progress toward the goal is measured. Progress
toward the goal is made. Most citizens would assume that this is what
environmental protection agencies and their leaders routinely do—identify environmental problems and opportunities, set goals for making
progress, direct attention and resources to the problem, make and measure progress toward the goal, and revise the strategy if it is not working.

Unfortunately, as any employee of an environmental regulatory
agency would tell you, this almost intuitive order of business is the
exception rather than the rule. Despite major federal and state environmental laws that set environmental goals, the decisions and compromises that get made during passage and implementation of the laws
often weaken the link between agency activities and environmental outcomes. In implementing these laws, both regulators and regulated parties tend to focus on activities and lose sight of the environmental outcomes sought. Although these activity-focused compromises are often
necessary and valuable in the short term, they can lose their value over
time if the focus on activities overwhelms attention to outcomes and the
connection between the activity and the environmental goal gets lost in
the implementation.

Perhaps the most striking example of this problem is the paltry state
of water quality information in the United States. To achieve rapid
advances in water quality, the 1972 Amendments to the Clean Water Act
concentrated on getting large wastewater dischargers to install equipment meeting national technology standards.[2] The law also included a
back-up strategy calling for states and the EPA to take additional actions
to meet water quality standards if the technology standards failed to
achieve them.[3] Yet almost thirty years after passage of the federal Clean
Water Act, water quality has been assessed for only 23 percent of the
nation's river miles, 43 percent of its lakes, and 32 percent of its estuar-
ies. Water quality data are available for only 5 percent of ocean shore-
lines.[4] How can federal and state agencies possibly meet water quality
standards if they do not even know how clean the waters are?

The system's concentration on activities seems to overwhelm its ability to clean up even those waters that have been assessed, only 40 percent of which currently meet water quality standards.[5] The problem is

that the program's early focus on controlling discharges from large sources through permits and routine inspection of permitted facilities has long consumed government attention. Maintaining this focus has left government agencies with limited additional resources to deal with other possible sources, even though the continued poor quality of assessed waters suggests that controlling only the permitted sources will be insufficient for meeting the standards. Government finally began to turn its attention to other sources in the late 1990s and early millennial years, primarily because environmental groups won a series of court cases compelling them to focus on the performance-focused provision of the law.[6]

At the same time, the EPA and states have honed their ability to measure activities. They can report how many permits have been issued, inspections conducted, enforcement actions initiated, and penalties assessed for wastewater treatment permit holders. Only one state, however, has actually attempted to track facility-specific and aggregate trends in discharges to the water to see if and how they have changed over time.[7] More attention is paid to ensuring that permits are renewed and inspections conducted than to tracking the individual and aggregate impact of permitted facilities on the environment.

Intergovernmental negotiations can also be extraordinarily activity focused, not because of venal intent on the part of any individual or organizational unit but because different EPA offices want to ensure accountability for the grants they send states. Before changes were made in 1995 to make the system more performance focused, each state was expected to enter into more than sixteen separate grant agreements with the EPA.[8] Each EPA headquarters program office that had grant money to send out to the states wrote a guidance document, instructing the EPA's regional offices about the national office's priorities and the commitments it expected the regions to secure from the states. A few regional offices then wrote their own guidance documents, articulating regional priorities, to complement those of the national office. The issuance of guidance documents for the multiple grants was neither synchronized nor predictable. As a result, states found it impossible to use their federal grant money in any strategic or coordinated manner to focus on environmental problems or deal with regulated facilities. They were too busy trying to accommodate the vagaries of the grant schedule and satisfy the intricacies of the numerous guidance documents. Instead, grant agreements focused on specific inputs and outputs to satisfy each annual guidance document, addressing details such as the personnel expenditure and the number of permits and inspections states promised to conduct in return for federal funds. Little, if any, mention was made of environmental issues.

The experience of Massachusetts in trying to conduct multimedia (air, water, and waste) inspections of regulated facilities exemplifies the frustrations that would arise when states tried to break away from the focus on activities. Multimedia approaches to environmental protection have long been advocated by national policy and program leaders, in part to avoid the problem of having a facility inspector from say, the water program, recommend a solution detrimental to the quality of the air. Despite national policy urging multimedia approaches that focus on environmental impacts, Massachusetts had to obtain prior approval from each of the EPA's separate grant-giving offices in the region and in EPA headquarters. It took Massachusetts more than three years to get federal approval to use federal funds for multimedia inspections.[9] The extensive time required for negotiating environmental outcome-focused changes exhausts all but the most ferocious performance advocate.

Counting activities is not a bad idea. It is, in fact, good operational practice. Studying how activity information is linked with outcome information can help program operators distinguish effective intervention strategies from those that are not. Moreover, in most cases, activities originally established as targets are selected because of logical assumptions about their connection to an environmental goal.

Over time, however, the activities become themselves the goal; the connection to the environmental outcomes they were designed to advance disappears. Offices and staff develop expertise in the activities and focus on what they know they can do and what others expect them to do, rather than assessing the efficacy of their own activities.[10]

Moreover, those managing activities assume great risk when they opt to analyze the legitimacy of their original presumptions about the activity-outcome connection. Who will commend an agency that takes the risk of assessing its activity-outcome assumptions if it discovers that its assumptions were wrong, and the agency's past work has had little impact? Although political supporters might be willing to defend an agency for objectively evaluating its own work, political opponents are likely to get more mileage lambasting the program for its ineffectiveness. The opponent will get the headline, decrying government waste, perhaps calling for a program's elimination; the defender, at best, will get a perfunctory one-line story noting his or her support for the bureaucracy. Not surprisingly, program managers might be wary of questioning activity-outcome assumptions.

Even political opponents have little motivation to press for objective evaluations of a program's effectiveness. They are just as well served by horror stories that serve their political needs as by carefully constructed evaluative analyses. Thus, unlike the private sector, where competition forces companies to revisit their assumptions about the links between their activities (for example, product quality, marketing campaigns) and outcomes (for example, profitability), few government agencies or legislators see much value in revisiting the activity-outcome link. It is politically safer to stay with the existing set of activities and not question original assumptions.

Nonetheless, too dominant a focus on activities and insufficient attention to the activity-outcome link steals time and resources away from measuring and making progress toward the final objective of environmental protection agencies—improving public health and the environment. Progress most likely gets made, but no one knows that for sure. Nor do the agencies have the ability to assess when, where, and why the progress is occurring. If no one asks whether activities that have always been done continue to be effective, few resources will be available to tackle more significant problems requiring different sorts of intervention.

This problem is not a secret deeply buried within the bowels of government. It is broadly recognized. Numerous high-level, multistakeholder, bipartisan groups have issued reports during the past decade sounding a common theme: the need for greater focus on environmental results and increased use of environmental performance information. The Enterprise for the Environment (E4E),[11] for example, recommended that the existing system be more "performance-based, information-driven, flexible in the means of meeting standards, open and transparent, and strictly accountable."[12] Two congressionally funded studies by the National Academy of Public Administration similarly recommend results-focused, priority-based, information-driven management of the environmental protection system.[13]

In recent years, many changes have been adopted to encourage a more performance-focused, information-driven environmental protection system. In May 1995 the EPA and leaders of state environmental protection agencies jointly committed to adopting a performance-focused environmental protection system, the National Environmental Performance Partnership System (NEPPS).[14] This system was adopted to get the EPA and states to use information about environmental and public health conditions and problems as the basis for determining annual (or biannual) work plans. Since 1995 thirty states have entered into some form of environmental performance partnership agreement.[15] Recent studies of NEPPS implementation praise NEPPS for allowing and encouraging both states and the EPA to focus more strictly on improving environmental outcomes than had previously been the case. The studies also find, however, that long-standing activity-focused routines have greatly hampered transition efforts.[16]

In 1995 the EPA also initiated Project XL to encourage performance-focused behavior by the regulated, as well as the regulators. Project XL offers companies and localities willing to deliver environmental performance superior to what would be achieved by full compliance with current laws and regulations more flexibility in complying with certain aspects of regulatory requirements. In one completed XL agreement, for example, the Intel Corporation agreed to achieve continually declining environmental emissions at one of its facilities at a rate in excess of what might otherwise be expected. It also promised to report publicly on its progress. In return, Intel was granted the ability to operate without seeking new permits for every production process change.[17]

By 2000 eighteen states and the EPA were experimenting with "performance track" systems. Although the programs vary, most seem to have two objectives. First, government seeks to reward regulated facilities with strong compliance and environmental track records and to encourage continuing and even stronger compliance and environmental performance in the future. Second, many performance-track experiments hope to motivate additional facilities to become strong performers in the future. To date, none of these efforts has made much headway in defining the performance that strong performers must exceed or finding incentives that are sufficiently enticing to invite a stampede of interest.[18] One significant impediment to performance-track efforts is the lack of generally accepted, facility-based environmental performance reporting standards.[19]

Interest in performance-focused environmental protection is not limited to the governments of the United States. Both the Netherlands and Denmark require environmental reporting from selected industrial sectors. Indonesia rates the environmental performance of companies. More than 300 companies worldwide produce corporate environmental reports; most include quantitative environmental performance information.[20]

Nor is interest in performance-focused governance limited to the environmental field. All but three of the fifty state governments require some sort of performance-based budgeting.[21] The Governmental Accounting and Standards Board began a project in the late 1980s to identify results indicators for twelve public services routinely provided by state and local governments.[22] Building on this effort, the International City/County Management Association and the Urban Institute began putting together a comparative performance measurement project for more than 200 local governments in 1995.[23]

At the federal level, Congress passed the Government Performance and Results Act of 1993 (GPRA), mandating that all federal agencies set performance goals, measure progress toward those goals, and report annually to Congress on that progress.[24] The GPRA builds on earlier efforts to shift the focus of federal agencies from inputs to outputs and finally to program results—real-world outcomes.[25] Several other countries have also mandated governmentwide performance management, including New Zealand, the United Kingdom, and Australia.[26]

Heightened attention to and the mandate for performance measurement at all levels of government in the United States and abroad reflect an unprecedented demand for improving the effectiveness of government programs. To some extent, the demand is driven by dramatic declines in citizens' confidence in government during the past several decades.[27] It is supplemented by the natural desires of those in government agencies who want to do their jobs well.

Performance management systems, and specifically, the increased use of performance measurement to run government programs and achieve improved social outcomes, hold particular promise for improving government performance. At the most basic level, outcome-focused, information-rich government holds great promise because it lets government agencies know whether or not they are accomplishing what they want to accomplish. It gives them information that enables them to do their jobs better. It allows and encourages those who work for government agencies to be more innovative and effective. It gives them the motivation and flexibility to apply their intelligence, experience, and ingenuity to pursue social gains. It allows them to be public sector entrepreneurs who look for serious problems and develop creative approaches to fixing them if existing approaches are insufficient.

Performance measures are valuable management tools because they provide a useful language for assessing progress, communicating priorities, coordinating across organizational units, and learning from experience. Further, they provide a useful language for aligning expectations with those outside government whose decisions affect an agency and for influencing those whose actions affect social outcomes. Finally, performance measures can engage citizens in fixing problems and can help citizens make smarter decisions when they need to make choices or purchases.

Although numerous examples exist of organizations and individuals using performance measurement to drive or guide improved performance, most government agency managers and workers still seem to be using performance measures primarily to fill out mandated annual reports. Interest groups are not paying attention to the content of the reports because they find so little in them useful. Legislators and other agency watchdogs are primarily monitoring whether reports are getting done, rather than debating whether an agency is doing the right things or brainstorming with the agency on how to accomplish objectives more effectively. Although there are a few noteworthy exceptions, most agencies that are using measures still seem to be focused on activity measures, rather than measures of "real world" outcomes.[28] That is certainly true for much of the EPA's GPRA reports.[29]

As suggested earlier, one reason why agencies may be collecting and reporting performance measures but not using them is fear. Some congressional advocates of the GPRA have clearly stated their hope that agency performance reports will provide ammunition to eliminate agencies or individual programs. Only the most daring or foolhardy government worker would deliver information that might contribute to the demise of his or her program, so many may intentionally, and very sensibly, try to deliver measurements that impart little useful information.

Another overwhelming problem is that few understand how performance measures can be used to improve government effectiveness. The politically appointed manager does not understand how measures can help him or her manage, especially in a political context. Performance measurement reports do not deliver re-election votes to incumbent presidents, governors, or mayors. They do not keep back the press of cantankerous legislators. They do not feed the media's need for a hot story. The time-scarce political appointee is likely to think, "Why bother, except to satisfy the mandate?" Career managers and the work force are even less enthusiastic. "We've seen this before," they say. "It takes a lot of time and doesn't deliver much in return. All it does is provide ammunition for our opponents. The less time spent on it, the better. This too will pass." The federal or state legislator interested in getting the agency's attention does not need performance measures. And few interest groups, hoping to find information to advance their cause, can afford the time to wade through the voluminous performance reports that governments deliver.

With so few enthusiasts, performance measurement and management may be on the road to failure. Unless the people in or affected by government programs begin to appreciate the enormous potential of performance information, mandated performance measurement could easily become just another activity requirement, a part of the problem it is intended to fix. Measurement fatigue will set in before performance gains are realized, indeed before people understand what public sector performance management means.

To avoid that danger, performance measurement needs to be useful to those who generate the measurements, those who are measured, and those who manage the system being measured. At its most powerful, it should also be useful to those outside an organization who are concerned that an agency makes progress toward its mission.

That is what makes the pledge to make the Charles River swimmable within ten years—dubbed the Clean Charles 2005 initiative—so intriguing. It works. It transforms performance measurement into a powerful performance management tool that is useful to a politically appointed manager, the career program manager, the program work force, the press, the public, and even regulated parties.

The Clean Charles 2005 Initiative: A Model

The Clean Charles 2005 initiative (hereafter the Charles initiative) exemplifies how outcome-focused performance measurement can be used to drive progress toward social objectives. Performance measurement enabled EPA New England's regional administrator, John DeVillars, to drive gains in water quality in the Lower Charles River. Setting a challenging but achievable performance goal effectively communicated DeVillars's priorities to those inside the agency and beyond. It energized staff, enlisted external allies, and placed gentle but effective pressure on those whose behavior needed to change. It allowed DeVillars and his staff to monitor progress toward the goal on a regular basis, making midcourse corrections as necessary. It established a motivating, but not punitive, accountability mechanism. After nearly a half-century of water quality too poor for safe swimming, dramatic gains in the quality of the water in the Lower Charles are now being realized. The Charles initiative provides a vivid example of how a government agency can use performance measures to get its job done.

The Charles initiative was born out of two enforcement actions affecting the river. Ken Moraff, an EPA lawyer working on the EPA's decade-long enforcement case against the Massachusetts Water Resources Authority (MWRA), was negotiating with the MWRA to control combined sewer overflow into the river. The MWRA was reluctant to make all the investments that the EPA wanted because it felt that its actions would not improve water quality enough to justify the investment, given all the other sources of river contamination. At the same time, Moraff was also about to initiate an enforcement action against the town of Brookline for illicit sewer connections to stormwater drains emptying into the Charles. Moraff took the Brookline case to DeVillars for discussion and sign-off, and DeVillars asked him to put the case in its environmental context.[30] He pressed Moraff to think about how resolution of the Brookline case would affect the quality of the river and whether the problems found in Brookline were likely to be evident in other communities. Without conceding to the MWRA's argument that fixing its combined sewer overflow problem was not going to make a difference, the EPA decided to look more comprehensively for sources of contamination to the Lower Charles.

Many different aspects of the Charles initiative are instructive for those interested in a better environmental protection system, as well as for those trying to use performance measures to manage the public sector more effectively (box 3-1).

Effective Performance Goals

Key to the success of the Charles initiative is establishment of a simple goal that resonates with the public and an equally simple method for communicating progress toward that goal. In his initial announcement in October 1995, DeVillars articulated a clear goal: the Charles River would be clean enough to swim in by 2005. Six months after announcing the initial goal, the EPA began reporting progress toward the goal

---

Box 3-1. *Model Qualities of the Clean Charles 2005 Initiative*

Key characteristics of goals
Simple, resonant, and understandable
Outcome focused
Time and location specific
Ambitious but feasible
Public

Key characteristics of progress measurements
Fresh (current)
Geographically and temporally frequent
Outcome focused
Credible
Audience appropriate (multiple measures for multiple users)
Readily available to meet needs

Key characteristics of how goals and measures are used
Regularly and interactively
To inspire and inform
To engage the media
To align expectations
To build collaboration and shared learning
For strategy accountability that is motivating, not punitive

---

using a simple grading system. On Earth Day 1996, the EPA awarded the Charles River its first grade, a D. By Earth Day 2000, the Charles River had brought its grade up to a B, like a good student showing steady improvement. Because the grades are so easily understood and the Charles River so familiar to the local community, the story is an obvious one for the media to report. What the Charles initiative recognizes is that simple performance goals and progress measurements are more than just bureaucratic indicators to be included in mandated reports. Rather, they are invaluable tools for communicating priorities and progress to staff, the media, and the public that, in turn, help managers drive continual progress toward the goal.

Goals Motivate

Simple, resonant goals can be motivating for the staff. Bill Walsh-Rogalski, current head of the Charles initiative, senses much greater staff energy and excitement associated with the Charles initiative and another results-focused project he manages than with other agency activities. "People are charged up about getting to results. They are willing to take risks and feel empowered to get things done. It is more challenging and more productive. It gets into psychology rather than management."[31]

The Clean Charles 2005 goal motivates for several reasons. First, goals motivate. Second, the Clean Charles goal taps into the motivational force of personal values. And finally, the Clean Charles goal excites the public, which can motivate agency staff.

People have a natural tendency to try to meet goals set for them. Social psychology research on the motivation of individual workers finds that workers given specific and challenging goals outperform those given a "'do-your-best' goal or no goal at all."[32] There are several reasons for this. "Goals provide us with a clear direction; inform us that we need to try hard; remind us that an end is in sight; and encourage us to think about the process of reaching that end."[33] Thus the simple act of establishing a goal, even without linking it to rewards, motivates improved progress toward that goal.

By honing organizational focus, goals can enhance organizational effectiveness. It seems reasonable to presume that the motivational effect of goals on individuals will translate to the organizations for which they work. The exception would be if individuals within an organization are working toward conflicting goals. In that situation, one worker's heightened motivation might offset that of another, wiping out the performance gain. If, however, organizational goals are clearly communicated, it increases the likelihood that workers and work units within an organization will focus on the organization's goals rather than their own.[34] Essentially, goals have a communication and attention-focusing function that is especially valuable for larger organizations.

Outcome Goals Are More Motivating

Goals can be even more motivating when they are outcome goals, what Walsh-Rogalski calls "results," if they align with workers' personal values or if they attract external attention that contributes to the motivational impetus.

Government agencies have the benefit of attracting many workers who want to serve the public and who believe in the general mission of these agencies. Setting an environmental performance goal allows environmental protection staff to do what they came to their agencies to do—improve the quality of the environment.

Outcome goals also motivate when they attract external attention, because external attention is motivating. Even many self-driven individuals find it useful to enlist external observers when they set targets. Indeed, Weight Watchers, Jenny Craig, and other diet-support companies are an entrepreneurial testimony to people's recognition that public exposure is a motivator for meeting performance goals. In the same way, media attention can increase the excitement for and pressure on government staff working on a project. It is affirming to get a good story in the paper about one's work, or to have a colleague from another organization offer commendation for progress being made. It can be even more affirming when that commendation is expressed as appreciation by friends and family for work that benefits the community. At the same time, it can be motivating to avoid the embarrassment of a story about the lack of progress toward a goal.

The sustained media coverage of the Charles River clean-up demonstrates that when government sets goals, it can be newsworthy. Boston's newspapers covered the initial goal-setting announcement.[35] They have given prominent play to the release of each annual progress report, covered major enforcement actions related to the goal, and reported major nonenforcement actions, such as new grant awards, affecting the river's water quality.[36] The *Boston Globe* dedicated a major Sunday magazine story to the "Renaissance on the Charles" and ran an op-ed by one of its columnists on the subject. It has also reported stories of occasional incidents, as when unusually high bacteria levels appeared.[37] These stories, which were more than small blips in the paper, have consistently received good coverage.

Press attention also helps staff secure resources to move the project ahead. In numerous ways, setting a public goal and public reporting at predictable intervals ensures that the agency remembers its environmental objective—improving the water quality of the river.

Media attention already drives behavior in government agencies but not always in ways that promise greater effectiveness. When government agencies establish outcome goals that are of interest to the media and commit to delivering on them by a certain time, and when they report progress toward those commitments, it increases the likelihood that media coverage will align with the agency's objectives. It increases the chances that agencies will be able focus their time and attention on addressing problems and pursuing the opportunities they want to address, rather than losing time responding to a hot news story about incidental items with little relative impact on social outcomes. By setting resonant outcome goals that catch the media's interest and reporting progress, government managers essentially enlist the media's assistance to make progress toward the goals.

Key Characteristics of Effective Goals

What is it about the Charles River goal that grabs the attention of the public and the press, strengthening its value as a motivational tool? The goal of a "Clean Charles by 2005" is powerful because it is stated in simple terms the public understands; people feel a personal connection to it. Part of that familiarity derives from the fact that cleaning the Charles is an outcome goal with real-world effects, and part deals with people's ability to imagine the benefits. The geographic and temporal specificity of the goal also adds to its power, because it helps the public recognize its connection to the outcome and allows the agency to tackle the goal in "bite-sized" pieces.

The Clean Charles goal is easy for the public to understand because it is defined in language used every day, rather than in words describing administrative processes. It is easier to appreciate the import of contaminated water flowing into the Charles during a heavy rain than to understand the relevance of a riverside community completing a storm-water management plan. Similarly, contrast the resonance of a report that the Charles River water quality has risen from a D to a B to the flatness of the activity-focused information that the EPA published in its *FY 1999 Annual Performance Report*. "Eleven states," the agency reported, "submitted upgraded non-point source programs for a cumulative total of thirteen, meeting EPA's goal."[38] Although both outcome and activity goals may be useful, people naturally grab on to the former; the latter lands with a bureaucratic thud.

To cut through the cacophony of information bombarding the public, agencies need to articulate goals in ways that encourage personal connection. Too often, goals are defined in ways that make them seem irrelevant. Translating unfamiliar goals to more familiar terms greatly enhances their motivating value for the public and agency staff, which contributes to the advancement of the goal. The public is more likely, for example, to understand and relate to the threat of "increased numbers of severe weather events, including droughts, floods, heat waves, and heavy snowstorms," than to the unfamiliar concepts of "climate change" and "global warming."

The Charles River goal especially grabs people's attention and inspires their hopes because it deals with an experience they know. They can imagine swimming or sailing in the river on a hot summer day. Even those who do not swim, sail, or row can envision an occasional stroll or bike ride alongside a glistening Charles.

Another way the Clean Charles goal is brought alive is its localization. A specific and limited geographic boundary for a goal enhances its familiarity. DeVillars did not promise that all rivers and lakes in New England would be swimmable by 2005. Had he defined the geographic scope of the goal in such a vague and broad manner, chances are no one would have believed him, or more important, paid attention.[39] By circumscribing the geographic scope to the Lower Charles River, the goal became more achievable and invited a strong personal connection from the river's abutters.

To illustrate the power of localization, compare how much more informative the Clean Charles goal is than the EPA's national goal for drinking water: "protecting human health so that 95 percent of the population served by community water systems will receive water that meets drinking water standards."[40] The EPA's annual performance report informs the American people that 94 percent of the population served by community water systems in 1999 received uncontaminated water, compared with a baseline of 83 percent in 1994.[41] It is laudable that the EPA set an outcome-focused drinking water goal and is annually reporting progress toward that goal. The same goal would be much more useful, however, if it included greater geographic clarity. Where do the people live who are served by contaminated systems? Of those, which systems—specifically—will be cleaned up before 2005 and which will remain in the still-contaminated 5 percent? Where are people who are not served by community water systems? Are any of them drinking contaminated or untested water? If so, where do they live?

If the EPA identified communities not meeting national standards, those targeted for improvement, and those not yet scheduled for attention, its annual report would be much more useful.[42] Goals assume greater meaning when broken down (disaggregated) into the component parts, such as geographic and demographic specificity, that make them more relevant.[43] The EPA, states, and localities could and should provide breakdowns in annual performance reports, presenting not only the aggregated goals and progress reports but also how each total breaks down to local goals. Geographic specificity greatly strengthens the value of performance reports for motivating change.

Limiting the geographic scope of the project not only makes the Clean Charles goal more "imaginable" for the public, it also makes it more manageable for the agency. As Moraff, the original Clean Charles manager, put it, "The issue of scale is important. We focused on improving water quality on a ten-mile stretch of the river. It is manageable. We can walk the Charles and look for pipes. The goal lets us deal with the problem in bite-size pieces."[44] Occasionally, the agency would extend its reach beyond the ten-mile stretch, but that occurred only when the EPA made a discrete decision to extend its reach, keeping the overall project scope contained. The goal of cleaning the Lower Charles so that it was safe for swimming was unquestionably challenging, but it was not so enormous that it overwhelmed those working on it. Goals that are too broadly defined can be demotivating because people working on the effort fear they cannot make the goal even before they get started. Cleaning the Charles by 2005 was certainly a stretch goal for the agency, but it was a manageable one.

Besides providing geographic detail, a specific and ambitious but realistic timetable makes a goal more resonant. The ten-year timeline for the Clean Charles goal is near term enough that people can imagine enjoying the benefits within their own lifetimes. At the same time, the time frame is long enough that it indicates to the community that this is a serious effort, not just a political splash. Ten years provides a sense that there is enough time for genuine progress.

Outcome Goals Allow Appropriate Action

Focusing on outcomes not only motivates, it also allows managers to manage. Systems that emphasize specific activities (for example, permits issued, inspections conducted) or resource utilization (for example, work years associated with fund allocations) tend to limit thinking about options for available activities and resource utilization. Focusing on outcomes invites people to use their wits and experience.[45] Before the Charles initiative, "EPA's approach had been to address each water-quality problem separately. One program addressed combined sewer overflows, another, stormwater rules—and so on. There was no coordinated look at the entire river and the problems contributing to poor water quality."[46] An outcome goal changes the way environmental agencies approach problems, compelling them to think—and constantly rethink—the nature and causes of the problem they are trying to fix. It invites them to tap the full continuum of tools at their disposal.

Since the inception of the effort, the agency has used a creative mix of enforcement, inducement, education, and information tools to improve the quality of the Charles. Triggered by the initial Brookline enforcement case, the EPA expanded its attention to include the other communities along the Lower Charles. The EPA sent letters instructing the communities to inspect their storm water pipes for illegal sewer connections. Numerous illegal hook-ups were found, including a ninety-unit apartment building directly discharging into the water. Rather than focus on penalizing the communities, the region instead negotiated agreements with the communities to eliminate the illicit connections by 1997. Although this approach did not add to the agency's traditional tally of enforcement penalties assessed, it consumed fewer resources per case, allowing the EPA to pursue more cases and resolve the environmental problem more quickly. (Penalties were assessed against two communities that the EPA believed had not adequately responded to the problem. These penalties were in effect suspended, however, on condition that the communities move quickly and aggressively to remove the remaining illicit connections, and in one case to implement storm-water controls beyond those required by law.)

Perhaps more interesting, the agency did not stop its effort at this point, as it would have done historically. It realized that it needed further effort by the communities to meet the 2005 goal, but that it lacked the regulatory authority to compel those efforts. So the EPA offered an inducement to the communities to get them to adopt storm-water management procedures. (Storm-water management procedures are generally "low-tech" but personnel-intensive practices, such as keeping debris out of sewers, adopting and enforcing "pooper scooper" laws, and removing junk from catch drains. They require significant changes in the way local governments handle their traditional public works functions.) To motivate the local governments to cooperate, the EPA proposed to sign a memorandum of understanding with each community, agreeing to waive the need to approve plans under forthcoming storm-water discharge regulations, which some projected might cost the communities $300,000 to $500,000 each. In exchange, the EPA wanted the communities to commit to early and voluntary adoption of effective storm-water management practices.[47]

Similar enforcement-led "stick-and-carrot" strategies were pursued with private sector organizations. In 1998 the EPA sent letters to 200 probable polluters, notifying them they had been identified as likely sources of problems (often, leaking underground oil tanks and faulty storm drains) and giving them two months to fix the problems. During that two-month period, the EPA and the state offered to help the polluters understand how to fix their problems, no questions asked. After that, however, if the problems were not fixed, the sources could expect a visit from inspectors and lawyers.[48] The notification received headline coverage in the paper.[49] Seeing the story, several consultants called the EPA and requested the list. The EPA was initially reluctant to provide it but changed its mind. It realized that its small inspection effort had successfully leveraged an enormously effective deterrence and environmental benefit.[50] In the EPA's own words:

The compliance assurance strategy—developed as part of EPA's Clean Charles 2005 Task Force—is unique in a number of ways including:
—It is the first time EPA has combined both assistance and enforcement efforts in one coordinated approach, targeting those efforts to the protection of one particular natural resource;
—It is the first time EPA has notified a broad universe of facilities in advance that they will be subject to aggressive inspections as of a certain date.[51]

When more traditional enforcement actions were needed, the EPA did not hesitate to take them. The agency took a major enforcement action against Boston University in 1997 for oil spills into the river in 1992 and 1996. As part of the settlement, the university agreed to pay $2 million to cover the cost of fines, clean-up, and environmental projects not related to the spill, as well as the costs of an independent audit of the university's environmental management practices. The EPA also initiated enforcement actions against the town of Milford for illegal sewer connections.[52] The enforcement actions not only imposed a financial burden on the violators, they also created a public relations problem. Milford, for example, earned the headline, "EPA Warns Milford of Fines, Suits Over Pollution of Charles River."[53]

These stick-and-carrot actions were just one part of a much broader effort that included more aggressive education, information, and technical assistance activities. The EPA was one of several sources providing financial support to the Charles River Watershed Association (CRWA) to collect and disseminate data on the river's water quality.[54] The agency also established a hotline for citizens to report spills to the river, contributed $1 million to scientific studies to help understand the sources of pollution to the river, and purchased the services of a consultant to provide technical assistance to localities on storm-water management. By 2000 the EPA was digging deeper and more creatively into its toolbox. It decided to reissue permits to six wastewater treatment plants on the Upper Charles, requiring reduced levels of phosphorous to control nutrient levels. It also ventured into the development and testing of new technologies, funding a consultant to test structural controls for storm water and to experiment with a curtainlike barrier to try to filter suspended solids and bacteria at a former public beach on the Charles.[55]

Environmental and other government agency staff have long struggled with the best ways to connect their daily work with the outcomes they seek to accomplish. They have struggled with ways to measure the effectiveness of their activities. They have worried that compliance assistance and education will undermine enforcement efforts or the perception of a strong enforcement presence. Agency reformers have lamented that personal allegiance to organizational "stovepipes" seems to stymie agency reform efforts. The Charles initiative demonstrates how starting with an outcome goal and organizing work around it—combining functional activities such as permitting, plan review, science, inspections, the threat of enforcement followed up by enforcement when needed—can push aside these concerns and barriers. Moreover, outcome-focused management does not require institutional reorganizations, which tend to consume enormous organizational energy. Much of it can be accomplished through greater use of teams and clear and strong authority granted to team leaders to manage those specialized personnel who can advance the goal, regardless of their office affiliation.

The reason the Clean Charles approach works so well is that the goal drives the selection of activities, not vice versa. This arrangement is in stark contrast to the way the EPA and state agencies normally work, starting with activities—such as permit reviews or violation-seeking inspections—and then deciding the most appropriate place to carry them out.

The EPA's focus on making the Lower Charles swimmable by 2005 not only helped the Charles but helped the EPA apply what it learned about sources of problems in the Lower Charles watershed to its clean-up of other rivers, as well. Moraff observes that the Charles initiative "helped the agency identify problems which were not being addressed by our existing programs. We had no idea that illicit connections were such a big problem. By focusing on the Charles we learned about generic problems, illicit connections and sewer deterioration, that were much bigger than we had previously thought. This not only helped us clean up the Charles, but other rivers as well."[56]

Effective Progress Measurement

The Charles initiative not only sets a goal for cleaning up the Lower Charles but also regularly measures progress toward that goal.

Feedback Motivates and Illuminates

The feedback provided by progress measurement serves as a continuous motivational force for the Clean Charles 2005 team. The measurement is perhaps more valuable, however, for its ability to illuminate where progress is being made and where it is not, because the information helps the team figure out more effective ways to meet its objective.

Undoubtedly, the media's attention to progress reports on the Charles is a powerful impetus for improvement. The EPA reports annually to an interested public on progress toward its long-term goal. The prospect of having to issue a report card each year for ten years, only one year apart, focuses the EPA and the Charles team on finding sources of river contamination that can be eliminated in the near term and the longer term. That they are released at least once a year instead of just at the end of the ten-year time frame keeps the goal from being treated as some far-off date by the people charged with managing the goal. That the high-visibility progress reports are only once a year, instead of every month or every quarter, affords staff time to act strategically.

Social psychology researchers have found that, even without the motivational value of external attention, providing individuals with feedback on their performance motivates them. Indeed, private feedback motivates even without setting an explicit goal or linking goals to rewards.[57] It motivates because people naturally like to do well. Researchers have found that it can be even more motivating when feedback is combined with goals, as is the case with the Charles initiative.[58]

Feedback not only motivates workers to work harder, it enables them to work more intelligently. "Key to our success has been comprehensive monthly sampling that lets us see how we are doing on a regular basis," says Moraff. "The Charles River Watershed Association picked up monthly monitoring samples [almost] each mile. The whole effort was driven by the data."[59]

Key Characteristics of Effective Feedback

What Moraff and the rest of the Charles River team discovered is the enormous power of fresh, frequent, outcome-focused, and credible feedback. Monthly monitoring reports at thirty-seven points along the river's eighty-mile stretch make the measurement information "actionable." The data reveal when and where problems are arising, triggering follow-up questions. They also more quickly indicate what works and what does not, inviting replication or discontinuation of specific intervention actions and programs.

An important characteristic of the data is their freshness and frequency. The monitoring reports contain fresh data; that is, the EPA and the public receive the measurement information soon after the measurements are taken. The data are also collected with relatively high temporal and spatial frequency; measurements are taken at frequent time and geographic intervals.

The frequency of the monthly monitoring reports allows the EPA to pinpoint sections of the river (between monitoring points) likely to have illegal sewer hook-ups into storm drains or other problems. The data enable EPA staff to detect a problem close enough to when and where it happens that the likely causes of the problem are easier to find and fix. Although the data do not explain why a problem occurs, the information gleaned prompts staff to ask "why" soon enough after the occurrence that the chances of finding the answer increase. For example, one time a monitoring report showed a high bacteria count at a city of Boston sewer outflow site. The EPA called the city to look at its sewer maps. After studying the map with the city, the EPA and city personnel went into the field, where they found a blocked sewer line. The city fixed the problem. Fresh and frequent performance measurement supports more accurate identification of the causes of river contamination.

The freshness and frequency of the monthly reports also make it easier for the agency to assess the effectiveness of different strategies to fix problems, because the monthly measures provide relatively quick feedback about whether or not an intervention worked. Following the correction of the blocked sewer in Boston, the monthly readings showed the bacterial surge had been eliminated. Similarly, the agency was able to monitor whether its efforts to eliminate illicit hook-ups to sewer systems had the intended environmental effect.

The Boston action is noteworthy because it illustrates not only how helpful frequent data reports can be but also how outcome-focused feedback changed the way the EPA reacted to the problem.[60] Governed by an activity-focused mentality, the EPA would traditionally have contemplated an enforcement response to this problem. Because of the relatively trivial nature of the legal violation and the costs associated with enforcement cases, it might never have initiated the action, leaving the environmental problem in place. Instead, the EPA worked with the community to eliminate the problem. (Had the city shown a past pattern of serious violations, the EPA might have decided the situation warranted initiating an enforcement action.)

Monthly monitoring reports are often not the only type of feedback information needed to inform an outcome-focused effort, especially since the cost of measuring every potentially important parameter of water quality on a monthly basis can be prohibitive. For the Charles River, the monthly information was complemented by data from other sources. The MWRA monitors the Lower Charles twice a year for a month-long period, and the state of Massachusetts tries to gather information on the river every five years as part of its watershed management program.[61] Those working on the Charles clean-up recognized that still other data were needed to consider several unanswered questions about the contribution of upstream and storm-water flows to the lower basin. As explained below, the way the Charles clean-up was being managed prompted the U.S. Geological Survey (USGS) to agree to collect and analyze some of the chief missing information.[62] Outcome-focused performance measurement, at multiple levels and for multiple purposes, has been essential to the success of the Clean Charles initiative.

To date, no one has questioned the credibility of the data. Several characteristics of the way the measures are collected and presented contribute to its credibility. Should anyone doubt the EPA's claims about progress toward its goal, collection of most of the data by independent third parties, the CRWA and the USGS, boosts data credibility. The fact that numerous parties conduct water quality sampling helps those working on the project cross-check the accuracy of their data. Although none directly overlaps, wildly inaccurate samples would be readily apparent.

Easy access to the data also strengthens their credibility. Those who want to know more about the river's water quality can find the websites on the Charles maintained by the EPA, the USGS, and the Charles River Watershed Association. At the EPA website, interested parties can see the underlying analysis that informs the annual grades, to see how the grades the EPA gives track the trends in water quality. At the CRWA website, people can read the monthly monitoring reports, while the USGS website provides real-time and trend data where tributaries feed into the river.

Performance Measurement for Public Use

Although the monthly monitoring reports and supplementary studies are extremely useful for stimulating and answering questions by federal and state environmental management staff about the causes of water quality problems and how to fix them, they are less meaningful for the general public. The average Jane and Joe have no idea how to interpret fecal coliform counts and phosphorous levels and they do not want to know. They simply want to know if the river is clean enough for swimming and boating and whether or not their tax dollars are being well spent.

The public wants performance information that helps it make decisions and choices on a daily basis. The Charles River Watershed Association recognizes that need and collects and packages some of its information accordingly. During the summer, it supplements monthly monitoring data with daily monitoring of sections of the river heavily used by boaters. It then translates that information for easy public consumption. It posts a colored flag at every boathouse along the Lower Charles, where the boaters need the information, as well as on the CRWA website. A blue flag signals that the waters are clean enough for safe boating. A red flag warns that they are not. This simple "point-of-use" information delivery mechanism not only guides individual decisionmaking, it reminds water enthusiasts that the health of the river is not a sure thing, inviting community vigilance.

The EPA also translates the detailed water quality monitoring information environmental agency staff use to a format more digestible by the public through its annual report card. To do that, it rolls up the monthly monitoring data into an annual grade. The simplicity of the annual grade makes it a powerful tool for communicating progress to the public, which makes it a valuable but gentle motivation tool for the agency. For those knowledgeable enough about river water quality to be concerned about the extra levels of contamination stirred up by heavy rains, the EPA breaks the annual information down into a few subcategories. It reports the percentage of time the Lower Charles meets state standards for wet weather flows and dry weather flows, and under each of those headings, for boating and swimming standards.

In 1998 the EPA began testing a new way to aggregate the detailed performance information it had, with hopes of accelerating river cleanup through the motivational value of public disclosure. It began aggregating the performance information it collected by jurisdiction, so it could issue grades for each town. As reported in the local paper, the EPA gave "a passing grade" to communities on the river east of Dover, "except for Weston, which got an F for failing to file an EPA-mandated plan for improving storm water runoff by sweeping streets, cleaning catch basins, and removing illegal sewer hook-ups to storm drains."[63]

Costs of Measurement

Readers may protest that while the Charles initiative offers a great example of how measurement can be useful, measurement is expensive. The Charles initiative suggests that cost may not be as prohibitive as feared. The CRWA's monthly sampling of the full eighty miles of the Charles River relies heavily on trained volunteers who follow quality-controlled protocols. The monitoring costs $3,500 a month, with the laboratory work provided at no cost by the MWRA.[64] As the Charles initiative also demonstrates, it is not necessary to measure everything at once. Monitoring that is fresh (current) and frequent in time and spacing can immediately help regulators spot problems, if they exist. Monitoring all communities at the same time may indeed require more funds than the public is prepared to provide. Decisions can be made about which areas get concentrated attention first, and which will follow.

Moreover, performance measures do not have to be fancy or costly to be useful. Former Maryland state senator Bernie Fowler demonstrated how simple the first step toward performance measurement can be. Every year since the 1950s, Fowler has walked into the Patuxent River to measure how deep into the water he can go and still see his sneakers.

The "Bernie Fowler Sneaker Index" gets reported annually in the paper and is tracked by the Chesapeake Bay Program.

Increased reliance on outcomes and performance measurement to drive environmental decisions can contribute to increased generation of useful performance measures. Raising public expectations for information about the quality of neighboring water bodies, especially in the age of the Internet, may raise public support for funding water quality measurement. Many citizens are likely to be surprised, for example, to learn that the quality of their local waters is not regularly tested, if tested at all. When they discover how little is known about the safety of their local river, it may increase popular support to pay for water quality monitoring, especially if the demand for recreational use of local water bodies increases. At the same time, once the EPA regional office set its sights on cleaning up the Charles, the generation of reliable measurements of river water quality became essential. In several enforcement cases involving actual or potential harm to the river, the EPA expected the violators to pay some of the costs associated with more accurately monitoring the environmental effects of their actions.[65]

In sum, the Charles River performance measures are enormously useful because they are fresh, frequent, outcome focused, credible, and readily accessible. They are useful because they are available in bite-sized pieces and can be rolled up into bigger chunks to meet the need, whether to inform a boating decision or motivate a jurisdiction. The performance measures are not perfect, but they are affordable, and despite their imperfections, they are very successfully guiding progress toward cleaning up the river.

Engaging the Public and Other Parties

Grabbing the public's attention motivates those inside the agency. Awakening the public's interest by setting a resonant goal does more than motivate staff, however. It helps enlist and engage the ideas, assistance, and cooperation of those outside the agency in a way that advances progress toward the goal. It can also focus the efforts of the interested public on a shared goal, allowing the agency to capture synergistic gains across organizations. To tap the energies and expertise of those who can or need to help, the agency must manage its outreach effort skillfully, including how it works with its partners and the way it reaches out to the media.

Before the Charles initiative, no one at the EPA felt responsibility for improving the river's water quality although everyone presumably cared about it. Outside organizations interested in working with the agency found few opportunities for genuine cooperation. The Charles River Watershed Association had long been looking for better ways to work with the EPA to clean the Charles, but in a Kafkaesque way could not find the right EPA person or organizational unit with whom to collaborate.

By the simple act of articulating the goal of a Clean Charles by 2005 and assembling a team to manage the goal, the EPA opened a door for collaboration with the community that had not previously existed. The Charles River Watershed Association and seven other nonprofits long committed to improving the river's water quality came running through the door as soon as it was opened.[66] The CRWA provided one of the most essential elements of the initiative—monthly water quality data. A second interest group helped build political support in one community, allowing local political leaders to adopt more aggressive storm-water management practices.

Publicly establishing a simple, resonant goal also simplified collaboration with other government agencies. The Massachusetts Executive Office of Environmental Affairs (EOEA) and the Department of Environmental Protection (DEP) already had a watershed plan for the Charles River basin.[67] Cleaning the Charles had long been a goal for the state. Unlike the Charles initiative, however, the state had never set a specific goal and timetable for the Charles. As part of the initiative, the EPA and the state agreed to split up responsibilities on the river, with the EPA focusing on the Lower Charles and the state focusing on the Upper Charles.[68] Among other contributions, the state provided additional monitoring information, participated in the review of combined sewer overflow plans, and provided loans for local water pollution abatement projects.

By setting a goal and measuring progress toward it, observes Kevin Brander, a state agency official, "EPA made people more aware of the efforts to clean the Charles, and they seemed to embrace it more. Gathering stakeholders helped bring more money to the Charles, because they made their presence felt through public forums. They also seemed to become more active in providing comments in the regulatory processes. We saw a higher level of participation." Moreover, notes Brander, "while work on the Charles speeded up, it did not seem to rob any resources from the other basins." Also, he says, increased attention to the Charles brought "praise to communities that did extensive work." [69]

The Massachusetts river basin coordinator invited the USGS to join the effort. Peter Weiskell, the USGS official heading the Charles study, reports that the Charles initiative "made a big difference in terms of our coming in because of the high level of commitment to this effort that EPA showed." Further, Weiskell believes, setting a goal and issuing an annual grade "absolutely helps the effort to clean the river because getting our water bodies to meet standards won't happen if you just focus on a few high-level actions. That is not the nature of the problem. It is much more widespread and diffuse, so the educational process and raising of consciousness in the community has to go on. This is a very good way to go to get our rivers to meet standards."[70]

Interest in meeting the Charles River goal is so high that others have also expressed a readiness to help. According to CRWA staff, the Army Corps of Engineers has volunteered support if it can help in some way.[71]

Not every government agency has joined the Charles initiative voluntarily. As noted earlier, the Massachusetts Water Resources Authority was involved from the beginning because it was under an enforcement agreement with the EPA to fix the combined sewer overflows spilling into the river. Despite the initial reason for its participation, the MWRA has been a full partner in the effort to clean the river. It provided initial financial support for the CRWA's monitoring efforts and continues, on a pro bono basis, to analyze the monthly samples that the CRWA draws from the river. The EPA press releases credit the MWRA for numerous actions it has taken to clean the river, including sewer separation projects and upgrades to treatment plants.[72]

Focusing on an outcome goal and measuring progress toward it may have led to an expanded and enriched scope of enforcement negotiations between the EPA and the MWRA. As noted earlier, the MWRA wants to implement a less costly and somewhat less protective improvement for dealing with the problem of combined sewer overflow than the EPA has sought, arguing that the marginal improvement realized from the more costly option the EPA wants does not justify the additional cost, especially given the other sources contaminating the water. Focusing first on the outcome led the EPA, the MWRA, and the state to contribute funds to get the USGS to conduct a study that could provide more relevant information. When the new data are analyzed, they will lead the EPA and the MWRA—under close scrutiny by many agencies and several active interest groups—to settle on the best strategy. If the data suggest that the changes the EPA wants will make a significant difference in overall water quality, the MWRA will be under significant public pressure to make the changes. If the data suggest otherwise, those at the table can roll up their sleeves to try to figure out what strategies would work better.

The cooperation of other local governments along the river also necessitated a bit of stick-and-carrot persuasion. Over time, however, the EPA is finding that the popularity of the Clean Charles goal helps convert what could be an ongoing antagonistic relationship into genuine collaboration. In some cases, it can even help local elected officials find the political support they need to authorize new expenditures. In the view of the current Charles River coordinator, Bill Walsh-Rogalski, "Communities are there because they are under some legal obligations, . . . but they have bought into the goal." Moraff concurs: "It was much easier to work with local officials because of the high visibility and popularity" of pursuing the Charles River goal.

The EPA has also used the visibility of the goal to compel the participation of private sector parties whose actions affect river quality. One important target has been the numerous universities along the river. Just the week before the annual Head of the Charles Regatta, the EPA announced punitive action against Boston University, "the largest ever federal environmental penalty against an education institution."[73] Harvard received far more complimentary coverage when it voluntarily launched a program to collect and treat storm water from campus runoff.[74] By 2000 a group of sixteen landowners along the river, including five universities, had formed the Clean Charles Coalition, "a voluntary association of industries, academic and research institutions . . . that have joined in support of a fishable and swimmable Charles River by 2005."[75] The coalition plans to provide mentoring assistance to help smaller sources of river pollution reduce their loads to the river.

In addition, local teachers have begun to get involved, working with a local nonprofit to create and test a watershed science and biology curriculum at eight area high schools.[76]

Environmental progress often depends on the cooperative efforts of numerous parties. The Charles initiative demonstrates how the establishment of a clear and resonant goal and timetable, complemented by credible outcome-focused performance measurement, can be a powerful tool for enlisting and engaging the cooperation of external parties who can help achieve the goal.

Finally, the EPA implicitly used its performance goal to clarify expectations with agency oversight bodies. By articulating his goal so publicly, DeVillars implicitly invited public and legislative support or opposition. If legislators did not like his goals, they could exercise their powers to stop him. If they did, they could join him at public events concerning the river, or even create their own events.[77]

In sum, EPA New England is using performance measurement to communicate to the public what the public wants and needs to know. Performance information disseminated via the media, online, and at the point of use informs everyday decisions. Performance information also invites the community to react if it feels the wrong goals have been chosen, progress is too slow, or the resources to address the problem are insufficient. Measurement is used to gauge success, communicate priorities and progress, inform decisions, stimulate inquiry, invite collaboration, build trust, motivate, influence allocation decisions, and stay focused on achieving the goal: a swimmable Charles River in 2005.

Management Matters

If the media had not given so much coverage to the Charles initiative, the agency's efforts to enlist and engage others in the effort would undoubtedly have been far less successful. Media attention to the water quality of the Charles was no accident; it resulted from skillful and intentional management by the region. EPA New England's approach to the goal of a Clean Charles by 2005 provides an excellent model of successful performance management, using performance measures to drive performance gains by "managing the measurement message" and "managing the measures."

Managing the Measurement Message

Public managers seldom welcome press attention to performance measurement. Most are aware of the media's increasingly negative coverage of government,[78] sometimes through all-too-painful personal experience. As noted earlier, a reporter's search for the sensational story can easily turn performance reporting into a distraction-generator, diverting senior management attention away from improving agency performance to correcting erroneous stories. As a result of those fears and a failure to appreciate the value of performance measurement information, many government leaders make no effort to interest the media in the story. The media, in turn, pay little attention to goal-setting announcements and performance reports.

A few more sophisticated agencies are beginning to realize that when people have so little trust in government, the release of performance measurement information can be a story in itself. Leaders of these agencies, not unlike corporate leaders talking with investment analysts and the trade press before releasing their quarterly and annual reports to the public, are taking the time to brief the media before the release of their performance information. In return for their efforts to educate the media about the meaning and import of the information in their performance reports, several have been rewarded with favorable stories.[79]

The EPA New England's Charles initiative suggests further steps government agencies can take to work with the media on government performance information. The initiative was carefully and intentionally structured to encourage a high level of media attention to tap the motivational and invitational benefits of publicity about the goal and the progress reports.[80] It suggests a model for how agencies can use performance goals and performance measurement to attract media attention to the government's performance and, more important, environmental performance.

EPA New England announced the goal of a Clean Charles by 2005 coincident with the annual Head of the Charles Regatta, an international rowing event that draws nearly 5,000 rowers and 300,000 spectators to the river.[81] The goal-setting event was set at Magazine Beach, a convenient location for Boston media outlets to reach the day before the regatta, when out-of-town visitors interested in the river swarm the area. Announcing the goal just before the event provided a natural news story that would interest locals as well as visiting rowers and friends. The setting of the press event provided a wonderful human angle to the story; local residents, some attending the event, had swum at the beach as recently as the 1950s. Local elected officials participated in the press conference, as did the Charles River Watershed Association, making it easy for the press to get quotations from a diverse group of sources.[82]

To get coverage of its annual progress reports and other stories, the EPA is following a similar formula. It uses the news value of a report card, a problem, or a noteworthy contribution to create a story. It times the story well, releasing the annual report card on Earth Day. Additional stories are released just before the regatta every year, which conveniently falls six months after Earth Day. In 1998, for example, "on the eve of the weekend Regatta," as the press account begins, the EPA announced a series of grants to improve river monitoring and real-time posting of river water quality information on the Internet and to help local communities better contain contaminated storm water running into the river.[83] A simple, resonant measure linked with some "newsworthy" event, sensitive timing, and good visuals have successfully attracted media attention to this government performance story.

EPA New England is not the only government agency to discover the potential for intentionally enlisting the press as part of its performance accountability system. When the Florida Department of Environmental Protection (DEP) issued the DEP's first-ever *Secretary's Quarterly Performance Report*, the secretary notified her division chiefs that they should "prepare a one page course of action . . . [for] each of the focus areas noted" to be shared with the governor and the press.[84]

Mayor Anthony Williams of Washington, D.C., elected as a management reformer in 1998, is also experimenting with enlisting the press as part of his feedback, motivation, and accountability system. Williams inherited a government with weak management controls and information systems. To address this problem, he took a bold step soon after he became mayor, announcing specific goals and timetables for the District government. For example, he established a pothole hotline and committed to fixing all reported potholes within seventy-two hours. Not surprisingly, local citizens called and wrote to the paper when potholes were not filled within the target time frame. This citizen feedback enables the mayor to learn very quickly when his government is not working as well as he wants it to, so he can tackle problems before they become too large.[85] Based on the success of his first round of public performance goals, Williams followed up with a second. In April 2000 he released public scorecards, posted online, committing himself and each of his deputy mayors to meet certain goals by certain dates.[86]

What the Charles River and these other examples show is that savvy government managers can enlist the assistance of the media in advancing public outcomes by selecting performance measures that resonate with the public, reporting on them regularly and understandably, timing progress reports and goal-related news to coincide with favorable news windows, and engaging the public as the government's watchdog, should government stray from its goal. Moreover, it demonstrates how attracting media coverage can help a government agency enlist and engage ready and reluctant partners who can contribute to better environmental quality.

Managing with the Measures

Picking simple, resonant, outcome-focused goals and progress measurements and getting publicity about them will not, by itself, lead to goal attainment. For measures to drive performance gains, managers must aggressively "manage the measures." They must become performance managers. Successful performance management requires senior managers to identify those goals that are their top priorities, repeatedly signal the priority placed on those goals, regularly monitor progress toward the goal, and work interactively with goal managers to explore the most effective strategies for making progress. The top manager also needs to designate a "goal manager" and project team responsible for driving progress toward the goal, and support that manager and team by providing personal time and ensuring the internal and external resources needed to implement the strategies. Moreover, agency managers must skillfully manage the enlistment and engagement process to influence actions that can affect the outcomes over which agencies lack direct control.

The region's top leader, the regional administrator, frequently talked about the Charles goal inside and outside the agency, regularly monitored progress, and interactively explored with the staff and the community best strategies for improving the river's water quality. By setting a measurable goal with a timetable, DeVillars not only signaled the priority he placed on the goal, he assumed public accountability for delivering on the promise. He reaffirmed his commitment and accountability each time he personally announced the annual grade of the river's progress. Assuming personal risk for attaining a goal indicated to those inside and outside the agency that the initiative was more than a press event: it was a top management commitment.

DeVillars managed the project in a highly interactive manner. He frequently sent staff notes with news clips and suggestions about the project and met with them as needed to brainstorm strategies.[87] When DeVillars asked staff about the project's progress, he wanted more than progress reports. DeVillars and the Charles River team debated intervention options likely to be most fruitful, given the information available. Walsh-Rogalski recalls one such discussion when DeVillars wanted to pursue one strategy and the staff strongly preferred another option. After considerable discussion to examine the reasoning, DeVillars deferred to the staff members' judgment, comfortable with their analysis and reasoning.[88]

As indicated earlier, DeVillars initially turned to Moraff, an enforcement lawyer in the agency already working on the Charles River case, to manage the Clean Charles 2005 project. Moraff was already a staff assistant to DeVillars and assumed the additional role of team leader for the project. The Charles River project team was small. It included Moraff, a compliance engineer with whom Moraff had been working on the MWRA case, and an agency expert on storm water.[89] Staff were added as needed. When Moraff was promoted to head the agency's enforcement office, DeVillars turned to Walsh-Rogalski, associate director of the region's site remediation program responsible for policy issues, to head the team.

There are several noteworthy aspects of DeVillars's designation of Moraff and Walsh-Rogalski as the team leaders. The first is simply the decision to designate someone to lead the Clean Charles effort, essentially serving as the goal manager. The second is the selection of someone with significant experience within the agency to take on the job.

Designating or identifying a goal manager may seem an obvious and trivial step, but it is a management task often overlooked. As with so many large (government and private) organizations, the EPA depends on an extensive field staff to deliver on its mission. Moreover, under many of its laws, the EPA delegates most program implementation responsibilities to states, maintaining responsibility for federal oversight and direct intervention when circumstances warrant. When the EPA sets national goals, it is assumed that each national program manager serves as a goal leader. Unfortunately, little effort is made to show how the national goals "cascade down" to regional and state goals, and how these "roll back up" to the national level. Thus headquarters, field staff, and states have a limited sense of connection to or responsibility for meeting national goals. Everybody is responsible, so nobody is responsible. As Moraff puts it, "It is a lot more comfortable when you have broader goals that a lot more people are responsible for, because if you don't make it, it's nobody's fault. With the Charles River project, we really put ourselves on the line."[90] Because DeVillars assigned them the job, Moraff and Walsh-Rogalski knew they and the Charles River team were responsible for achieving the goal. Knowing clearly where the buck stops pushes them to make progress continually, staying focused on the score and constantly rethinking their game strategy.

In selecting his goal manager, DeVillars chose wisely by tapping individuals deeply familiar with the EPA culture. Moraff and Walsh-Rogalski both have many years of experience working in the EPA regional office. This helped them figure out how to tackle the cultural shift from activity-focused management to outcome-focused management. They brought to the pursuit of their goal an understanding of the jurisdictional problems they would inevitably encounter working outside the traditional patterns of the system, allowing them to anticipate and address problems before they arose, or at least recognize a problem when confronted by it.

DeVillars and the Charles River team have also taken great care in managing the process of collaboration. The EPA convenes its partners on a quarterly basis. The meetings are used to encourage learning across organizations and brainstorm strategies for action. Partners review the data being gathered and discuss what the data suggest and the questions they raise. The meetings provide a forum for local governments to share what they are learning about eliminating illegal connections and implementing storm-water management activities. The meetings also offer an opportunity for coordination. While he was regional administrator, DeVillars attended many of these meetings. Sometimes he served as cheerleader, motivating everyone with reports of the progress being made. Sometimes, offering his ideas and resources, he challenged others to contribute theirs. On a few occasions, he used the "bully pulpit value of quarterly meetings . . . for the areas where EPA lacks legal control."[91]

There has never been a separate budget dedicated to advancing the Charles River goal. The region and its partners draw funds from whatever sources they can find to get the work done. When additional resources have been needed, the staff has turned to the regional administrator to find the needed support, whether from internal funds or outside assistance. The staff has made no attempt to secure a dedicated budget, sparing it the time needed to engage in the formal budget process. Instead, the team has opted to focus on developing and implementing strategies to reach their goal. Performance measurement, in this case, directly informs resource allocation decisions being made by the regional administrator, but there is no formal connection between the measurements and the budget.[92]

That there is no discrete budget for the project is noteworthy for several reasons. It requires that the larger organization have discretionary or flexible funds available for projects such as this one. Also, many discussions of performance measurement and management assume a direct link between performance results and the budgeting process, yet no formal link was ever made or implied in the Charles project. Funds have been found to meet specific needs as they have arisen.

DeVillars's leadership has been key to the success of the Clean Charles 2005 experience. This is not surprising. Nearly every book, article, or report on effective performance measurement and management asserts that senior-level management attention is an essential ingredient. Unfortunately, senior management attention to performance measures is often the exception rather than the rule. Agency leaders do not seem to understand how outcome-focused performance management can help them.

What the Charles initiative shows is why agency leaders ought to pay more attention to performance management. The establishment of a resonant goal with a timetable helped DeVillars win press coverage and popular support for his priority. It helped him communicate his priority to the organization quickly and with minimal organizational trauma. Organizational leaders have few tools as effective as goals and performance measures for moving their priorities. In theory, they can use the annual budget for this purpose. In practice, however, budgets are ill-equipped for the job. Budget decisions occur only once a year, and an enormous lag time occurs between an agency leader's decisions about funding priorities and fund availability. The lag makes it hard to maintain the momentum for change. Moreover, agency leaders do not always get their priorities funded. They first need to fight for their budget priorities within the executive branch. Assuming they survive those battles, they then need to win support from the legislature. Even after budgets are appropriated, they often still have difficulty tracking whether actual spending aligns with intended spending. Agency leaders can communicate priorities and drive change more immediately and effectively by setting outcome goals, designating goal managers, regularly tracking progress toward those goals, and engaging managers interactively to explore strategies to advance toward the goal.[93] For managers who do not have discrete budgets appropriated or allocated and are expected to manage a complicated matrix organization, as is the case with the EPA's regional administrators, performance management can be even more helpful.

The Charles 2005 initiative also shows that successful performance management does not have to start at the very top of an organization. Leaders of individual units, such as a regional office or a project team, can also use performance management fruitfully to drive priorities and achieve performance gains.

Accountability

Performance measurement, we have seen, can be a powerful tool helping agency managers and staff improve performance. The discussion so far has said little about the value of performance measurement for enhancing accountability. Yet accountability is often considered a primary reason for performance measurement.

The Government Performance and Results Act of 1993 states clearly its "accountability expectation" for federal agencies. Its first listed purpose is to "improve the confidence of the American people in the capability of the Federal Government, by systematically holding federal agencies accountable for achieving program results."

The Joint Agreement signed by the EPA and the states creating the National Environmental Performance Partnership System says, "We must . . . enhance our accountability to the public and taxpayers."[94] Similar language can be found in state and local performance policy documents.

Accountability can mean many different things. For some, it means ensuring the absence of corruption. Highly specific laws, regulations, and policies that characterize many government programs today evolved from an effort to prevent "the politics of personal favoritism and gain from meddling in the administrative decisions about personnel, procurement, finance, and service delivery."[95] For others, accountability is about ensuring that government delivers to its citizens what they want and are prepared to fund. For many performance measurement advocates, accountability is about rewarding good performance and penalizing poor performance, applied to organizations and individuals.[96] Many apply the concept of performance rewards and penalties to organizations or programs, calling for increasing funds for those with strong performance and jettisoning or cutting funds for those that perform poorly.[97] Others apply it to individuals. Numerous state education reform efforts promise bonuses for high-performing teachers.[98] Some threaten job loss for consistently poor performers.[99]

The challenge posed by these accountability mechanisms is that poorly structured systems can seriously undermine the performance-improving effects of using goals and measurement.[100] Accountability mechanisms designed to boost accountability expectations might interfere with performance improvement in several different ways.[101] Several examples are presented here for illustration, although others are certainly possible. First, accountability mechanisms designed to ward off corruption can prevent agencies from operating in an outcome-focused manner, inhibiting creativity and productivity-enhancing innovation that lead to performance gains. Accountability mechanisms designed to reward or penalize performance can also create problems. Problems can arise, for example, when the reward-to-penalty ratio is perceived as unfair, when incentives are directly linked to outcomes although accurate outcome measurement is difficult, when the allocation of rewards encourages competition although cooperation is warranted, and when program budgets are used to deliver the penalty or rewards.[102]

Process-Focused Accountability

Government systems to ensure accountability against fraud or abuse usually demand accountability for the process, rather than for results. These traditional accountability mechanisms have not been updated to support performance-focused programs. They track inputs, activities, outputs, expenditures, or strict adherence to written rules rather than trying to ensure responsible efforts to deliver promised outcomes,

Consider one example of the way abuse-avoiding accountability mechanisms can create unwanted effects. Government watchdogs often treat accountability as the ability to count, literally, the dollars the government has granted to another organization to make sure the money has been spent precisely as promised. Less attention is paid to whether or not the money achieved the purpose for which it was provided. The EPA program that provided federal funds to local governments to construct wastewater treatment plants vividly illustrates this dollar-counting focus. Years after the federal government terminated the construction grants program, the EPA visited localities to make sure every dollar charged to the federal grant was allowable under the grant conditions.[103] The audits often took place several election cycles after the funds were spent. As a result, the grant-winning elected official on whose watch the mis-spending occurred would reap political rewards for bringing in federal funds, while subsequent officials would bear the political cost of finding local dollars to repay often unexpected, unallowed costs.

In another example, current federal environmental grant regulations strongly signal a continued emphasis on process accountability. Among the barriers slowing a rapid and robust transition to the National Environmental Performance Partnership System—designed to make EPA-state partnerships more focused on the environment and less on process requirements—are the EPA's current grant regulations, including the grant regulation written for performance partnership grants. The regulation requires states to report, among other information, work-years purchased with federal dollars. "An approvable work plan must specify the estimated work years and funding amounts for each work plan component"[104]

This provision would make it hard for a state to undertake a project, such as the Charles initiative, that uses fresh and frequent performance measurement to guide, and regularly revise, its selection of appropriate strategies. Imagine, for example, that newly available monthly water quality measurements suggest a state's outreach or enforcement efforts in a given area are not having the anticipated effect. The state might want to change the activities it funds with federal dollars, perhaps shifting funds from staff time to the purchase of a promising new piece of equipment. Because the state would have made specific "work-year" commitments in its grant agreement with the EPA, its ability to make a midcourse change in its intervention strategy would be significantly slowed by the need to get approval for changes to its work plan. A similar problem would arise if a state lost a larger than expected number of key personnel at one time and decided to hire consultants to get the work done. Not surprisingly, many states decide that the battle to become performance focused, at least with federal funds, is not worth the effort. They concede to negotiating inputs and activities in their performance partnership and other annual agreements with the EPA.

In sum, although tracking expenditures and preventing corruption are very important, many of the mechanisms adopted to protect against ethical trespasses have evolved into overly rigid, prescriptive, and wasteful constraints. Updated control systems need to be established that are equally effective but do not interfere with performance-improving efforts.[105]

Formal Link between Outcomes and Personal Consequences

Even if traditional accountability systems are updated to be more performance focused, incentive systems designed to promote performance accountability can also threaten the performance-improving benefits of performance measurement. Tension can arise when explicit links are established between outcome results and personal rewards or penalties. Creating these links, long common in the private sector, represents a significant departure from past practice in the public sector. A leader of the U.S. Coast Guard's pilot GPRA project captures the anxieties that can arise in shifting to an outcome-focused organization:

> One of the central—and most difficult—issues presented by the Government Performance and Results Act is the shift in focus from inputs, activities, and outputs . . . to *outcomes*. . . . Consider what outcomes are: they are not what you do as an organization, they are the real-world effects of what you do. They are, by definition, things you don't control. . . . managers are often reluctant to risk accountability for things outside their control. Outcomes also commonly cut across organizational lines. A variety of programs will influence outcomes in areas like safety and environmental protection. . . . Maybe more significantly, the search for outcome-oriented goals is a process of examining the very basis for your existence. Measurement in this environment can be very threatening.[106]

When managers or workers feel unfairly threatened by an incentive system, they very sensibly "push back" to protect themselves. This is exactly what happened with New Zealand's effort to build accountability into its management reforms. Under New Zealand's reform program, managers enter into a "purchase agreement" between each department and the relevant minister. If a department fails to meet its performance targets, the manager can lose his or her job. Since managers are given hiring and firing discretion, the jobs of midlevel managers and other employees may be at risk as well.[107]

Fearful of losing their jobs, New Zealand's managers have resisted being held accountable for results they cannot control. They have been willing to accept accountability in their management agreements only for that which they can control, outputs.

> New Zealand focuses on outputs because they provide a reliable basis for enforcing managerial accountability, not because they are

the most important indicator of government performance. Accountability is facilitated because the supply of outputs can be directly attributed to the performance of chief executives and their departments; outcomes, by contrast, tend to be influenced by many factors, some of which are likely to be beyond the control of the relevant department.[108]

Regrettably, the New Zealand solution puts the government right back where it started before it tried to adopt a performance-focused system, counting activities. The reversion to "bean-counting" compelled by a highly structured, high-stakes performance agreement threatens to send New Zealand down the same activity-focused path that prompted performance-focused government reform worldwide. New Zealand could end up effectively and efficiently delivering to its citizens products they do not want, failing on an important dimension of public accountability: that government delivers to its citizens what they want and are willing to fund, not what government officials want or know how to deliver.

Reward-Penalty Ratio

"Doesn't the private sector also have trouble controlling all the variables affecting outcomes?" you might ask. "Don't private firms have to deliver strong performance in a competitive marketplace even when they cannot control all the variables? Indeed, isn't survival in a climate of uncertainty essential and inevitable?" This is undoubtedly true. In the private sector, however, high risks tend to be balanced by tremendous upside potential (most evident in financial markets). The companies and employees that are most at risk often stand to reap the greatest rewards. Most public sector organizations, however, lack the ability to earn huge profits and share performance gains with their employees. New Zealand managers can lose their jobs if their performance is poor, but they have little promise of earning bonuses or profit sharing if their performance is good. Indeed, New Zealand has even found it difficult to deliver increased budgets to strong-performing organizations as the reform effort originally envisioned.[109] The bottom line is that most public sector incentive systems seem biased toward the negative. As public management expert Robert D. Behn observes, "I bet I know what the managers who are to be held accountable think. I bet they believe, from their own empirical experience, that holding people accountable means that when they fail they are punished and that when they succeed nothing significant happens."[110]

Measurement Problems

Problems also arise when accurate outcome indicators are difficult to collect. How do you count changes in chest pains or headaches associated with environmental improvements? And what happens when outcomes can only be measured long after the relevant government intervention, such as reductions in reproductive problems associated with promulgation of a new environmental regulation or the effect of early childhood day care programs on employability? When those seeking accountability want to use some form of measurement as the basis for awarding incentives even when measurement difficulties arise, they often retreat to using effort or activity indicators as surrogates. The problem with using effort or activities to decide rewards or penalties is that unless all relevant dimensions of effort and activity can be measured and their relative importance accurately assessed, the reward system will motivate the wrong allocation of effort for getting the best job done. It will inevitably drive workers to do more of those reward-earning activities that can be measured at the expense of those that cannot. Activities that cannot easily be measured but that may be crucial to success, such as thinking or answering questions, will be given short shrift.

Competitive Rewards Impede Cooperation

Incentive systems that are designed to boost the motivation and accountability of individual workers can also impede performance improvements when cooperation among workers is needed and incentives are based on comparative performance. Consider, for example, an incentive policy that allows only a small subset of workers within each organizational unit to earn bonuses. The argument often given for such a structure is that not everyone can be a top performer. Indeed, some observers take it as a given that incentive systems that reward a large percentage of the work force must be handing out bonuses indiscriminately, losing the desired incentive effect. It is not hard to imagine a competitive tension arising among workers when rewards are limited to a small percentage of people in the organization. When employees should be cooperating and sharing information with one another to improve performance, they may instead be trying to devise ways to make their own performance look good compared with that of their colleagues.[111]

Penalty Undermines Program Objectives

One version of performance accountability calls for linking budgets to program performance, rewarding strong programs with increased funding and penalizing weak ones with funding cuts. This is seen as the public sector equivalent of the financial rewards that strong performing companies enjoy. Yet cutting funds for weak government programs is likely to hurt program beneficiaries more than it hurts those who run the program. Unlike the private sector, most government agencies hold a monopoly on the delivery of public services in their area. An alternate supplier is usually not available to pick up the slack of a poorly performing government organization. At the same time, strong performing programs may not always warrant increased funding. Sometimes budgets should be cut for programs that have accomplished their objectives and be redirected to unaddressed needs. Budgets are ill-equipped to serve as a performance incentive mechanism.

Accountability Mechanisms Needed

As these examples demonstrate, poorly structured accountability mechanisms can be a barrier to improved performance. If the accountability system seems unfair, workers are likely to try to protect themselves. They can leave the government, pursuing opportunities that seem more just. They can try to hide within the organization, refusing management jobs and just biding their time, having lost their motivation because of an unfair evaluation system. They may try to change the nature of the measures used as indicators of performance or try to manipulate the measures in deceitful ways. In such circumstances, performance measurements no longer improve government performance. They become the objective itself, with workers sensibly trying to protect themselves or extricate themselves from the system.

Despite the potential dangers of many of the mechanisms used to ensure accountability, effective accountability controls are needed. Citizens need to know that government is doing what its citizens want it to do and are willing to fund, not just doing what government officials want or know how to deliver. Citizens also need to sense that the goals of government agencies closely match the expectations of citizens. They need comfort that government agencies and their employees are working diligently and, it is hoped, intelligently to achieve performance improvements. They need and deserve reasonable assurance that government officials are avoiding self-dealing and fighting waste. And when government regulates other parties, citizens need assurances that those being regulated are being held accountable to perform in accordance with laws and the public interest.

Indeed, especially in the regulatory area, there is great concern that the move to performance-focused systems will dismantle the already weak accountability systems that exist, without replacing them with something equally or more effective.[112] Advocates of performance-based management frequently tout its ability to provide "flexibility with accountability."[113] Opponents fear that performance-focused efforts will successfully deliver states, locals, employers, and even the federal government greater flexibility but fail to deliver improved social outcomes.

Fears about the loss of accountability are well founded. They grow from years of experience with, and debates about, performance-focused systems. Opponents fear that many advocates of performance-focused changes are not interested in improved performance but have jumped on the performance bandwagon hoping to win support for state-specific or even site-specific performance standards that have historically been weaker than national standards in most states.[114] This struggle was at the core of the debates about the use of technology or performance standards in the 1972 Amendments to the Clean Water Act and continues today.[115] Opponents know that many environmental laws already allow companies the flexibility to adopt practices that will deliver performance superior to technology standards. Few companies, however, will pursue that option because it raises performance expectations for all facilities, not just the one for which the company seeks to make changes. The companies know that performance-focused systems usually require increased outcome measurement and reporting, yet even as states and regulated entities call for decisions to be based on stronger science and embrace the notion of performance-focused systems, they have also resisted efforts to increase measurement and reporting requirements.[116] And opponents know that both the EPA and states hate to take the political heat associated with setting performance standards and conducting performance assessments, as evidenced by their delays in setting and implementing water quality standards until forced to do so by court decisions.

A Performance-Focused Model for Accountability

The Charles initiative suggests a model showing how performance measurement can deliver the accountability the public seeks, without impairing the performance-improving aspect of measurements. The initiative shows how performance measurement can be used to improve alignment with citizen and managerial expectations and motivate staff, even when an agency does not directly control all the variables affecting outcomes. It also illustrates how the agency can work with the regulated community in a performance-focused way, affording flexibility while strengthening accountability. The model will not fit all circumstances, but it begins to point the way toward effective performance-improving accountability mechanisms.

Consider the government's ability to deliver to its citizens what they want and are prepared to fund. The traditional mechanism presumed to align public expectations with government work in democracies is the electoral process. If citizens do not like the basket of policies and products the government is producing, they can remove governmental leaders at the next election. The practical problem with this approach, of course, is that it forces citizens to make choices about a big bundle of goods and does not give individual agencies much feedback about whether or not they are getting it right.

By announcing the goal of a Clean Charles in 2005, EPA New England unbundled the goods, implicitly inviting citizens to comment on a specific goal. Citizens do not have to wonder what the agency is trying to do or how it is trying to do it, because the EPA gives them that information explicitly. If they do not like it, they can write letters to the agency, the newspaper, or their elected representatives. If they like the goal but feel the agency is handling the project poorly, they can similarly make their views known. If they think another goal should have higher priority, they can readily express that view, as well. Citizens do not have to wait until the next election to make their views known to influence the government's choice of priorities and actions to advance those priorities.

Goals do not automatically enhance public accountability. If goals are framed too vaguely or in a way the public does not understand, the public is unlikely to pay much attention. Although the agency satisfies external mandates for performance measurement, it does not build public accountability. Because the Charles goal is so clearly articulated, is outcome focused, and has geographic and time specificity, the public pays attention. Catching the public's attention strengthens public accountability.

The Charles initiative also suggests a way to motivate improved performance without dysfunctional consequences. The high-stakes penalties and low-return rewards used in New Zealand logically compel self-protective behavior. They drive those being measured to press for accountability for outputs they know they can control rather than for the outcomes they should be trying to influence. Rewards linked to inexact measurement are also likely to compel self-protective behavior, distorting decisions about effort and resource allocation toward that which can be measured easily rather than that which needs to be done. Rewards limited to only a few individuals for accomplishments that require cooperation are likely to stifle needed cooperation.

The Charles initiative motivates without these dysfunctional effects by making it easier for staff members to understand how their work aligns with the reasons they came to the EPA in the first place. The initiative motivates simply by providing feedback, which taps intrinsic motivational forces.

At the same time, the Charles initiative uses the motivating value of rewards and penalties but does so judiciously. For staff, it primarily employs the gentle but effective incentive of the delight of managerial and public approval combined with the fear of internal and public embarrassment. The Charles experience suggests that the media can be enlisted to become part of an incentive system that reports fairly and regularly, without the gratuitous and unfair journalistic swipes feared by so many government officials. If government officials give the media something to watch, make the story easy to report, predictable in its timing and, if possible, linked to community events, the press is likely to report it. This, in turn, creates a gentle and effective pressure on the agency to get the job done.

What will happen if the EPA fails to make its final goal or meet the timetable? It is possible that the agency would be terribly embarrassed, and that the leadership might get thrown out, if elected, or asked to resign, if appointed. I suspect this will not be the case if a program is structured as the Charles initiative has been. The initiative has made goals, strategies, and progress transparent to the public and revised strategies as appropriate. The public has been supportive of the project to date. My guess is that the public will remain supportive even if the goals are not met, as long as the transparency of the program remains solid, the strategies are cogent, and the goals address the concerns of the community.

When we think of performance-focused accountability, we tend to assume that agencies should be held accountable for attaining their goals, or rewarded or penalized based on the level of performance attained. It is time to change that assumption. It makes more sense to hold performance-focused agencies accountable for selecting goals that resonate with the public, collecting and accurately analyzing information about progress toward the goal, developing and following cogent strategies, and sharing relevant information with the public in a way it can and will want to understand.

Outcome-focused accountability does not necessitate a strict and explicit link between the attainment of outcomes and rewards or penalties. DeVillars never explicitly linked personnel rewards to improvements in the water quality of the Charles, although effective performance managers have since enjoyed career advances.

The Charles initiative necessarily employed a more aggressive incentive system to motivate local governments and the private sector. Unable to tap the intrinsic and nonmonetary rewards that can motivate employees and because local governments and private firms are expected to take actions that have significant costs, the Charles initiative readily employs the threat of financial consequence for failure to act. Performance-management and performance-focused, information-driven environmental protection strategies depend on facility-specific performance obligations linked with penalties for those who fail to meet their obligations. At the same time, the use of resonant public environmental goals introduces public opinion into the accountability equation. By so doing, the Charles initiative has been able to sway actions more quickly and provide greater protection than current laws require.

In sum, the Charles initiative suggests that performance measurement and management can enhance government accountability to the public without impairing the performance-improving aspect of measurement. A clearly articulated and resonant goal with a timetable grabs the public's attention and invites it, between elections, to comment on what government is doing. Regularly scheduled, event-linked progress reports let the press, public, managers, stakeholders, and staff know how close to attainment the goal is and keep the pressure on everyone to meet the goal. Outcome-focused goals and fresh, frequent outcome measurements that allow staff to see how their actions affect outcomes enlighten and heighten motivation. Regular interactive meetings with managers and informed stakeholders encourage constant thinking and rethinking of strategy, based on updated information. Independent measurement and measurement by multiple parties ensure credibility of the progress reports. At the same time, focusing on outcomes can encourage performance gains beyond those likely to be realized by simply relying on traditional compliance assurance methods.

Is the Charles River an Exception?

The Charles River is the jewel in the crown, I have been told. It lends itself easily to this sort of high-visibility enterprise. Doubt has been expressed that this approach can be applied to environmental areas or concerns that are less well known.

The Lower Charles is indeed a special river. It is edged on one side by the city of Boston and a park designed by Frederick Law Olmstead, the nation's most famous landscape architect. On the other are two of the nation's leading universities, Harvard and the Massachusetts Institute of Technology. Unlike the mighty Mississippi, though, the Charles River holds no unique standing as a river of national significance. It is primarily valued by those who live near it. All over America, in places like Cleveland and Washington, D.C., rivers once valued primarily for their commercial contributions are increasingly appreciated as recreational assets. Americans today are migrating toward coastlines because of their love of water.

In communities across this country, there are thousands of Clean Charles 2005 projects waiting to happen. Indeed, there are communities where they already have. In 1987 the Chesapeake Bay Program set a goal of reducing nutrients by 40 percent by 2000. Like the Charles initiative, it has regularly measured and reported progress toward the goal since that time and aggressively reached out to engage governments, nonprofits, and the private sector in finding solutions to achieve the goal. By 1997 the Bay program reported that its goal was in sight.[117]

Many states already pursue a watershed approach. Too many of these efforts, however, fail to set time- and place-specific goals or to use fresh and frequent progress reports. As a result, they miss the motivational and enlistment power of performance measurement.

The potential for "managing the measures" to improve environmental quality is not limited to water. The Clean Air Act requires states to manage their air sheds to meet goals and timetables and sanctions states with heavy penalties if they fail to meet them. Indeed the effectiveness of goal setting, progress reporting, and effective incentives is affirmed by improving air quality trend lines.[118] One could imagine even greater effect on, and less contention about, improving air quality if the discussions about strategy moved from government-to-government negotiations to a more open process. This is exactly what the mayor of Tulsa, Oklahoma, did in the 1990s. Fearing that Tulsa would exceed the ozone standard for a third time, forcing the city into a "non-attainment status" under the Clean Air Act that would have severely curtailed new economic development projects, the mayor decided to "manage the measures" more aggressively. She moved the discussion about strategy out from the halls of government to the community that could help fix the problem. She reached out to local experts, nonprofits, regulatory partners, and the regulated community, and together they reviewed relevant data, monitored progress, and brainstormed strategies to avoid federal penalties. And just as DeVillars held his staff accountable for the cogency of its strategies rather than strictly accountable for achieving outcomes, the EPA agreed to a similar accountability arrangement with Tulsa. It designated Tulsa its first Flexible Attainment Region, recognizing that the city's plan for reducing ozone levels was solid, even if it did not satisfy every detail of its outcome goal.[119]

The Charles initiative should not be the exception. It is not hard to imagine government using goals and regular performance measurement to enlist community support to keep a local beach open all summer, improve water quality in a near-by lake, guarantee drinking water that exceeds national standards, or increase visibility from a mountain. The Charles initiative offers a vivid example of how performance-focused, information-driven environmental protection can be applied across the country.

How the Charles Initiative Fits into an Agencywide System

Of course, the Clean Charles 2005 model is just one piece of what a larger performance-focused, information-driven environmental protection system could be. Ideally, the Charles initiative would fit neatly into an EPA-wide performance management system, where information about environmental goals and environmental progress is broadly known, regularly reviewed, and becomes the basis for strategy development, tactics formulation, and resource allocation. This target-focused performance management system would complement increased use of environmental performance measurements in other ways, such as informing consumer choices and citizen decisions and tapping the motivational and learning potential of comparisons.[120]

Significantly increased reliance on performance measurement will not happen overnight, but progress can be made immediately. The Charles initiative should and could fit neatly into the EPA's agencywide GPRA report, alongside information about similar performance-focused efforts to clean other water bodies across the nation. It could also fit neatly into the state-EPA performance partnership agreement.

Unfortunately, despite the passage of the GPRA and the adoption of the National Environmental Performance Partnership System, the Charles initiative is treated as an exception rather than as a model to be replicated. While the Charles River project is highlighted in its own box in the EPA fiscal year 1999 Performance Report, it is not placed in context.[121] The EPA makes no effort to "roll up" the performance gains of the Charles with those of other water-quality-improving efforts across the country. In fact, the EPA appears to have considered, and abandoned, this possibility. In its annual performance report to Congress, the EPA described annual performance goal and measure number 16 as follows: "More than 220 communities will have local watersheds improved by controls on combined sewer overflows and storm water."[122] The report goes on to inform the reader that the "EPA is not yet able to measure actual improvements in watersheds; therefore this goal has been dropped after FY1999."[123] Rather than encourage the regions and states to measure their water quality by maintaining a relentless focus on outcome goals and measures, the agency opted instead to retreat to the familiarity of activity counts. Its proposed new measure settles for a simple tally of the number of communities that "implemented requirements in Storm Water Phase I permits and/or CSO Long-Term Control Plan."[124] This activity-focused indicator imparts little useful information to the general public.

Federal, state, and local environmental regulators can and should immediately push for a relentless focus on environmental and public health outcomes to determine activity selection, not the other way around. Environmental outcome targets should replace activity targets for regions and states. These new targets could be established in an iterative top-down, bottom-up process or in the reverse order. The EPA's national program offices might propose a few important national goals for environmental and public health improvements with timetables. They could then work with the EPA regional offices, who would work with each of the states (and territories, tribes, and localities, as appropriate) to sort out how these aggregate goals cascade down to each region and state. States would negotiate with regions, and regions with head-quarters, a few ambitious but feasible environmental targets and timeta-bles, just as major corporations do when they set corporate goals and negotiate expectations with their organizational subunits.[125] The EPA performance report should then be enhanced to provide location-specific information, perhaps through on-line links, so that communities can more easily find information about local environmental conditions and the nature and status of efforts to improve them.

When environmental targets are not possible because the existing state of the measurement is inadequate, the EPA and state performance plans could set targets for improving information quality. The perfor-mance report would report progress on improving the quality of envi-ronmental information. When funding levels are insufficient to allow the necessary information gathering, performance plans could make that clear so that those living in communities where water and air quality are not tested can know it.

Because unexpected events inevitably arise, the EPA, its regions, and the states should not be held strictly accountable (that is, specific rewards linked to specific outcomes) for achieving all the outcome goals they set. As with the Charles River team, regions and states should be held accountable for developing and pursuing cogent strategies. They should also be responsible for effectively disseminating information about their efforts and progress to the public.

The headquarters offices of the EPA should be responsible for organiz-ing and presenting performance information in a way that supports regional, state, and local performance-focused decisionmaking. Head-quarters should also work with the regions in examining the performance information to assess and revise intervention strategies and to facilitate cross-area learning. The EPA regions should similarly support the states.

The EPA and states could also enhance the availability of point-of-use performance information. Although it may be too costly to fly flags daily at every beach and boat launch site in a state, it would not be too costly to post available information on a website and indicate with a permanent sign at every location where current water quality informa-tion can be found. Local weather stations and newspapers already carry air quality reports. They might be willing to report other forms of envi-ronmental information as well.

The time for increased use of environmental performance measure-ment to drive environmental gain has never been better. Federal and state legal mandates now require the EPA and most state environmental protection agencies to set outcome-focused goals and generate annual performance reports or submit some performance budgeting information. At the same time, dramatic improvements in information collection, processing, and dissemination technology make widespread use of performance information remarkably affordable and technically feasible. Yet unless the people in, or affected by, government programs, and especially government leaders, begin to recognize the value of outcome-focused performance measurement as a management tool they use regularly in their strategic and daily decisions, measurement fatigue will set in before the power of performance measurement is realized. This opportune moment may pass and not return again for decades.

The Charles initiative demonstrates how valuable performance measurement can be. The initiative works because it focuses attention on a specific outcome goal and, by so doing, engages the interest of many people. It works because the public performance goal and measurements of progress toward the goal are more than just numbers; they serve as focal points and a rallying cry and a constant reminder to check back and verify the effectiveness of the strategy and revise it if necessary. It works because it defines a common agenda across organizational boundaries. It works because fresh and frequent measurements are used on a regular basis to shape decisions about what activities to do. It works because point-of-use performance information informs consumer decisions. It works because individual and organizational leaders are aggressively managing according to the measures, within the agency and beyond its borders. Finally, it works because annual report cards, publicity about individual components of the effort, and regular meetings with concerned parties enhance the agency's accountability, without being unduly or unfairly punitive. The Charles initiative successfully uses environmental performance measurement to motivate changes leading to measurable gains in environmental quality, which is, after all, its *raison d'être*. Let us hope others will learn from its lesson and rapidly follow with more performance-focused, information-driven environmental protection strategies.

Notes to Chapter 3

1. U.S. Environmental Protection Agency (EPA), region 1, "EPA Gives Charles River a 'B' and Announces Innovative 'Curtain' at Magazine Beach," EPA New England press release 00-04-14, Boston, April 14, 2000.

2. Technology standards specify the type of equipment or process that regulated parties are required to use. In contrast, a performance standard would specify the minimum water quality that discharged wastewater would need to exceed.

3. Oliver A. Houck, *The Clean Water Act TMDL Program: Law, Policy, and Implementation* (Washington: Environmental Law Institute, December 1999), pp. 3–6.

4. U.S. EPA, "Water Quality Conditions in the United States: A Profile from the 1998 National Water Quality Inventory Report," EPA-841-F-00-006 (June 2000), p. 1. Oliver A. Houck notes that the quality of this annual assessment has been questioned by the Public Employees for Environmental Responsibility, "Murky Waters, Official Water Quality Reports Are All Wet: An Inside Look at EPA's Implementation of the Clean Water Act," in Houck, *The Clean Water Act TMDL Program,* p. 8.

5. Only 40 percent meet water quality standards for fishing and swimming. U.S. EPA, "National Water Quality Inventory" (2000).

6. Houck, *The Clean Water Act TMDL Program.* The lawsuits compel states and the EPA to establish total maximum daily load (TMDL) limits for contaminants to the receiving waters.

7. Maine Department of Environmental Protection, "Use of PCS Data," undated presentation. This is a one-time report that Maine prepared to assess the value of this sort of analysis, using data from 1993 to 1996. If other states are doing this type of analysis, it is not widely known.

8. In 1995 the EPA and states created the National Environmental Performance Partnership System (NEPPS) to address these problems. In addition, in the EPA's appropriations language, which includes grant funding for the states, Congress allowed the EPA to combine multiple grants into a single combined grant if requested by the appropriate state (and occasionally local) authority.

9. The effort to adopt multimedia inspections was known as the Blackstone Project. Conversations with Pat Deese Stanton, Massachusetts Department of Environmental Protection; and with Pat Meany and Stephen Perkins, EPA, region 1.

10. Robert K. Merton, *Social Theory and Social Structure* (Free Press, 1968), pp. 251–54.

11. E4E was convened by two-time EPA administrator William Ruckleshaus and involved a broad-based bipartisan membership, including four former EPA adminstrators, several members of Congress, two governors, a mayor, leaders of national and regional environmental organizations, senior executives of large companies, and several state environmental agency directors. Several members, a few from environmental groups and a few from businesses decided not to sign the final report.

12. Center for Strategic and International Studies, "Bi-Partisan Group Announces Recommendations to Improve the Environment," press release announcing the release of *The Environmental Protection System in Transition: Toward a More Desirable Future,* final report of the Enterprise for the Environment (Washington, 1998).

13. National Academy of Public Administration, *Resolving the Paradox of Environmental Protection* (Washington, September 1997); and National Academy of Public Administration, *Setting Priorities, Getting Results* (Washington, 1995).

14. Carol M. Browner and others, "Joint Commitment to Reform Oversight and Create a National Environmental Performance Partnership System," policy memorandum signed at the EPA "All-States" meeting by Carol M. Browner, administrator, EPA; Tom Looby, director, Office of Environment of the Colorado Department of Health and cochair of the State/EPA Capacity Steering Committee; Fred Hansen, deputy administrator, EPA; and Mary Gade, director of the Illinois EPA and cochair of the State/EPA Capacity Steering Committee, May 17, 1995.

15. U.S. EPA, Office of Reinvention, *The Changing Nature of Environmental and Public Health Protection: An Annual Report on Reinvention*, EPA100-R-98-003 (March 1998), p. 8.

16. The National Academy of Public Administration recently sponsored several evaluations of the National Environmental Performance Partnership System. The studies basically concluded that NEPPS has resulted in progress toward environmental performance-focused approaches. More discussions between the EPA and states have to do with problems in the environment and how to fix them than with whether or not a state is willing to do what the EPA wants it to do. At the same time, the studies found that the activity-focused culture of both states and the EPA seriously slowed progress. National Academy of Public Administration, *environment.gov: Transforming Environmental Protection for the Twenty-First Century*, research papers 11–14, vol. 3 (Washington, 2000).

17. U.S. EPA, "Project XL Progress Report: Intel Corporation," EPA 100-R-00-005 (December 1999).

18. Michael Crow, "Beyond Experiments," *Environmental Forum*, vol. 17 (May–June 2000), pp. 19–29.

19. Shelley H. Metzenbaum, "Information Driven," *Environmental Forum*, vol. 17 (March–April 2000), pp. 28–41.

20. Allen White and Diana Zinkl, "Green Metrics: A Global Status Report on Standardized Corporate Environmental Reporting," paper prepared for CERES (Coalition for Environmentally Responsible Economies), annual conference, 1998.

21. Julia Melkers and Katherine Willoughby, "The State of the States: Performance-Based Budgeting Requirements in 47 out of 50," *Public Administration Review*, vol. 58 (January–February 1998), pp. 66–73.

22. Governmental Accounting Standards Board and the National Academy of Public Administration, "Report on Survey of State and Local Government Use and Reporting of Performance Measures—First Questionnaire Results," Washington, September 30, 1997.

23. Governmental Accounting Standards Board and the National Academy of Public Administration, "Report on Survey of State and Local Government Use and Reporting of Performance Measures"; and Urban Institute and Interna-

tional City/County Management Association, *Comparative Performance Measurement* (Washington: ICMA,1997).

24. *Government Performance and Results Act*, P.L. 103-62.

25. Harry P. Hatry, *Performance Measurement: Getting Results* (Washington: Urban Institute Press, 1999). For a more complete description of these early federal efforts and a discussion of the lessons associated with them, see General Accounting Office, *Performance Budgeting: Past Initiatives Offer Insights for GPRA Implementation*, GAO/AIMD-97-46 (March 27, 1997).

26. For New Zealand, see Graham Scott, Ian Ball, and Tony Dale, "New Zealand's Public Sector Management Reform: Implications for the United States," *Journal of Policy Analysis and Management*, vol. 16 (Summer 1997), pp. 357–81; and for other nations, see Donald F. Kettl, "The Global Revolution in Public Management: Driving Themes, Missing Links," *Journal of Policy Analysis and Management*, vol. 16 (Summer 1997), pp. 446–62.

27. Joseph S. Nye Jr., Philip D. Zelikow, and David C. King, eds., *Why People Don't Trust Government* (Harvard University Press, 1997).

28. One noteworthy exception is the Coast Guard. See Richard Kowalewski, "Using Outcome Information to Redirect Programs: A Case Study of the Coast Guard's Pilot Project under the Government Performance and Results Act," U.S. Coast Guard Office of Marine Safety, Security and Environmental Protection, April 1996. In general, the GPRA material of the U.S. Department of Transportation is more outcome focused than that of most other federal agencies.

29. The sections of the EPA's GPRA reports pertaining to air are a noteworthy exception.

30. DeVillars was recused from the MWRA case because he had previously chaired the MWRA board. Moraff did not discuss that case with him.

31. Interviews with Bill Walsh-Rogalski, U.S. EPA, region 1, summer 2000.

32. Nancy R. Katz, "Incentives and Performance Management," a paper prepared for the Executive Session on Public Sector Performance Management, Harvard University, Kennedy School of Government, 2000. The discussion that follows on the effect of goals and information on motivation and performance is informed by Katz's paper. References cited by Katz are noted here. Assertions about the relationship among performance, information, motivation, and outcome changes that are not footnoted are just that—this author's assertions, based on observation and, I hope, logic and common sense.

33. Katz, "Incentives and Performance Management," p. 1. Katz cites the research of G. Latham and T. Lee, "Goal Setting," in E. Locke, ed., *Generalizing from Laboratory to Field Settings* (Lexington, 1986), pp. 1–118; and E. Locke and G. Latham, *A Theory of Goal Setting and Task Performance* (Prentice-Hall, 1990).

34. Robert S. Kaplan and David P. Norton. *The Balanced Scorecard: Translating Strategy to Action* (Harvard Business School Press, 1996). See also Robert S. Kaplan and David P. Norton, *The Strategy-Focused Organization* (Harvard Business School Press, 2001).

35. Scott Allen, "Charles Cleanup Gets New EPA Push: Focus This Time Around on Pollution Prevention," *Boston Globe*, October 22, 1995, p. 33. U.S.

EPA, "EPA Sets Clean Up Goal for Charles River by Earth Day 2005," EPA New England press release, October 22, 1995.

36. Evie Gelastapolous, "BU Agrees to Pay $2 Million for Charles River Spills," *Boston Globe*, October 9, 1997, p. B5; Peter J. Howe, "EPA Warns Milford of Fines, Suits Over Pollution of Charles River," *Boston Globe*, September 27, 1996, p. B5, and "U.S. Eases Pressure on River Cleanup; Progress Is Seen along the Charles," *Boston Globe*, May 17, 1998, p. B1.

37. Peter J. Howe, "Renaissance on the Charles," *Boston Globe Magazine*, October 5, 1997, p.14; Derrick Z. Jackson, "A Clearer Picture on the State of the Charles," *Boston Globe*, May 29, 1996, p. 13; and Peter J. Howe, "Bacteria Levels Soar on the Upper Charles; Sewer Leaks in Milford Suspected," *Boston Globe*, September 7, 1996, p. B.7.

38. U.S. EPA, Office of the Chief Financial Officer, *FY 1999 Annual Performance Report*, EPA 190-R-00-001 (March 2000), p. 27.

39. In fact, according to the *State of the New England Environment*, 96 percent of New England's assessed rivers, streams, lakes, and ponds are swimmable. The report does not, however, indicate the percentage of the lake and pond acres and river and stream miles that have been assessed. U.S. EPA, region 1, *State of the New England Environment Report, 1970–2000*, EPA 901-R-00-001 (March 2000), p. 15.

40. U.S. EPA, Office of the Chief Financial Officer, *EPA Strategic Plan*, EPA 190-R-97-002 (September 1997), p. 29.

41. U.S. EPA, *FY 1999 Annual Performance Report*, p. 22.

42. Sec. 114 of P.L. 104, 182, the Safe Drinking Water Amendments of 1996, requires community water systems to notify their customers annually about water quality. This is a significant development in building a performance-focused, information-driven environmental protection system.

43. Hatry, *Performance Measurement*, pt. 3.

44. Interviews with Ken Moraff, U.S. EPA, region 1, summer 2000.

45. See, for example, Allen Shick, *Spirit of Reform: Managing the New Zealand State Sector in a Time of Change, A Report Prepared for the State Services Commission and The Treasury, New Zealand*, August 1996 (www.ssc. govt.nz/Documents/reform1.htm [December 9, 2000]).

46. Jody Perras, "Reinventing EPA New England: An EPA Regional Office Tests Innovative New Approaches to Environmental Protection," Learning from Innovations in Environmental Protection Research Paper 14 (Washington: National Academy of Public Administration, June 2000). Perras has written an excellent case study of the Clean Charles 2005 program and several other innovative programs tried in EPA, region 1.

47. E-mail from Walsh-Rogalski, February 22, 2000.

48. Abraham McLaughlin, "EPA Floats New Program to Save America's Rivers," *Christian Science Monitor*, March 5, 1998, p. 3.

49. Peter J Howe, "Charles Cleanup Targets Polluters: Firms Given Deadline to Make Needed Repairs," *Boston Globe*, March 2, 1998, p. A1.

50. Interview with Moraff, summer 2000.

51. "EPA Details Aggressive Pollution Prevention and Enforcement Strategy for the Charles River," EPA New England press release 98-3-1, March 2, 1998.

52. Howe, "Bacteria Levels Soar," Boston Globe, September 7, 1996, p. B7.

53. Peter J. Howe, "EPA Warns Milford of Fines, Suits Over Pollution of Charles River, Boston Globe, September 27, 1996, p. B5.

54. The Charles River Watershed Association has posted a spreadsheet showing Charles River water quality since October 16, 1995.

55. U.S. EPA, region 1, "EPA Gives Charles River a 'B'."

56. Interview with Moraff, December 2000.

57. Katz cites the work of M. Enzle and J. Ross, "Increasing and Decreasing Intrinsic Interest with Contingent Rewards: A Test of Cognitive Evaluation Theory," Journal of Experimental Social Psychology, vol. 14, no. 6 (1978), pp. 588–97; and J. Harackiewicz, "The Effects of Reward Contingency and Performance Feedback on Intrinsic Motivation," Journal of Personality and Social Psychology, vol. 37, no. 8 (1979), pp. 1352–63.

58. Katz, "Incentives and Performance Management."

59. Interview with Moraff, summer 2000.

60. See also Kowalewski, "Using Outcome Information"; and Malcolm K. Sparrow, The Regulatory Craft (Brookings, 2000).

61. The Massachusetts Executive Office of Environmental Affairs and the Department of Environmental Protection adopted a watershed approach to managing the state's water resources in 1993, two years before the Charles initiative was launched. Under the state's watershed management plan, the state tries to review each watershed basin on a five-year cycle, gathering information in the first year, monitoring the second, assessing in year three, implementing control strategies in the fourth year, and finally, looking back and learning in anticipation of starting the cycle again. The state issued an assessment report on the receiving waters of the Charles in February 2000. Interview with Kevin Brander, Massachusetts Department of Environmental Protection, July 2000.

62. The USGS has set up monitoring equipment at five different locations on the Charles River to collect a steady stream of information about water level, temperature, and salinity. It also gathers information on bacteria, biological demand, metals, nutrients, and suspended solids.

63. Peter J. Howe, "Swimming in the Charles Is Goal," Boston Globe, April 24, 2000, p. 1.

64. Interview with Kathleen Baskin, Charles River Watershed Association, September 2000.

65. In negotiated settlements, both Conrail and Genzyme agreed to provide funds to the Charles River Watershed Association to support its monitoring work. A third settlement, with Boston University, enlists the Charles River Watershed Association to help BU control its storm-water discharges.

66. Boston Harbor Association, Charles River Watershed Association, Conservation Law Foundation, Friends of the Muddy River, Restore Olmstead's Waterway, Save the Harbor/Save the Bay, and Watertown Citizens for Environmental Safety.

67. Massachusetts also designates a river basin coordinator for each watershed.

68. The state, however, did not set a specific goal or timetable for the Upper Charles. It continued to follow its five-year watershed action plan, assessing watershed quality once every five years.

69. Interview with Brander, July 2000.

70. Peter Weiskell, U.S. Geological Survey, August 2000. The USGS study is being supported financially by the EPA, the Massachusetts DEP, the MWRA, and the USGS.

71. Interview with Baskin, September 2000.

72. U.S. EPA, "EPA Gives Charles River a 'B'."

73. Gelastopolous, "BU Agrees to Pay $2 Million."

74. Pete J. Howe, "US Eases Pressure on River Cleanup; Progress Is Seen Along the Charles," *Boston Globe*, May 17, 1998, p.B1.

75. www.cleancharles.org

76. U.S. EPA, "EPA Gives Charles River a 'B'."

77. Public management scholar Mark Moore has proposed that police chiefs similarly use performance measurement to clarify expectations with their authorizing environment, the political oversight apparatus. Mark H. Moore, "Police Accountability and the Measurement of Police Performance," Harvard University, Kennedy School of Government, November 11, 1991.

78. Thomas Patterson, *Out of Order* (Vintage Books, 1993).

79. See, for example, Stephen Barr, "DOT's Full-Throttle Performance," *Washington Post*, April 4, 2000, p. A27.

80. Interview with John DeVillars, August 2000.

81. Howe, "Renaissance on the Charles," p. 14.

82. See, for example, Howe, "Swimming in the Charles Is Goal."

83. Peter J. Howe, "As Charles Stars, New Cleanups Vowed," *Boston Globe*, October 16, 1998, p. B4.

84. Florida Department of Environmental Protection, *Secretary's Quarterly Performance Report*, vol.1 (October 31, 1997); and memorandum from Secretary Virginia Wetherill included in "Briefing Materials for Presentation to Governor Lawton Chiles, Florida Department of Environmental Protection, Secretary's Quarterly Performance Report," December 2, 1997.

Florida began issuing quarterly performance reports on October 31, 1997. These reports set a new standard for environmental agency performance measurement because of their comprehensiveness, transparency, and useful detail. Wetherill's successor, David Struhs, has continued the reports, although printed copies are no longer available, only the online version. In May 2000 Struhs announced plans for major improvements to future reports. An interim report was posted on Florida's website on November 2, 2000. Some improvements have already been made, including more trend analysis than previous reports and the presentation of outcome information with its supporting activity information.

85. Lyndsey Layton, "Pothole Proof Rolling In; Growing Stack of Hubcaps Shows a 3-Foot Gap in Credibility," *Washington Post*, April 7, 2000, p. B3.

86. Carol D. Leonnig, "For District Voters, A Way to Keep Score," *Washington Post,* April 21, 2000, p. B2. See also District of Columbia Office of Communications, "Mayor Unveils Finalized City-Wide Strategic Plan and Accountability 'Scorecards'" District of Columbia press release, April 20, 2000.

87. Interviews with Moraff and Walsh-Rogalski, summer 2000.

88. DeVillars's interactive approach was a small-scale version of a highly successful interactive performance management system used by former New York City police commissioner William Bratton to achieve dramatic reductions in crime rates. Armed with fresh, frequent, detailed crime statistics and activity information broken down geographically and showing week-to-week, month-to-month, and yearly trends, Bratton and his management team instituted regular meetings with precinct commanders to discuss their proposed intervention strategies. Each precinct commander was expected to be thoroughly familiar with statistics for his or her own precinct and to have developed a cogent action plan based on the information. The meetings were also used to the tap the expertise of other precinct commanders who might have tried similar tactics in their precinct and to secure assistance from central office units, as needed. This system is known as Compstat and has been replicated by other police departments, as well as the New York City Corrections and Parks Department. See John Buntin, "Assertive Policing, Plummeting Crime: The NYPD Takes on Crime in New York City," case C16-99.1530.0, Kennedy School of Government, 1999. See also Dennis C. Smith, "What Did Public Managers Learn from Police Reform in New York? COMPSTAT and the Promise of Performance Management," paper prepared for presentation at the nineteenth annual research conference of the Association of Public Policy Analysis and Management, Washington, 1997.

89. The compliance engineer was Brian Pitt, and Jay Brolin was the expert on storm water.

90. Interview with Moraff, summer 2000.

91. Interview with Walsh-Rogalski, summer 2000.

92. The EPA's regional offices do not have separate budgets. Regional administrators have a small amount of discretionary funds available for geographic initiatives and administrative projects. Most regional funding is passed through the stovepipes of the EPA's national headquarters offices and arrives at the regions with "activity-strings" attached, greatly complicating outcome-focused endeavors.

93. Shelley H. Metzenbaum, *Making Measurement Matter: The Challenge and Promise of Building a Performance-Focused Environmental Protection System,* case C16-99.1530.0 (Brookings Center for Public Management, October 1998), p. 25.

94. Browner and others, "Joint Commitment to Reform Oversight," cover letter.

95. Robert D. Behn, "The New Public-Management Paradigm and the Search for Democratic Accountability," paper presented at the eighteenth annual research conference of the Association for Public Policy Analysis and Management, 1996.

96. This form of accountability is often described as principal-agent account-ability. Principal-agent theory has received extensive attention from economists. According to Schick, this theory greatly influenced the architects of New Zealand's government reform efforts.

97. See, for example, testimony of Virginia L. Thomas, hearings on *The Government Performance and Results Act and the Legislative Process of House Committees*, before the Subcommittee on Rules and Organizations of the House Committee on Rules, 106 Cong. 2 sess., March 22, 2000 (www.house.gov/rules/rules_thom10.htm [December 18, 2000]).

98. See, for example, *Plan for the Implementation of AB1114: The Certified Staff Performance Incentive Act* (approved by the State Board of Education at its December 1999 meeting), California Board of Education.

99. The Texas system, for example, authorizes the education commissioner to remove the management and teachers of schools for consistently poor performance.

100. Robert D. Austin, *Measuring and Managing Performance in Organizations* (Dorset House Publishing, 1996).

101. Herman B. Leonard, "Four Divergent Challenges for Performance Management," paper prepared for the Kennedy School of Government Executive Session on Public Sector Performance Management, June 2000.

102. The difficulty of structuring effective reward systems has received great attention over the years. The father of total quality management approaches, Edward Deming, warned against misuse of measurements to create fear in the work force. See W. Edwards Deming, *Out of the Crisis* (Massachusetts Institute of Technology, 1986), pp. 73–74, esp. p. 76. See also Thomas B. Wilson, *Innovative Reward Systems for the Changing Workplace* (McGraw-Hill, 1995).

103. See, for example, "EPA Office of Inspector General Semiannual Report to Congress, October 1, 1995 through March 31, 1996; Construction Grants (www.epa.gov/oigearth/396sct1d.htm. [December 18, 2000]).

104. U.S. EPA, "Environmental Program Grants—State, Interstate, and Local Government Agencies," 40CFR, parts 35, 735, *Federal Register*, vol. 66, January 9, 2001, pp. 1726–48.

105. Robert Simons, "Control in an Age of Empowerment," *Harvard Business Review*, vol. 73 (March 1995), pp. 8–88.

106. Kowalewski, "Using Outcome Information to Redirect Programs."

107. Scott, Ball, and Dale, "New Zealand's Public Sector Management Reform: Implications for the United States," pp. 357–81.

108. Schick, *Spirit of Reform*, sec. 7, p. 2.

109. Ibid.

110. Robert D. Behn, "Linking Measurement and Motivation: A Challenge for Education," in Paul W. Thurston and James G. Ward, eds., *Advances in Educational Administration*, vol. 5 (London: JAI Press, 1997), p. 17.

111. Wilson, *Innovative Reward Systems for the Changing Workplace*.

112. Rena I. Steinzor and William F. Piermattei, "Dialogue: Reinventing Environmental Regulation via the Government Performance and Results Act:

Where's the Money?" *ELR News and Analysis,* vol. 28 (October 1998), pp. 10563–76.

113. President Bill Clinton and Vice President Al Gore, "Reinventing Environmental Regulation," *National Performance Review* (Washington, March 1995), p. 14.

114. James M. McElfish Jr, "Minimal Stringency: Abdication of State Innovation," *Environmental Law Reporter,* vol. 25 (January 1995), pp. 10003–07.

115. See Houck, *The Clean Water Act,* chap. 2.

116. See, for example, *Troy Corp. v. Browner,* 120 F.3d 277 (D.C. Cir. 1997); *National Mining Assoc. v. Browner,* Civil Action No. 97-n2665 (D. Colo.); and *Dayton Power and Light Co. v. Browner,* Civil Action No. 1: 97CV03074 (D.C. Cir). The Toxics Release Inventory is a national database identifying facilities, chemicals manufactured and used at those facilities, and annual accidental and routine releases of these toxic substances. The EPA TRI-expansion rule requires companies to report on chemicals released to the environment that are not currently reported to the community and to apply existing TRI reporting requirements to several specific industrial sectors not currently required to report their releases.

117. The Chesapeake Bay Program, "State of the Bay," conclusion (www.chesapeakebay.net/pubs/sob/conclusion.pdf [December 18, 2000]).

118. www.epa.gov/airtrends/

119. U.S. EPA, Office of Air and Radiation, "Flexible Attainment Region Case Study: Tulsa, Oklahoma," November 19, 1998.

120. Metzenbaum, "Making Measurement Matter," 1998.

121. U.S. EPA, *FY 1999 Performance Report,* p. 26.

122. Ibid., p. A-3.

123. Ibid.

124. Ibid.

125. Discussions during Kennedy School of Government's Executive Session on Public Sector Performance Management, Harvard University, 1998–2000.

CHAPTER FOUR

Regulatory Reform on the World Stage

GRAHAM K. WILSON

R egulatory reform is a familiar topic to Americans, but it is by no means an exclusively American topic. The Organization for Economic Cooperation and Development monitors regulatory reform on its website, and a visit to that site suggests that member countries are indeed interested and engaged in regulatory reform.[1] Their interest is rooted in the attempts of policymakers to reconcile several strong and conflicting demands common to most if not all advanced industrialized democracies.

A Continuing Demand for Regulation

First, as numerous public opinion polls have demonstrated, the public demands high levels of environmental and consumer protection. Environmental interest groups in the United States have become an established and important part of the Washington scene, while a high proportion of American citizens describe themselves as environmentalists. A similar story can be told in Britain, where membership in the Royal Society for the Protection of Birds (RSPB), which is essentially an environmental group, exceeds the *combined* membership of all the political parties. As in the United States, where much of the energy of the environmental movement was directed into campaigns against pesticides, European environmentalists are deeply concerned about the environmental consequences of new technology. Environmental groups supported by prominent individuals (such as the prince of Wales in Britain) have argued that bioengineered products such as corn seeds used widely in the United States are a threat to popular species such as the monarch butterfly. Concerns about the safety of products and food are also equally prominent in the United States and in Europe. Anyone who doubts that there is a continuing demand for strict regulation in the United States should remember the numerous indignant questions from newspapers, politicians, and members of the public demanding to know why regulators had not prevented the accidents involving Ford SUVs allegedly caused by their Firestone tires disintegrating at speed. There were immediate congressional inquiries into why automobile safety regulators had not been more vigilant. The entire British regulatory system experienced a crisis of credibility in the 1990s because of the "mad cow" problem. It was discovered that a brain disease, bovine spongiform encephalopathy (BSE, or mad cow disease) that destroys the brain, contrary to the advice scientists gave the British government was capable of leaping the "species barrier" from cattle to humans. About eighty Britons have died from "mad cow disease," hundreds of thousands of cattle were slaughtered as a precautionary measure, and for a period the European Union (EU) banned the export of British beef not only to other members of the EU but to anywhere in the world; farmers' incomes plummeted. As with the Firestone tire crisis in the United States, consumers demanded to know why regulators had failed to protect them and, even worse, had assured them that the risk of BSE being transferred to humans was nonexistent.

Mad cows have even caused friction between the EU and the United States. In the aftermath of mad cow disease, European consumers, highly skeptical of claims by scientists that there are no grounds for concern, have resisted strongly the use of growth hormones or genetically altered food stuffs, resulting in serious trade disputes with the United States. In Britain, protesters wearing white overalls have attacked crops planted with genetically altered seeds. European attitudes on these issues have approached levels of intensity (or, to their opponents, hysteria) more commonly associated in the past with American environmentalism. Whereas Europeans had once considered themselves more sophisticated than Americans in realizing the inevitability of risk in life, Europeans now seemed to be hostile to risks, for example, from genetically altered food, that Americans find negligible and entirely acceptable. Demands for high levels of environmental and consumer safety translate not only into demands for stricter regulation of domestic producers but into demands that imports be equally safe. So American farmers, having totally satisfied the traditionally strict regulators in the United States of the safety of genetically altered corn or beef from cattle that have been given artificial growth hormones, find their products banned from the EU. Although the United States suspects that the EU is engaging in disguised trade protectionism in the aftermath of mad cow, the political costs for EU leaders of allowing genetically altered food to enter their markets would be high. In short, the demand for regulation to protect the environment and consumers and the consequences of that demand have not diminished but have become international.

Competitiveness

The second pressure acting on almost all government today arises from business's legitimate concerns about costs. Intensified economic competition within countries and internationally in the era of globalization has made business even less tolerant than in the past of regulations that impose unreasonable costs. How far globalization is accountable for the intensification of competition in the advanced industrialized economies can be debated. Undoubtedly, some of the increase in competition is national rather than international, resulting in an intensified quest by businesses for an optimal or at least lower-cost environment. The *New York Times* recently reported that the rate at which business is relocating within the United States is more than double the rate at which it used to relocate in the recent past; more than 11,000 businesses relocate each year.[2] Yet we undoubtedly live in an era in which international trade has been facilitated by enormous technological and policy changes. Containerization, roll on–roll off (ro-ro) shipping, mail, faxes, cheap international phone calls, and air cargo services have facilitated the trading of goods, from automobiles to fresh fish, that were once relatively hard to transport across oceans. Governments have worked through the General Agreement on Tariffs and Trade (GATT) and later the World Trade Organization (WTO), to lower trade barriers to levels not seen since World War I; before being superseded by the WTO, GATT facilitated the lowering of tariffs on manufactured goods by 96 percent from their levels in the late 1940s to a level today at which they are an insignificant influence on trade.

Much of the increase in competition may be a regional rather than a truly global phenomenon, with the largest increases in trade, for example, being within North America (including Mexico) or with the EU rather than between, for example, Africa and Europe.[3] Yet this fact, rather than making globalization less important as a source of increased competitive pressure, arguably makes it more important. At the start of the twentieth century, when international trade was at levels not surpassed again until the 1990s, it often involved, as the law of comparative advantage would have predicted, countries exporting goods that they were proficient at producing and importing those whose production was ill-suited to them. A classic example dates from the midnineteenth century: Britain exported manufactured goods and imported cheap food. International trade today involves countries importing products they make themselves, often quite well. Automobiles, for example, are both manufactured in the United States or EU and imported from countries such as Japan. Commercial jet aircraft are both produced in the United States and the EU (by Boeing and Airbus Industrie) and imported into the United States and the EU, so that some American airlines buy Airbus planes, and some European airlines buy from Boeing. Not surprisingly, every advanced economy has been experiencing a sharp increase in competitive pressures, and everywhere business has become highly resistant to any avoidable increase in their costs, including through regulation. Business executives may recognize the inevitability of regulation, but they are more determined than ever to avoid excessive regulatory costs.

Internationalization

The third development that has complicated the regulatory environment has been that policymakers have been confronted with the need to reconcile domestic regulations with an increasingly global environment. Major corporations have no wish to be confronted with significantly different regulations in every country in which they operate. The integration of national markets without the integration of regulations could confront business with serious practical difficulties. More important, the effective abolition of tariffs in trade in manufactured goods in the final Uruguay Round of GATT in 1995 focused attention on nontariff barriers to trade. Environmental regulations have sometimes been interpreted as disguised protectionism. The United States has argued that EU

measures against beef produced with growth hormones or cereals produced from genetically altered seed are merely novel means by which to
pursue the long-standing goal of protecting EU farmers from American
competition. In several controversial cases, international bodies have
ruled that American regulations or laws designed to protect the environment conflicted with international trade law. In the most recent of these
major cases, the successor body to GATT, the World Trade Organization, ruled that the United States broke international trade law by ban-
ning shrimp imports from countries that did not require fishermen to fit
turtle exclusion devices (TEDs) to their nets. The TEDs prevent turtles
being caught in their nets and drowned; unfortunately, TEDs cost fishermen a significant amount of money, and the fishermen in question
were typically very poor. The shrimp-turtle dispute, like the earlier
tuna-dolphin case brought against the United States under GATT, highlighted the tension that can exist between international trade policy and
environmental regulations. Finding forms of regulation that are consistent with international trade law became another major concern for
policymakers.

Crises of Regulatory Systems

A fourth development has been that established approaches to regulation have been increasingly called into question. In the United States,
faith that further progress can be achieved in environmental protection
through traditional "command-and-control" approaches has declined.
Criticisms of command-and-control regulation take many forms. As in
any area of regulation, some people contend that the payoff from
increased regulation in environmental protection is not worth the economic costs imposed. There are critics, however, who contend that traditional regulation serves poorly the cause of environmental protection
that they fully support.[4] Their criticisms take several forms. Some complain that traditional regulations too often specify the exact approaches
that business must adopt to reduce pollution. Individual enterprises free
to choose their own approach rather than one spelled out by government might be able to achieve a greater reduction in pollution, as well as
avoid significant, unnecessary cost increases. For decades critics have
pointed out that by imposing controls rather than seeking cooperation,
government invites resistance not compliance.[5] Finally, friendlier critics
of traditional regulation contend that traditional regulation may have

succeeded in the past by reducing pollution from fixed-point sources such as smokestacks, but it is ill-suited to deal with major issues from nonpoint sources, such as runoff from farms.

After a long period in which attacks on command-and-control regulation were seen as little more than sophisticated arguments on behalf of corporations against regulation in general, arguments for alternative approaches today can be found even among environmental and consumer groups. There is even an acronym—NSMD (nonstate market directed) for approaches that do not depend on government. An example of an NSMD approach would be encouraging the spread of sustainable forestry practices through environmental groups encouraging consumers to purchase forest products identified with a "green label." The companies whose products receive this designation from environmental groups can expect to obtain a somewhat higher price for their products than companies whose products lack the label. Government is not involved in this process at all. Acceptable practices and enforcement procedures are agreed directly between environmental groups and the industry in question.

We should not assume, however, that regulatory systems in other countries have been immune from criticism or crises. Criticisms of regulation in the United States have usually focused on what has been seen as its excessive legalism and adversarial character.[6] Yet the American system has comparative advantages. It is conspicuously more transparent and welcoming to citizen groups than are regulatory systems in Europe. The European approach has rested in part on widespread acceptance of the belief that government agencies, supervised by democratically accountable politicians and officials, can be trusted to protect the public good. It is precisely this belief that the mad cow crisis undermines. The repeated assurances from food safety regulators, first in Britain and then in the EU more generally, that BSE posed no threat to humans who ate beef were false.

Common Challenges but Different Starting Points

Advanced industrialized nations have experienced similar challenges to their environmental regulatory regimes. However, as a large body of academic work establishes, the regulatory regimes of advanced industrialized countries have differed considerably. Although these regulatory regimes differ in many respects, some of the most important are the degree of cooperation as opposed to legal compulsion or flexibility involved. Studies dating back to the 1980s noted clear differences between the United States and European countries.[7] Regulatory enforcement in the United States tended to be legalistic and inflexible. In such apparently unlikely settings as social democratic Sweden and pre-Thatcherite Britain, regulations were developed in a more consensual manner and enforced with a great willingness to overlook accidents and to try to forgive error as long as good faith attempts at compliance were being made. All major standards introduced by the Occupational Safety and Health Administration (OSHA) were bitterly opposed by business in every forum possible, including the federal courts; the British equivalent of OSHA, the Health and Safety Commission, made regulations through friendly, cooperative discussion among the representatives of labor unions, employers, and government. The OSHA inspectors in the United States issued fines whenever they saw a violation of standards; British health and safety inspectors saw their task as educating and encouraging employers to adopt safer, healthier practices and believed that cooperation, not punishment, was the best strategy.[8] British practice has been to rely significantly on data from pharmaceutical corporations in evaluating the safety of new products and to leave it to the medical profession to determine their efficacy; the Federal Drug Administration (FDA) has insisted on voluminous submissions, running into hundreds of thousands of pages from the manufacturers of new pharmaceutical products, but has not been willing to place trust in the evidence submitted to it. As David Vogel noted, there were "national styles of regulation," and the United States was clearly an outlier.[9]

The reasons why the United States has been an outlier have been much debated by the authors cited above. Vogel and Kelman emphasized differences in culture between the United States and Europe, particularly in attitudes toward government. European business executives were more accepting of government authority and less combative than their American counterparts. Others placed greater emphasis on institutional differences between the United States and Europe. The fragmentation of American interest groups in general, and business groups in particular, contrasts with the neater pattern found in other advanced industrialized democracies. In the United States, numerous organizations compete to be regarded as the voice of business; a minimal list would include the Chamber of Commerce, the National Association of Manufacturers, the Business Roundtable, and the National Federation of Independent Business. In most advanced industrialized democracies, a single organization is the authoritative voice of business to which trade associations representing individual industries are affiliated; corporations in turn join the appropriate trade associations. As Mancur Olson argued, it is easier to arrange statesmanly compromise between government and an "encompassing" interest group that has in effect a monopoly in representing a sector of society such as business or labor rather than between government and fragmented and competing groups, none of which can afford to put any national interest ahead of its members' interest.[10] Wilson also took an institutional perspective. He argued that the fragmentation of power between institutions in the United States created a game without an ending; corporations that were disappointed in the outcome of discussions with a regulatory agency in the United States had numerous opportunities to contest it in Congress, the courts, and higher up in the executive branch (for example, with the Office of Management and Budget). European business has had fewer opportunities to contest the decisions of government departments because legislatures and courts are weaker; European business has therefore been more attuned to seeking agreement with government agencies, and those agencies have been willing to "pay" for business cooperation in enforcing regulations by adopting a more conciliatory approach than their American counterparts.[11] These different perspectives are not necessarily incompatible and were all based on a shared belief that the United States was an outlier in regulatory unreasonableness.

It might be thought, therefore, that it was primarily the United States that needed regulatory reform. European nations, accustomed to more consensual and cooperative regulation, had less need for reform. In fact, regulatory reform has been an important issue in Europe as well as in the United States. Britain provides an interesting example of a country that once seemed to avoid the alleged American problems of undue legalism and excessive cost in regulations but now experiences many complaints about regulation. The complaints have been sufficiently numerous and vociferous that the Labour government in Britain has established a regulatory impact unit (RIU). The government requires regulatory impact assessments of risks, costs, and benefits to be attached to proposals to ministers that would affect business, charities, or voluntary organizations. Departments are expected to consider using a nonregulatory approach. The RIU is also charged with examining the impact of regulations on small business and assessing the cumulative burden of regulation.[12] Yet the problem has not disappeared. The director general of the Institute of Directors (a British business lobby) has accused the government of having "a mania for regulation," and small business rates regulation as the second most serious problem facing it and says that regulation requires fourteen hours a month of paperwork.[13]

Why has regulation become an issue in a country whose regulatory reasonableness was once contrasted with the opposite attitude in the United States?

First, the country has moved toward a more legalistic, American-style approach in some areas. There has even been a shift toward the use of criminal law to make corporate officers personally responsible for environmental or other disasters, such as railroad crashes. The rise of public interest groups in Europe, which naturally demand access to regulatory decisionmaking, also makes it less likely that the old cozy relationship between regulators and affected industries can be maintained.

Second, as we have seen, the mad cow crisis has also undermined faith in the former, more consensual, style of regulation, encouraging a shift toward stricter approaches. Rightly or wrongly, the mad cow crisis was interpreted as a consequence of overly friendly relations between the Ministry of Agriculture, Fisheries, and Food (MAFF) and the food industry (including agriculture).

Third, and perhaps most important, the EU has been the source of a massive number of regulations. European corporations have found that besides the national regulatory agencies (which have not disappeared), they are now increasingly controlled by EU regulators whom they do not know and have difficulty influencing, and with whom they are less likely to develop collaborative relationships. Why is the EU the source of such voluminous regulation? Giandomenico Majone has argued that as the EU has limited ability to impose taxes, it is drawn instinctively to adopting regulations that it has the undoubted capacity to enact. Regulations serve the dual purpose of dealing with a problem and simultaneously increasing the power of the institutions of the EU.[14] Some of these regulations are designed to remove impediments to a single European market; ironically, in the course of promoting market freedom, these regulations have involved legislating on the most mundane questions of everyday life, such as what can be described as a sausage or as chocolate! Other European regulations have been directed at placing a common floor of environmental and consumer protection and safety regulations under the integrated European market. Whatever the motivation for enacting them, however, regulations have the dual effect of making life more complicated for business and the institutions of the EU more prominent (as opposed to those of its member nations). This development has been all the more troubling for European businesses because the regulatory style of the EU had shown distinct signs of being more legalistic and less consensual than most European national styles of regulation. EU regulation has prompted the same reaction against remote and uncomprehending authority as is a familiar part of the American scene. Only recently and probably because of fears about competitiveness has the EU moved toward greater flexibility.

Types of Regulatory Reform

A common assumption in the United States has been that the obvious answer to the problem of excessive regulation is simply to deregulate. If regulators had less power, or if they had to pass a series of demanding cost-benefit tests before instituting new regulations, the problems of excessive regulation would be solved. There are two difficulties with this approach. First, as noted earlier, every indicator available to us—the findings of opinion polls, as well as attitudes of elected officials—suggests that the public wants high levels of environmental protection and regulation. Arguing for simple deregulation is almost certainly not viable politically. Second, pushing for deregulation alone will be resisted by environmental groups and will therefore result merely in continuation of the Great Regulatory Wars in which the United States has been engaged for several decades. It would be valuable to find more constructive alternatives.

International experience suggests a variety of approaches to regulatory reform. They differ considerably but have generally meant some self-regulation and cooperation between regulators and government. We might array these approaches on a spectrum. At one end is a highly explicit bargain between industry and regulatory authorities. At the other end is an implicit and undefined arrangement or bargain.

The most explicit bargain between regulatory authorities and industry is the compact approach used in the Netherlands. In pursuit of fulfilling its commitment to implement the Kyoto Agreement on greenhouse gases, the Netherlands decided that rather than introducing extensive new regulations, it would negotiate an agreement with Dutch industry. The agreement or compact signed by the Ministry of Economic

Affairs, the Ministry of Housing, Spatial Planning, and the Environment, plus the provincial authorities on the one hand, and the Confederation of Netherlands Industry and Employers (VNO-NCW), associated trade associations (such as the Netherlands Chemical Industry Federation, VNCI), and individual corporations on the other, established a cooperative approach to achieving the Kyoto targets.[15] Industry undertook to achieve the highest standards in the world within five years. The standards were defined by a joint industry-government benchmarking commission, and attainment or nonattainment of the standards was determined by an independent nongovernmental auditor. In return, government would undertake not to impose any burdensome taxes (such as an energy tax) on the industries cooperating, and in a side agreement, representatives of industry and government agreed on a relatively short (two-page) list of equipment investments that would qualify for a tax allowance.

Why would industry in the Netherlands sign an agreement committing it to the highest, and presumably therefore most expensive, standards in the world? The first reason offered is the commonly stated argument that pollution represents resources lost to industry; pollution prevented equals money saved. Yet though this argument is often advanced, it has rarely been sufficient motivation for industry to prevent pollution, perhaps because the costs of pollution prevention exceed the costs saved. Probably more important were the plausible threats of government action if industry did not cooperate. In the absence of the compact, new taxes or regulations might have been adopted. Individual corporations deciding whether to sign the compact or not were aware that corporations that signed the compact were less likely to be inspected rigorously by government agencies. In the words of one government official, "All those inspectors who aren't inspecting signatory corporations have got to go somewhere."[16] The Dutch government had the prospect of achieving through the compact significant improvements in environmental performance without the political or administrative costs that would have resulted from pursuing the goals through additional regulation.

Perhaps as important in the Dutch case as the motives for participating is the importance of strong trade associations in facilitating cooperation. Strong trade associations could negotiate agreements with government that their members would honor. A similar story can be told of Norway, where thirteen trade associations, representing 44 percent of stationary energy use in manufacturing, made a voluntary agreement with government to reduce energy use, and therefore emissions; the companies the associations represented were eager to avoid regulation or carbon taxes. Six hundred companies are covered; the program provides information and benchmarking. Again, the existence of strong trade associations capable of making authoritative commitments on behalf of their members and helping to enforce them was crucial.[17]

A second approach to regulatory reform is the EMAS (Eco Management and Auditing System) adopted by the EU in 1995. The EU, as noted earlier, had begun to acquire a reputation for American-style legalistic and inflexible regulation. Given its concerns about uncompetitiveness ("eurosclerosis"), the EU was eager to try different approaches. Moreover, the European Commission realized that it lacked the resources to fulfil its original goal of evaluating and harmonizing the numerous different national environmental protection laws and regulations. EMAS offered industry the prospect of self-regulation monitored by an independent auditor. Corporations using EMAS would monitor and try to improve their environmental performance, which would be assessed by an auditor, usually employed by the trade association and approved by the government. Although bargains between governments and industry are not necessarily part of the EMAS system, they frequently are linked to it. For example, in the Environmental Pact of Bavaria, the government of Bavaria undertook to reward industries adopting EMAS with "appropriate relief from obligations imposed by regulatory law."[18] The agreement allowed "companies registered as audited sites within the scope of EMAS to be relieved of reporting and documentation obligations, of controls and monitoring by the supervisory authorities and of approval procedures in a degree equivalent to the responsibility they themselves have assumed."[19]

Again one might ask why business would choose to be part of EMAS. Corporations that adopt EMAS are no doubt motivated by a desire to achieve an enhanced public image and reductions in production costs by ending waste that contributes to pollution. However, the main appeal of EMAS is that it substitutes a more flexible and collaborative type of inspection for government regulation. Better EMAS than national or EU regulation might be the reasoning of those adopting it. EMAS is available to manufacturing and extractive industries, and though it requires monitoring of outcomes, the EMAS framework does not specify performance levels to be attained.

A third approach to solving the problems of regulation is ISO 14000.

ISO 14000 is technically a series of standards (ISO 14000, 14001, 14004, 14011, and 14012) promulgated by the International Standards Organization, a nongovernmental organization based in Geneva. The United States is represented in ISO by the American National Standards Institute and by interest groups that participate in ISO's Technical Assessment Groups (TAGs). ISO is not an environmental organization; most of its standards are highly technical and uncontroversial, covering product and parts specifications. The ISO 14000 approach differs from the ones discussed so far in that ISO is focused purely on processes, not outcomes. Corporations that wish to obtain an ISO 14000 certificate must agree to monitor their own environmental performance, develop plans to improve their performance, assess how far they have succeeded in fulfilling those plans and, once the initial plan has been fulfilled, develop plans for further improvements. ISO 14000 therefore aims at continuous self-monitoring and improvements by corporations in the environmental sphere. Corporations must also be in compliance with the environmental regulations and standards of countries in which they do business. The two greatest weaknesses of ISO 14000 are that it does not mandate any performance level and does not require external reporting or validation by independent experts. It can therefore be regarded as much less demanding than EMAS. ISO 14000 was based on a British standard (BS 7750) that did require the reporting of results to an external registry; this feature was dropped, however, at American insistence.[20] American business, operating in an environment in which it is dangerous legally to admit to polluting, could not afford to provide government agencies or people who might sue them with admissions of less than perfect performance.

Yet ISO 14000 has been growing rapidly outside the United States and more recently within it. What has been driving ISO 14000 forward? Paulette L. Stenzel suggests several plausible explanations as to why corporations seek ISO 14000 certification. These include significant cost reductions as preventable pollution that is a form of waste is eliminated, a good public image for the corporation, improved relations with financial institutions who, when making loans, are sensitive to environmental risks in clients' projects, and possible relief from regulatory or even criminal proceedings against the corporation under environmental laws. Regulators and prosecutors may see ISO certification as showing a company's good faith, attributing its misdeeds to error, not profit-maximizing intent.[21]

The most interesting feature of ISO 14000 is how it has been promoted by business itself, especially by large corporations. Clearly, ISO 14000, as a self-enforced and voluntary system focused on processes rather than outcomes, has great appeal for business. Although uptake of ISO 14000 has been slow in the United States, it has increased recently, at least partly because it has been promoted by large corporations. In 1999 the Ford Motor Company announced that it was requiring its suppliers to be ISO 14000 certified by the end of 2001, and Ford was followed by General Motors within weeks.[22] This produced an intriguing situation of role reversal in which state governments (for example, Wisconsin) offered businesses workshops and seminars on how to comply with regulatory requirements imposed by the private sector!

Why should large corporations be so keen to promote ISO 14000? Almost certainly one of the factors at work was fear that environmental standards in general and ISO 14000 in particular might otherwise become in practice a trade barrier. A previous set of ISO voluntary standards, ISO 9000, had become a de facto condition for doing business in Europe. ISO 14000 looked set to follow. One Ford executive remarked that if American industry did not adopt ISO 14000, it would find itself shut out of Europe.[23] It might be argued, therefore, that even the highly voluntary, self-enforced ISO 14000 had an element of being developed to ward off regulation by government.

Different Countries, Different Ways

It is obvious that the appeal of different means of dealing with the pressures evident in all countries for great regulatory flexibility differ considerably from one country to another. Even merely within Europe, for example, as table 4-1 shows, there are marked variations between Germany and most other countries in the relative appeal of EMAS and ISO 14000. Clearly, there must be reasons why Germany is much more likely than other countries to use EMAS. Clearly, there must be reasons why the Netherlands has adopted an approach very different from that of the United States. Why, in the face of common challenges, has the response of countries differed so much?

The approach adopted by the Netherlands is clearly part of a much larger neocorporatist approach to policymaking. This approach has been celebrated in recent years as the Polder model, a model of highly consensual decisionmaking in which government, employers' organiza-

Table 4-1. *Eco Management and Auditing System versus Industrial Standards Organization 14000, 1999*

Nation	EMAS	ISO 14000
Germany	2,238	1,450
Sweden	165	645
France	34	365
United Kingdom	71	1,009
Netherlands	23	210
Italy	13	166

Source: Wisconsin Department of Natural Resources, Office of the Secretary, November 1999.

tions, and unions attempt to reach a common position on major social and economic policy issues. The Polder model has been credited with reforming the labor market of the Netherlands to make it much more flexible and reforming the Dutch welfare state (for example, to end the abuse of disability pensions). In the view of its admirers, the Polder model achieved for the Netherlands the same advantages of economic flexibility that the Thatcher reforms achieved for Britain but without the political and social unrest that Thatcher provoked. The model of regulatory reform in the Netherlands, with its highly flexible approach, is built, therefore, on a practice of policymaking very different from that of the United States. Major economic organizations are used to being incorporated by government into partnership in governance, sharing in the responsibility of tackling serious economic problems. The highly centralized employers' organizations and unions—in contrast to their relatively weak and fragmented equivalents in the United States—provide suitable building blocks for this type of policymaking. Frequent past collaboration on many policy issues engenders trust among major economic organizations, which facilitates solving new problems. Finally, the neocorporatist approach, illustrated by the Dutch approach to regulatory reform, rests on deeply implanted values in Dutch society that prize social harmony. Perhaps this drive can be traced back to the need to solve, after the sixteenth century, the challenges of living in a religiously divided society. Few countries place such emphasis on social harmony.

The extensive use of EMAS in Germany also relates to general features of German society. Germany is described memorably by the political scientist Peter Katzenstein as having a weak state in a strong society.[24] German economic organizations—such as unions, employers' organizations, and others—have long been important in the governance of policy areas as varied as health care and industrial training. German industrialists had, as far back as the nineteenth century, adopted forms of self-regulation on industrial safety though which workplaces were inspected by officials of trade associations. This mode of self-regulation was adopted to forestall moves to introduce government regulation. EMAS is in many ways the latest of a long series of measures in which unwelcome government involvement is forestalled by forms of industrial self-governance. Yet industrial self-government could not be achieved unless economic organizations had the necessary unity and authority. In relatively few advanced industrialized democracies do employers' organizations have the unity and standing that they do in Germany. EMAS has built on this tradition.

Ironically, precisely these highly organized features of Dutch and German society have facilitated the adoption of more flexible forms of regulation. It is often supposed in the United States that the fostering of purely market-based forms of social relationship will accomplish greater flexibility and reasonableness in regulation. The Dutch and German examples point to the possibility that the more highly organized the society and economy, the greater the opportunities for flexibility and cooperation. Yet even if this argument is true, there is in practice no way in which other countries could create the conditions that have fostered regulatory flexibility in the Netherlands and Germany. Britain, for example, lacks the strong, unified, and authoritative employers' organizations that Germany possesses. In only a few advanced industrialized economies is there the established pattern of neocorporatist policymaking that could be used effectively to achieve regulatory reform in the Netherlands.

Part of the appeal of ISO 14000 is that it is readily adapted to a variety of social and governmental settings. As a self-administered procedure voluntarily adopted by corporations, ISO 14000 requires neither the strong trade associations nor the neocorporatist habits of EMAS and the Dutch approach. Indeed, the question about ISO 14000 is whether there are any conditions under which it *cannot* be adopted, as opposed to conditions under which it can. Astonishingly, in view of the voluntary and undemanding nature of the program, there are indeed arguments that ISO 14000 poses problems for American corporations. It certainly is true that in the United States ISO 14000 certification lags behind that in Europe. North America accounts for only 5.5 percent of ISO 14000 certificates, compared with 54 percent for Europe and 32 percent for Far East countries. Although ISO 14000 certification in the United States has been increasing, in the latest period for which figures are available, the eighth cycle of certification (to the end of 1998), the United States gained 212 certificates, compared with 277 in the United Kingdom, 299 in Germany, and 829 in Japan.[25] If, as American executives have often claimed, they are eager to find a more flexible but equally effective alternative to command-and-control regulation, why has ISO 14000 certification lagged in the United States?

A probable explanation is that, as Pietro Nivola would have predicted, the adversarial and legalistic American environment stands in the way of reform.[26] Paula Murray has pointed out ways in which following ISO 14000 procedures may more legally difficult for American corporations than for their overseas counterparts. Corporations cannot necessarily keep privileged in legal proceedings the material that they compile in assessing their own performance under ISO 14000 procedures. Murray notes that the EPA and the federal Department of Justice have aggressively opposed laws adopted by states that make materials gathered by corporations during EMS procedures privileged, and she concludes that "the confidentiality issue will continue to hamstring the efforts to create meaningful environmental management systems that are compatible with the letter and spirit of ISO 14000."[27] Murray notes that although the EPA claimed to be willing to work with corporations committed to self-regulation, its major experiment with ISO 1400 procedures, a trial with Lucent Technologies, almost broke down because of the EPA's determination not to accord privileged status to material gathered by Lucent during ISO 14000 exercises. Until the United States can assure its corporations that implementing ISO 14000 will not result in providing evidence for litigants or prosecutors to use against them, corporate enthusiasm for it will be attenuated.

Can the United States Join the Reform Movement?

Obviously, there are severe challenges to the United States in adopting regulatory reforms that have been very successful within the EU. In brief, regulatory reform has been facilitated in Europe by strong business associations that have long-standing, close, collaborative relationships with government. In these settings, relatively untroubled by legal constraints, government has been able to devolve onto business organizations and corporations the responsibility for tasks such as environmental protection and remain confident that business will take this responsibility seriously. Although it has been common to criticize the more "organized" forms of capitalism found in Europe for contributing to lower growth rates and higher unemployment than have prevailed recently in the United States, they have also facilitated the adoption of more flexible forms of regulation that may satisfy continuing popular demands for effective environmental and consumer protection and business demands for minimizing regulatory cost.

One can state the argument more fully by asking a puzzling question: why has the United States, the country in which demands for regulatory reform first emerged, proved such a difficult setting for regulatory reform? One might also wonder whether this situation can be changed.

Many factors impede reform in the United States. First, the United States has always prided itself on being governed "by laws not men." Countries that have had an easier time of creating more flexible regulatory regimes have done so against a background of being prepared to give government officials discretion. All the older comparative studies of regulation emphasized that the flexibility of, for example, British safety and health inspectors was exercised against a background in which they were granted considerable power and authority. The acceptance of the authority of the state is a prerequisite for, not a barrier to, regulatory flexibility. Recall that in the Netherlands government officials were allowed to negotiate a two-page list of pollution-reducing equipment that qualified for a tax allowance. It is unlikely that such a list could have been negotiated in the United States without extensive efforts in Congress and the courts by manufacturers and suppliers of equipment not included to force their product onto the list. Yet the fact that rules are comparatively difficult to draft in the United States does not detract from their popularity. In the United States—and perhaps increasingly in countries, like Britain, that had previously tolerated official discretion—the tendency has been to try to minimize the scope of administrative discretion by writing rules more and more tightly, thus negating the commonsense flexibility at the heart of regulatory reform.

The structure of the interest group system in the United States has also been a problem. More flexible regulation in the Netherlands and Germany has been achieved because authoritative interest groups enjoy a virtual monopoly on representing their sector of society or the economy. In the United States, in contrast, interest groups compete to represent a sector of the economy or society. Who represents business in the United States? Is it, for example, the Chamber of Commerce, the Business Roundtable, the National Association of Manufacturers, or the National Federation of Independent Business? Competition among interest groups in the United States not only reduces their authority but makes it very hard to negotiate and operate the sort of flexible regulation found in the Netherlands. As the Chamber of Commerce discovered when it tried to reach a compromise with the Clinton administration on health care reform in 1993, a willingness to compromise is often portrayed by competitors (in that case the National Federation of Independent Business) as a sign of weakness. A similar problem afflicts public interest groups. The numerous environmental interest groups compete with one another for contributions and foundation money. Proclaiming a belief that most corporations are run by reasonable people whom it is sensible to trust is not generally an effective strategy for an environmental group trying to raise money.

Regulation in the United States has also been a contested, conflictual process. Although we now witness a number of attempts, even by the EPA, in Project XL, for example, to develop more cooperative relationships with the regulated, such experiments contrast with decades of conflict and suspicion. Erasing this legacy will not be easy.

Yet this is a moment in which more reform seems possible. Currently, large American corporations are exerting extensive pressure to develop ISO 14000. The reasons are related to the fact that regulatory reform is so conspicuous on the world stage. Fear of being at a competitive disadvantage with corporations overseas that enjoy more flexible regulatory systems combines with fear that failure to adopt ISO 14000 will result in exclusion from countries, notably, the members of the EU, that may come to treat it as a condition for doing business. Large corporations are not the only force for change, however. American states have nearly always enjoyed a reputation for more flexible and collaborative regulation than the federal government. Businesses used to find state occupational safety and health regulators more congenial to deal with than federal regulators. Now fourteen states have been pushing for adoption of EMS approaches and rewarding corporations that do so with regulatory relief. The state of Wisconsin is well advanced in an important experiment, Green Tier, that will attempt to involve not only corporations but public interest groups in an attempt to build collaborative approaches to regulation. The Wisconsin experiment will be very important in determining whether significant regulatory reform based on collaborative approaches is possible in the United States.

The answer will be of interest to more parties than the United States. As global economic integration proceeds, the need to find a system of regulation that does not become a nontariff barrier to trade is pressing. Yet no global system can exist without the full participation of the United States. A global system of regulation without the United States is, to use the well-worn simile, like *Hamlet* without the prince of Denmark. Any prospects for global progress that ISO 14000 offers will not be achieved unless it is applied in the United States.

The Impact of International Organizations

The 1990s witnessed great controversy about the impact of international organizations on regulation. American environmental groups reacted with anger to two rulings in particular. The first was by a disputes panel of GATT in the so-called tuna-dolphin case, the second by its successor body, the WTO, in the shrimp-turtle case.[28] From the perspective of GATT and the WTO, the United States was adopting sweeping and broad-brush regulations that these rulings found were nontariff barriers and therefore contrary to international trade agreements. In the United States, both cases aroused fears that international organizations were diminishing the country's ability to impose laws that raise environmental standards. In practice, such fears were overstated. In neither case did the United States simply comply with the rulings; American environmental groups were able to insist on Latin American countries adopting dolphin protection measures as the cost of the United States complying with GATT's ruling in their favor, and the United States has yet to comply with the WTO ruling on the shrimp-turtle case. Yet ironically the United States has protested vociferously over the failure of the EU to remove promptly the bans on the import of beef from the United States produced with artificial growth hormones and has been similarly angered by EU opposition to the use of "hush kits" to extend the life of older heavily polluting aircraft that do not comply with noise regulations. In these cases, it is the United States that complains bitterly that supposed health or environmental concerns are merely window dressing for economic special interests, such as European farmers or aircraft manufacturers using nontariff barriers against competitors.

Most of the discussion of the impact of international organizations on regulation has therefore concerned the related issues of whether trade agreements have reduced the sovereignty of nation-states and whether nations' capacity to protect the environment has been diminished. Yet this controversy also has implications for regulatory reform that have not been adequately addressed. In most respects, the controversies are likely to improve the scientific basis of regulations. As in the beef hormone controversy, for example, regulators will be under severe pressure to demonstrate a compelling scientific case for their actions; regulations based on a generalized fear that a substance or process might have health implications run the risk of being challenged in international organizations and domestically. Although defendants in WTO cases (as in domestic legal proceedings) will try desperately to find science to fit their case (the EU and artificial growth hormones is an example), the rigorous scrutiny that complaining governments will bring to bear on alleged nontariff barriers will make obfuscation more difficult. However, judging whether nontariff barriers are merely posing as sound regulation often depends on whether domestic and foreign competitors are seen as receiving identical treatment. Many proposals for regulatory reform have been based on a strategy of giving more discretion to trusted corporations. It is easy to see how domestically based corporations might be regarded more favorably than foreign-based ones. Foreign-based corporations might also have trouble adapting to the nuances of informal understandings. Dutch officials were nonplused when American oil companies flew in what one Dutch official described as "a plane load of lawyers" to examine an environmental compact that the Dutch understood to be a gentlemen's agreement rather than a legal document.[29] Yet relations between host governments and foreign corporations can be good, sometimes better than between domestic corporations and their government. Moreover, corporations themselves might be more involved in discussing and preventing the use of regulations as unfair barriers to trade. One point that is certain, however, is that proposals for regulatory reform will have to keep international organizations in mind. It is easy to see how some regulatory reforms could be misunderstood as nontariff barriers.

International Self-Regulation

Achieving more collaborative forms of regulation within the framework of nation-states might seem difficult enough. To hope for collaborative forms of international regulation might seem utopian indeed. As we have seen earlier, one of the best alternatives to government regulation has come in countries where business organizations have shouldered responsibility for preventing pollution or unacceptable business practices through what has been called "private interest government."[30] A convenient summary of the conditions under which industry accepts such responsibility is provided by Karsten Ronit.

> According to the "private interest government" approach, associations have to fulfill certain basic criteria to serve as private interest governments and to be accepted by government. . . . key preconditions for establishing and running such arrangements are: a monopoly in the organization of a given interest category; an avoidance of an unacceptable degree of free riding; a capacity to achieve compliance among members; and finally, a capacity to sanction violations of those rules.[31]

It seems to go almost without saying that such conditions do not apply internationally. How could business organizations achieve monopoly, prevent free riding, impose sanctions, and win the compliance that Ronit emphasizes?

Yet there are pressures pushing international businesses toward self-regulation. First, as J. M. Ayres has described, social movements critical of business have proved surprisingly adept at using the new technologies, such as the World Wide Web, often associated with the globalization of business.[32] Protesters have coordinated campaigns across continents, so that readers of magazines in Germany, for example, have organized to boycott publications on paper from German companies that use pulp from forests in British Columbia that are not operated on a "sustainable forestry" basis. Such international movements can embarrass and defeat corporations, even if the *legal* basis for regulating the corporation lies in another country where the corporation has the requisite political power to win a victory for itself. British political scientist Grant Jordan has illuminated these processes in his study of how

Shell was forced to retreat from its plan to sink an outdated oil storage facility used in its North Sea fields in deep water in the Atlantic.[33] Everyone agreed that the British government had the power to regulate Shell; the British government then led by John Major approved the plan and even defended it against criticism in meetings of EU heads of governments. Prime Minister Major left one such meeting to discover that his willingness to take the heat for Shell had been in vain; Shell had abandoned the plan because protests against it in Germany and the Netherlands had proved too powerful. Similarly, pressure against clothing firms in the United States has led to changes in working conditions in third world countries whose governments had no wish to impose stricter requirements on foreign investors. The global corporation is globally vulnerable to protests. Internationally connected new social movements can put pressure on corporations, not necessarily in the country where the legal power to regulate lies, but where their own strength (and the corporation's vulnerability) are greatest. Warding off these criticisms often means that companies must adopt codes of conduct for themselves and their suppliers that manifest a commitment to high standards.

A second impetus has been the need to stabilize markets. The international shipping industry made serious attempts to create organizations that would limit excessive competition and maintain standards.[34] A surprising cooperation has emerged between international pharmaceutical companies and regulators in Europe, the United States, and Japan, in part because the industry was frustrated by the difficulty of marketing products across numerous different national regulatory systems.[35]

A third impetus toward international self-regulation has been to avoid government regulations that might (as the pharmaceutical industry has experienced) be different in different countries and market disrupting. One of the best schemes was developed in the dyes industry, which formed ETAD (the Ecological and Toxicological Association of Dyes and Organic Pigments Manufacturers) in 1974. ETAD adopted a code of ethics in 1974, which it revised and strengthened in 1989, 1993, and 1997. ETAD applies the code globally, thus covering third world countries with little regulatory capacity of their own, and has even expelled companies for noncompliance. The pharmaceutical industry has also developed and applied self-regulatory processes on the marketing of drugs through its International Federation of Pharmaceutical Manufacturers Association (IFPMA), at least in part to ward off action by governments coordinated by the World Health Organization (WHO).[36]

A further impetus to international self-regulation comes from government. Governments, it might be argued, always have an incentive to transfer the political and administrative costs of regulation to others. When regulatory issues are international, they run the risk of complicating diplomacy between states. Given the importance of the relationship between the United States and its European allies, neither side benefits from disputes about the use of artificial growth hormones in beef production or similar topics taking on undue importance in government-to-government dealings. David Aaron, deputy secretary of commerce for trade in the Clinton administration, has suggested that governments will devolve the settling of trade disputes to corporations and business organizations.[37] An early example of this trend was the agreement between the EU and the United States to use a "safe harbor" process for data gathered by U.S. corporations in Europe that were potentially in violation of EU regulations protecting privacy more strictly than does the United States. Under the safe harbor process, American business organizations certify that U.S. corporations protect the privacy of Europeans adequately.

International self-regulatory arrangements may foster the growth of domestic business organizations. International self-regulatory schemes often presume that there is a strong enough domestic business organization to implement them. Domestic business organizations (as in the data protection scheme) may be given specific responsibilities in international agreements. If the domestic business association is not strong enough to fulfil these responsibilities, there will be pressures for it to become so unless the corporations in the relevant industry are few enough in number to play this role themselves. American corporations, generally not accustomed to entrusting major responsibilities to business associations, may be anxious to retain the responsibility for implementing international voluntary regulation. American corporations have a good record, by and large, in developing internal company strategies for pursuing regulatory policy goals. American corporations are much more likely than, for example, Canadian firms to have developed internal policies and procedures.[38]

American corporations may also prove adept at handling international self-regulation. As already discussed, while it would be an exaggeration to say that the world has developed an "international civil society" composed of multiple groups and interests, the world has moved somewhat in that direction. Effective if informal international social movements concerned with human rights, the environment, and poverty have developed; these groups have been effective in pressuring corporations to adopt policies to promote their goals. Agreements between international movements and corporations are often of the NSMD (nonstate market directed) type, bypassing governments altogether. This is not a situation in which Japanese or European companies are likely to feel comfortable; they are used to dealing with governments, often through business organizations. American corporations, in contrast, are used to social movement politics, accommodating demands from feminist, racial minority, and environmental groups. An American corporation's experience of negotiating with Jesse Jackson's PUSH movement is more relevant to international negotiations between social movements and corporations than experience of cozy discussions between a business peak organization and a government department in a European country. It might be that the American genius for informal politics is well suited to the emerging practice of international voluntary regulation.

Conclusion: From Governing to Governance?

There is astonishing ferment in the discussion of regulatory reform on the world stage.[39] It is certainly true that globalization has fostered increased concern about anything that raises costs for corporations, including regulation. Yet the initial assumption made when globalization first became a popular topic—that a simple move toward deregulation would ensue—seems misplaced. It is far more likely that, as the demand for regulation remains high, nations will continue their attempts to find more flexible, less costly modes of regulation compatible with both competitiveness and public confidence.

If there is any one theme that links developments around the world, it is the attempt to mobilize resources outside government, as well as inside, to supplement and sometimes replace approaches that rely on law and regulation with approaches that rely on what might be called private sector governance. Private sector governance can take the form of voluntary activity (though often motivated by a fear of government regulation) to pursue regulatory goals such as environmental protection. Individual firms, trade associations within countries, or even international organizations representing an industry globally can encourage the spread of "best practices." Yet in the new world of regulation, not just multilayered government but what is in effect government by a variety of organizations becomes common. Associations and even companies like governments in effect create and enforce policies intended to achieve regulatory goals such as environmental protection. Regulatory requirements may be imposed by private sector organizations or even by individual corporations (such as Ford and General Motors). As was true after the imposition of ISO 14000 by Ford, businesses may even find that government agencies, far from being the source of regulatory requirements, are now allies in learning how to deal with requirements imposed by the private sector. A new, and in some respects more complicated, mode of governance results. That new mode of governance consists not just of a dichotomy of government regulators on the one hand and the regulated on the other, but of a complex web of governance regulatory agencies joined by private sector organizations in pursuing regulatory goals. Countries that are adept at achieving public-private partnerships may be especially advantaged in this process. All, however, will experience intriguing new modes of governance, as public and private authority, as well as the global and the local, become ever more intertwined.

Notes to Chapter 4

1. www.oecd.org/subject/regdatabase>

2. *New York Times*, July 23, 2000, p. A1.

3. Richard Wade, "Globalization and Its Limits: Reports of the Death of the National Economy Are Greatly Exaggerated," in Suzanne Berger and Ronald Dore, eds., *National Diversity and Global Capitalism* (Cornell University Press, 1996).

4. For summaries and evaluations of some these criticisms, see Organization for Economic Cooperation and Development (OECD), *Reducing the Risk of Regulatory Failure: Challenges for Regulatory Compliance* (Paris, 2000); and National Academy of Public Administration, *Resolving the Paradox of Environmental Protection: An Agenda for Congress, EPA and the State: A Report for Congress* (Washington, 1997).

5. Donald F Kettl, "Environmental Policy: The Next Generation," *Brookings Policy Brief* 37 (October 1998).

6. Eugene Bardach and Robert Kagan, *Going by the Book: The Problem of Regulatory Unreasonableness* (Temple University Press, 1982); and Pietro Nivola, *Comparative Disadvantages? Social Regulations and the Global Economy* (Brookings, 1997).

7. Ronald Brickman, Sheila Jasanoff, and Thomas Ilgen, *Chemical Regulation and Cancer: A Cross-National Study of Policy and Politics* (Washington: National Science Foundation, 1982); Steven Kelman, *Regulating Sweden, Regulating America: A Comparative Study of Occupational Safety and Health Policy* (MIT Press, 1981); Graham K. Wilson, *The Politics of Safety and Health* (Oxford: Clarendon Press, 1985); and David Vogel, *National Styles of Regulation* (Cornell University Press, 1986).

8. Wilson, *The Politics of Safety and Health*.

9. Vogel, *National Styles of Regulation*.

10. Mancur Olson, *The Rise and Decline of Nations: Economic Growth, Stagflation and Social Rigidities* (Yale University Press, 1982).

11. Wilson, *The Politics of Safety and Health*.

12. Minister for the Cabinet Office's statement on government's new approach to regulatory control (www.cabinet-office.gov.uk/regulation1999/jcspeech.htm).

13. "The End of the Affair," *Economist,* August 19, 2000, p. 49.

14. Giandomenico Majone, *Regulating Europe* (London: Routledge, 1996), and "The Regulatory State and Its Legitimacy Problems," *European Politics,* vol. 22 (January 1999), pp. 1–24, and *The Development of Social Regulation in the European Community: Policy Externalities, Transaction Costs, Motivational Factors* (San Domenico, Italy: European University Institute, 1995).

15. *Energy Efficiency Benchmarking Covenant,* July 6, 1999.

16. Interview, the Hague, October 1999. In this and other citations in this chapter, interviewees were promised anonymity as a condition for agreeing to the interview.

17. OECD, *Reducing the Risk of Regulatory Failure,* p. 27.

18. Bavarian State Chancellery, *Environmental Pact of Bavaria*, Munich, 1999.

19. Ibid., D.III.2, para.1.

20. Naomi Roht-Arriaza, "Shifting the Point of Regulation: International Organization for Standardization and Global Lawmaking on Trade and the Environment," *Ecology Law Review,* vol. 22 (1995), pp. 480–539, esp. p. 506.

21. Paulette L. Stenzel, "Can the ISO 14000 Series Environmental Management Standards Provide a Viable Alternative to Government Regulation?" *American Business Law Journal,* vol. 37 (Winter 2000), pp. 237–98.

22. For discussions of why "big business" has been pushing ISO 14000, see Stanley Fielding, "High Gear?" *Global Business,* vol. 1 (February 2000), p. 63; "Autos and Chemicals Drive Certification," *Chemical Week,* April 5, 2000, p. 42; and "Profiting from ISO 14000," *Chemical Week,* September 29, 1999, p. 83.

23. Interview, October 1999.

24. Peter J. Katzenstein, *Industry and Politics in West Germany: Towards the Third Republic* (Cornell University Press, 1989).

25. *The ISO Survey of ISO 9000 and ISO 14000 Certificates* (Geneva: ISO, 1999), pp. 6, 7.

26. Nivola, *Comparative Disadvantages?*

27. Paula C. Murray, "Inching Towards Environmental Regulatory Reform—ISO 14000: Much Ado about Nothing or a Reinvention Tool?" *American Business Law Journal*, vol. 37 (Fall 1999), pp. 35–59, esp. p. 37.

28. The tuna-dolphin case concerned American bans under the Marine Mammal Protection Act on imports of tuna from countries that had failed to enact laws or regulations preventing the accidental killing of dolphins while catching tuna; the shrimp-turtle case concerned similar bans under the Endangered Species Act on imports of shrimp from countries that failed to require turtle exclusion devices on shrimp fishing nets. For an analysis of the tuna-dolphin case from an environmentalist perspective, see Richard W. Parker, "The Use and Abuse of Trade Leverage to Protect the Global Commons: What We Can Learn from the Tuna-Dolphin Conflict," *Georgetown International Environmental Law Review*, vol. 12 (Fall 1999), pp. 3–123.

29. Interview, the Hague, 1999.

30. Wolfgang Streeck and Philippe C. Schmitter, *Private Interest Government: Beyond Market and State* (London: Sage, 1985).

31. Karstin Ronit, "Analyzing Domestic and International Business Self-Regulation in the New Millennium," paper presented at IPSA XVII World Congress, August 2000.

32. J. M. Ayres, "From the Streets to the Internet: The Cyber-Diffusion of Contention," *Annals of the American Academy of Political and Social Sciences*, November 1999, pp. 132–43.

33. Grant Jordan "Indirect Causes and Effects of Policy Change: The Brent Spar Case," *Public Administration*, vol. 76 (Winter 1998), pp. 713–40.

34. Daniel Marx Jr., *International Shipping Cartels: A Study of Industrial Self Regulation* (Princeton University Press, 1953).

35. David Vogel, "The Globalization of Pharmaceutical Regulation," *Governance*, vol. 11 (January 1998), pp. 1–22.

36. Karsten Ronit and Volker Schneider, "Global Governance through Private Organizations," *Governance*, vol.12 (July 1999), pp. 243–66.

37. Nancy Dunne and Dan Lerner, "Role for Business in Trade Disputes," *Financial Times*, April 3, 2000, p. 12.

38. OECD, *Reducing the Risk of Regulatory Failure*, p. 78.

39. Ibid.

CHAPTER FIVE

The Civic Sustainability of Reform

CHRISTOPHER H. FOREMAN JR.

Pervasive mistrust and disagreement face anyone aspiring to reform environmental policy. Environmentalists disparage the credibility of self-interested "polluters," and businesses despair of satisfying the environmentalists' demands, which they often perceive as profoundly unreasonable. Everyone is suspicious of environmental agencies, and the agencies themselves often display tension across the state-federal divide.

Many critics say that environmental policymaking is insufficiently democratic. "Enhancing stakeholder participation" is a reform mantra, but there is no reason to believe that simply bringing more players into the game will, by itself, yield environmental choices that are more palatable or more cost effective. There is no guarantee that even earnest efforts to make the game more accessible will be successful. If the effort fails, or seems insufficient, enhanced cynicism and mistrust might easily result. But even a highly participatory process that extracts "consensus" through logrolling and vague statements of aspiration may only replicate the evasive imprecision common in legislation.[1]

Mistrust affects every level of environmental policymaking. Its historical roots antedate the creation of the U.S. Environmental Protection Agency (EPA) and the enactment of the landmark laws the agency enforces. Indeed, the modern environmental movement arose in the 1960s on a foundation of mistrust. Environmental enthusiasts of the late 1960s believed the system they faced was systematically rigged, by narrow material interests and short-run thinking, against the public interest cause they championed. By 1980 environmental awareness was firmly embedded as a public value.[2] Since then, developments in American politics have complicated the problem of mistrust and disagreement. Moreover, the early struggle to raise public consciousness and enact fundamental legislation has long since given way to a contentious era of policy implementation on many fronts. The nature of the environmental threat was once the main source of angst, but today environmental programs are a source of controversy. Do these programs work well or poorly? Should they be reformed, and if so in what way? The more we try to do, the more programmatic pitfalls stimulate argument and disappointment.

This chapter first reviews developments in the past two decades that have created such a challenging political context for would-be reformers. The discussion then moves to whether and how citizens can be more effectively and productively included in environmental initiatives, thereby directly addressing one of the primary anxieties about reinvention (beyond the simple fear that it may allow more pollution). Can reinvention be rendered democratically legitimate and substantively effective? What can environmentalists tell us that might conceivably help propel reinvention, despite the strong reservations many environmental advocates have about it?

The Managerial Model and Its Limits

During a recent conference on environmental reinvention, one participant briefly addressed the American political system's obsession with accommodating new categories of stakeholders in policy processes. The moment passed quickly, but the question raised is worth reviving:

> What's ironic is the shift in the way that some of our programs have gone, where you need a stakeholder process to assure the public interest. I mean, I lost something somewhere along the way. I . . . thought that's . . . why we elected members of Congress and . . . people [to] various offices around the country, and . . . why Congress then delegated some authority to act on the public's behalf through executive agencies.[3]

As the commentator was doubtless aware, support for this "textbook" managerial model of policymaking began evaporating a long time ago.[4] In the 1960s public interest advocates were actively rejecting the notion that the demands and needs of citizens flowed neatly into a legislative process and thereafter into implementation by politically neutral agency experts.[5] The regularly superior political position of business interests in traditional economic regulation helped to make environmental activists unwilling to trust in such processes to defend the ecology and the public health. Only an ever-vigilant and energized citizenry could keep regulators dutiful and business power (that is, "polluter" power) at bay.

One profound result was the passage of statutes enabling citizens to bring environmental lawsuits. Environmental activists believed that such provisions would bolster the stringency of regulation. As R. Shep Melnick has observed, "Previous statutes had required citizens wishing to sue administrators to show that they had suffered direct, concrete harm at the hands of an agency. Almost all the regulatory laws passed in the 1970s, though, authorized 'any citizen' to file suit against administrators either for taking unauthorized action or for failing to perform 'nondiscretionary' duties."[6] Richard J. Lazarus and Stephanie Tai comment that such provisions resulted from congressional "awareness that government enforcement resources would necessarily be insufficient (and unreliable) to establish the credible threat needed to promote compliance."[7] In other words, the government could not be relied on to achieve protection unless aided by an empowered and attentive citizenry. Greater access to the courts was also partly the result of an inclination by judges to grant standing to a wider array of litigants than previously. Moreover, the new empowerment of citizen activists was in line with a trend in the politics of regulation that dramatically lowered, during the 1960s and 1970s, the cost of obtaining effective access to the political process overall.[8]

Long before the advent of the Reagan presidency and its antigovernmental rhetoric, citizen suit provisions (such as sec. 304 of the Clean Air Act) clearly manifested activist mistrust of traditional regulatory apparatus. The primary environmental statutes were also enacted under conditions of divided government, encouraging a dynamic of "one-upmanship" between President Richard Nixon and his political rivals in Congress. Stringent deadline-laced statutes have been common (though the deadlines have regularly proved overly optimistic and have been repeatedly extended).[9]

But while useful for "action-forcing" and "action-blocking," litigation is inappropriate for some important purposes. It is not suited to a delicate balancing among interests and values when technical uncertainty, citizen mistrust, and the desire for flexibility are all keenly felt. States, communities, and an array of advocates must struggle harder than ever to reconcile competing needs and perspectives, a process that judges can do little to facilitate. More broadly, national institutions in general (lacking adequate authority, technical understanding, and trust) are hard pressed to find solutions that will satisfy diverse and often polarized clienteles.

Tensions in Post-1980 Environmentalism

The past shapes the future, for it is the foundation on which we build (or from which we depart). The 1970s yielded environmental statutes and regulatory structures anchored in a skeptical citizen scrutiny of both agency and business behavior. The 1980s and 1990s witnessed deepened mistrust on at least three fronts. First, the presidential election of 1980 brought to Washington an administration determined to tame the regulatory beast, especially in environmental policy. In tandem with Reagan's ascent, critics of environmental policy, especially in the American West, objected to what they viewed as unfair encroachment on accustomed local prerogatives by Washington "land grabbers" (that is, bureaucracies responsible for managing federally owned land or enforcing federal rules). Second, a confounding and often boisterous new grassroots activism, directed against toxic chemical production and waste disposal, demanded a place at the environmental policy table. Finally, as state environmental programs developed greater capacity and a more refined sense of their own needs, priorities, and possibilities, tensions rose between state and federal authorities.

Regulatory Relief

The Reagan presidency broke new ground in promoting antigovernmentalism as a governing doctrine. The Republican Party had long been more forthrightly "pro-business" than its rival, which of course regularly accommodated organized labor as a major constituency. But in declaring, in his first inaugural address, that "government is not the solution to our problem; government is the problem," Reagan made a rhetorical appeal (directed, on that occasion, toward the nation's continuing economic crisis) that went beyond anything previous Republican presidents had embraced. Excess regulation emanating from Washington, Reagan believed, was at least partly responsible for the economic malaise in which the country found itself.

Reagan (and later George Bush) pursued highly visible, and enormously contentious, efforts to rein in federal regulation, with environmental policy implementation taking center stage.[10] Because he lacked the congressional and public support necessary for rewriting landmark regulatory legislation more to his liking, Reagan pursued a firmly administrative strategy anchored in appointments, budgets, and White House regulatory review. But Reagan's top environmental appointments proved especially controversial. They included James Watt as secretary of the interior, Robert Burford at the Bureau of Land Management, and Burford's "ideological ally and longtime personal companion," Anne Gorsuch, at the EPA.[11] As head of the Mountain States Legal Foundation, founded by conservative businessman and philanthropist Joseph Coors, Watt would become "a leading advocate for western energy, ranching, and development interests battling against federal environmental restrictions" intent on (as Watt testified) "defend[ing] individuals and the private sector from illegal and excessive bureaucratic regulation."[12]

Burford and Gorsuch had been activist conservatives in the Colorado legislature, charter members of an alliance the Colorado media had nicknamed "the crazies."[13] Watt would quickly establish a national profile very much in accord with the "Colorado crazy" image. He staked out controversial positions on such matters as wilderness development (which he did not think oxymoronic), made enemies by the basketful, and seemed not at all to mind. He firmly cast himself as a charter member of the so-called Sagebrush Rebellion, a loose alliance of western-state conservatives angered by the Carter administration's initiatives that restricted the private use of public lands.

Whatever other troubles his conservative views and blunt-spoken approach may have generated, Watt at least managed to avoid large-scale institutional scandal. Gorsuch would be much less fortunate on this score, becoming mired in a well-publicized and deeply politicized 1982–83 saga fueled by charges of politically motivated maladministration, especially in the nation's new Superfund hazardous waste cleanup program. No fewer than five subcommittees of the House of Representatives weighed in with critical oversight hearings. Rita Lavelle, assistant administrator for hazardous waste and emergency response, was asked to resign, refused, and was fired by President Reagan. (She later went to prison for having lied to Congress.) By the spring of 1983, with nearly all of the EPA's top appointees fired or forced out, the agency stood nearly decapitated, and the Reagan administration deeply embarrassed. The White House was compelled to launch a serious effort at political damage control, retrieving the respected William Ruckleshaus, the EPA's original administrator, to run the agency a second time.[14]

These events were merely the most extreme in a long history of adversarial relations between business-oriented conservatives on the one hand and environmentalists and their allies on the other. The nation now enters a new century, more than a decade beyond the Reagan presidency, but the same kinds of relationships (and rhetoric) had endured in less dramatic form throughout the Clinton presidency. Since 1995 Republican politicians have held an increasingly powerful institutional base from which to challenge the EPA. During the Clinton era they attempted this most directly through the appropriations process, proposing to attach restrictive provisions to money bills and the committee reports that accompany them, to the chagrin of the groups that meticulously track the environmental policy process.[15] To environmental advocates, such initiatives (which often mandate additional analytic requirements for ferreting out regulatory costs) all too often appear to be little more than "sand in the crankcase" masquerading as reform.[16] With the presidency of George W. Bush, however, Republican policymakers have an unprecedented opportunity to redefine environmental policy to their liking, though the Senate filibuster and public opinion remain formidable barriers to policies perceived as radically deregulatory.

The challenge is that the public has consistently viewed environmental protection very favorably (though less so when some aspect of it, such as vehicle emissions inspection and maintenance programs, imposes a palpable burden directly on citizens). All sides claim the cherished mantle of "environmentalist." Yet the mass public seems largely unaware of the vast progress made against pollution in America since 1970.[17] Perhaps partly for this reason it is harder than it would otherwise be to justify departures from stringency and relatively easier than otherwise to portray any proposed shift as a capitulation to polluters. The mass public may have only a dim memory of the Reagan administration's initiatives and scandals. But environmental advocates have far stronger recollections and, moreover, readily discern echoes of Watt and

Gorsuch in recent challenges to stringency. To put it briefly and mildly, neither "relief" nor "reinvention" has proved broadly compelling to the mass public or to environmental advocates, and past efforts at relief contaminate today's prospects for reinvention. This challenge remains, even as the party more uniformly allied with business interests controls the White House and the House of Representatives. Being effectively tarred with the "antienvironmental" brush would undermine the conciliatory image that George W. Bush has sought to project.

Toxic Terror

Besides current partisan and ideological tensions, one must add the challenge posed by the rise of an aggressive environmental populism, including the racially charged variant of it known as environmental justice (that is, the greater procedural involvement and substantive fairness sought for low-income and minority communities). Because such advocacy plainly thrives on mistrust of business and government, coping with it is among the more daunting political difficulties environmental policymakers face. Indeed, environmental populism's underlying diagnosis of what ails environmental policy appears at odds with the emphasis and tone of much "next-generation" analysis.

On the one hand, task forces and policy research organizations worry mostly about performance measurement, rationalized priority setting, and more flexible compliance regimes.[18] On the other hand, environmental populism (or "ecopopulism") stresses a strong and diverse public voice and equitable treatment.[19] Furthermore, environmental populists frequently exhibit strong skepticism toward the scientific inquiry and data gathering that reinvention advocates want improved as a pathway to reform.

Although these two perspectives stand in significant tension, they need not be viewed as polar opposites, which is at least one source of hope for rapprochement. Next-generation rationalizers clearly recognize the desirability of citizen participation and the need for democratic legitimacy. A 1995 report by the National Academy of Public Administration observes that "the Toxic Release Inventory . . . has provided community groups with an important, albeit imperfect, foundation for working with local industries."[20] Ruckleshaus, an important proponent of next-generation thinking, explicitly calls for "greater reflection of the essential democratic values of our society; and greater fairness, in avoiding undue risks or expenses for any one portion of the population."[21]

DeWitt John of the National Academy of Public Administration observes that the new "civic environmentalism" seeks regulatory flexibility but also demands citizen engagement.[22]

Environmental populists can often accept the need for science-based decisionmaking provided that the community in question is comfortable with (and, ideally, has a role in) data gathering and assessment. Unfortunately, suspicion of the scientific and public health establishments (combined with the inadequacy of traditional epidemiology for resolving many environmental controversies) can make the gulf separating science and grassroots activism exceedingly difficult to bridge.[23] A seemingly benign term often favored by business representatives and their allies— "sound science"—masks a minefield of disputed facts and value premises (as in the enduring debate over the so-called precautionary principle).[24]

Environmental populism's origins lie deep in America's postwar development, rooted partly in social inequalities that did not yield to the end of the Great Depression and partly in industrial externalities addressed neither by the discharge-control schemes crafted in the early 1970s nor by traditional conservation.[25] The triggering event was the discovery of leaking toxic waste in the Love Canal neighborhood of Niagara Falls, New York. Love Canal made citizens, the media, and policymakers aware of the "ticking time bomb" of toxic waste sites.[26] It propelled a Democratic Congress and president to enact waste cleanup legislation only weeks before Republicans arrived to claim the White House and the Senate. Later, in Times Beach, Missouri, national attention turned to toxic waste again, culminating in a dramatic federal buyout offer to an entire neighborhood, just as the EPA scandal was forcing the newly married Anne Gorsuch Burford from her job as administrator.

Consciousness of the threat posed by toxic chemicals added a new acronym to America's political vocabulary: NIMBY, or "not in my backyard." As complex cleanups stalled, costs escalated, and naively crafted siting processes broke down when put to the test of real-world implementation, students of policy for toxic substances have cast about aggressively for effective solutions.[27] Meanwhile, citizen advocates have sought empowerment through a combination of protest, litigation, lobbying, and information dissemination. Today any community's "right to know" its emissions and discharge burden is forcefully invoked by a wide variety of policy actors, from the EPA administrator to the smallest cash-strapped neighborhood group. Mistrust is inherent in such a milieu.

State-Federal Tensions

By the 1990s many state governments had accumulated vast experience in environmental policy, through the partnership role for which federal statutes provide and by dint of their own initiatives. As far back as the Carter administration, state environmental officials had often complained about "what they considered to be an overbearing and unnecessary federal presence that signified a lack of confidence in their capacity to administer environmental affairs."[28] By 1993 state environmental commissioners had formed the Environmental Council of the States (ECOS), grounded in the recognition that

> long before the pressure for devolution of environmental programs gained momentum, states were performing the overwhelming majority of environmental protection functions in the nation. Through delegated federal programs and state-developed programs, states issue most of the permits, initiate most of the enforcement and compliance actions, and develop many of the innovative ideas for dealing with environmental issues.[29]

It is in the state-federal relationship that challenges of mistrust and disagreement are perhaps most vexing, because they go to the heart of ongoing policy implementation. Tensions among congressional leaders, between Congress and the White House, or between business leaders and environmental activists are to be expected, perhaps even encouraged. Such tensions may inhibit statutory change and create a predictably adversarial and, to some, unsavory political discourse, but they do not necessarily corrupt or burden the vital work of day-by-day decisionmaking and policy implementation. But if levels of government mistrust one another or find it hard to work together, the result could be potentially more serious, since there is no way to evade or postpone the need for an effective working relationship.

As environmental policy has become more complicated for federal decisionmakers, so has it also for state officials. Relative success nationally against point sources and mobile sources of pollution has made even more starkly evident at the state level the difficulty of tackling suburban sprawl or agricultural and urban runoff. Hazardous waste sites are an abiding concern for citizens, but only a relative handful of them rise to the level of active federal intervention, leaving the states as the primary decisionmaking and response venue.

Emergent community demands for environmental justice prompted a vigorous search for ways to pour new wine into old statutory bottles.[30] One reason is that proposed federal legislation on environmental justice has not fared well.[31] The recently evolved status of Title VI of the Civil Rights Act as a major policy instrument for environmental justice is a source of tension between state authorities and the EPA (and between community activists and the political establishment) that did not exist during the Reagan-Bush era. In March 1998, ECOS pronounced the EPA's interim environmental justice guidance on Title VI "not workable," launching a contentious search for common ground and new language.[32] Although the EPA released a new version of the guidance in June of 2000, the effort to retrofit Title VI as environmental policy remains problematic.[33]

The broader terrain of reinvention has also shown signs of intergovernmental strain. By September of 1997 the EPA and ECOS had reached a draft agreement on principles governing regulatory innovation, but only after differences over how much flexibility states would enjoy, and how they would include stakeholders, had caused the EPA to withdraw an earlier proposal and temporarily suspend participation in negotiations.[34] In killing the original draft, the EPA deputy administrator commented that he was "exceedingly surprised and really shocked" by the discretion the states were asking for.[35]

Nevertheless, state-level environmental innovation has been prolific (though, not surprisingly, uneven among states) and a powerful driver of national environmental policy. The late political scientist James Lester sorted states into four categories—progressives, strugglers, delayers, and regressives—determined by their relative mix of commitment and institutional capacity.[36] Variations in civic support underlie these categories and condition the prospects for effective cooperation. When EPA officials speak of their "partnership" with state officials, the label most properly refers to a variety of relationships anchored importantly in such categories. The National Academy of Public Administration, recognizing state-level differences in capacity and political will, argues that EPA's approach ought to vary accordingly:

The principle is simple: one size does not fit all. Those states that are capable and willing to take over functions from the federal government should have full operational responsibility. . . . In those states without the capability or the political will to assume responsibility, EPA should continue to exercise intensive oversight. And for those states falling between the two extremes, EPA should try to enhance their capabilities and help move them toward full delegation.[37]

In 1995 the EPA and the states established a National Environmental Performance Partnership System (NEPPS) intended to drive a more cooperative, flexible, and performance-based regime of environmental protection. Results of this voluntary initiative to date appear mixed.[38] The overall effort has been severely hampered for many reasons (including the predictable difficulty of pursuing a performance-based, multimedia approach to pollution through institutions long accustomed to focusing on *activities* undertaken in a single medium).

Most striking is how little NEPPS appears to have grappled with the challenge of citizen engagement. A recent assessment of seven states participating in NEPPS prepared for the National Academy of Public Administration found that only Texas and North Carolina had done much to address the civic dimension. Otherwise, "public participation has not been an integral element of state NEPPS programs."[39] A second NAPA assessment precisely echoed the first, declaring that "most of the states covered in our study obtained very little public participation . . . [in the drafting of their performance partnership agreements (PPAs)] or in any other aspect of the NEPPS process."[40] Most state efforts were judged "desultory and ineffective."[41] Even national environmental groups seem to have had little interest in NEPPS.

Reinvention Obstacles and Conventional Alternatives

The preceding discussion raises serious questions about what might be called the "civic sustainability" of environmental reinvention at each of the three levels of governance where reinvention must find support: national, intergovernmental, and local. It is imperative at all three levels that reinvention find support (or at least tacit consent) from the public and from civil society. When are we likely to see support, indifference, or opposition, especially within the diverse "environmental community"?

The most straightforward obstacle reformers face is the perception that environmental reinvention might allow shirking of responsibility by business or government, resulting in environmental degradation, unacceptable health risks, or an unnecessary stalling of the war against pollution. The draft state-federal reinvention agreement killed by the EPA in February 1997—the agency and ECOS would finally agree on a statement of guidelines and principles the following September—had drawn criticism from environmentalists for failing to promote a cleaner environment along with cheaper environmental controls.[42] Efficiency alone has never been a compelling value to activists or to the public, and it remains politically anemic as a basis for environmental reinvention.

Consider briefly Project XL, perhaps the Clinton administration's major environmental reinvention initiative. Like NEPPS, Project XL (for eXcellence and Leadership) was launched in 1995, shortly after the Republican takeover of Congress. Project XL was offered as a vehicle to permit firms "to test innovative ways of achieving environmental protection at both the facility and the community levels if they can demonstrate that the proposed changes will yield superior environmental performance."[43] Project XL has enjoyed mixed success (including some instructive failures). A significant hurdle has been that environmental and community activists often do not believe that specific proposed projects can reliably generate adequate pollution reductions or the kind of vigorous citizen oversight they seek.

In November 1996 the EPA signed an agreement with Intel Corporation, the leading maker of computer chips. The EPA described the agreement as "a facility-wide pollution cap," ensuring that the firm's Chandler, Arizona, site would remain a minor source of air pollutants. "The EPA, Arizona, and Maricopa County agreed to allow Intel to change equipment and processes and build new facilities without air permit reviews, as long as emissions stay below the plant-wide limits. The project also consolidates Intel's reporting and publishes environmental results on the Internet."[44] All this did not sit well, or nearly well enough, with the Silicon Valley Toxics Coalition, which branded the agreement "a sweetheart deal for environmental de-regulation." The coalition's bill of particulars included the following:

—The air pollution limits allowed were "2 to 50 times less stringent than existing limits and the standards do not protect against chronic health problems."

—The permit in this instance "is based on what Intel can get away with rather than how clean Intel could be. Instead of setting limits based on state of the art, Project XL bases its limits on numbers designed to escape EPA's regulatory jurisdiction."

—Intel is "not even required to monitor air emission or the performance of its scrubbers; there is no way to independently verify whether Intel is meeting its commitments."

—The agreement "would de-regulate some pollutants currently regulated."

—The stakeholder process for developing the deal was "fundamentally flawed" because Intel picked the stakeholder group, which "includes only minimal Chandler community representation and no fabrication worker representatives from the plant." Such stakeholders as did participate "lacked the time, resources, independent technical assistance, and decision-making authority to ensure that the deal would increase protection of public health and the environment."[45]

These criticisms of the Intel deal seem fairly representative of the reservations that led some environmental advocates to deride XL as standing for "eXtra Leniency." Less than two years after the program was announced, the EPA hosted a meeting of environmental and citizen groups, several of them critical of Project XL. As the *Washington Post* reported, critics were "concerned that the agency doesn't really know what to extract from a company in return for offering regulatory flexibility . . . [and] that stakeholders [would] be reduced to mere observers in the process of coming to agreement with companies, rather than full participants."[46]

In January 1997 the Weyerhaeuser Corporation signed an XL agreement with the EPA providing for emissions and waste reductions at its pulp manufacturing facility in Oglethorpe, Georgia. In exchange the EPA and the state allowed "process modifications without prior approval, streamlined the wastewater permit renewal process, eliminated unnecessary sampling, and allowed annual certification to replace monthly reporting."[47] But David Hawkins of the Natural Resources Defense Council (and former Carter administration EPA assistant administrator for air programs) worried that the agreement would not achieve significant reductions beyond what the law would soon require.[48]

Other civic problems bedevil Project XL and reinvention. One widely shared perception is that these efforts originated as a Clinton administration attempt to blunt Republican criticism and forestall damaging regulatory rollback, rather than a serious commitment to transform the way environmental protection is pursued. (This perception is damaging even though it almost certainly distorts the history and motivations

underlying reinvention efforts.) Another problem is that reinvention initiatives, such as Project XL and the industry-sector-based Common
Sense Initiative (CSI) also pursued by the EPA, lack a sufficient ground-
ing in environmental statutes, thus creating greater exposure to, or at
least fear of, litigation.[49] Finally, putting opponents into a room and
forcing them to talk to each other may not, by itself, yield much substantive change. Indeed, a breakdown in talks, such as occurred on the
CSI petroleum refining sector subcommittee at the end of 1996, may
only deepen mistrust.[50]

Well-publicized progress in environmental protection since 1970 may
also hamper support for reform. Many significant victories over pollution have relied on conventional approaches: tough enforcement, stringent national standards and end-of-pipe controls, strict liability, and
wholesale phase-outs such as occurred with chloroflourocarbons
(CFCs), polychlorinated biphenyls (PCBs), and leaded gasoline. Accordingly, some reinvention skeptics emphasize that more flexible and per-
formance-oriented approaches may only work reliably in tandem with
more traditional methods, or when an old-fashioned regulatory "ham-
mer" looms in the background.[51]

With the appropriate doses of political compromise and regulatory
flexibility, conventional policymaking need not always bog down in
recrimination and litigation. Consider, for example, the EPA's program,
announced in December 1999, to regulate mobile sources of ozone and
airborne particulate matter.[52] The rules were trumpeted by the *New
York Times* as a major environmental and political victory for President
Bill Clinton, who announced "the costliest environmental regulations of
his presidency . . . without facing major criticism."[53] Trust may be
unimportant (or at least far less important than raw self-interest and
creative compromise) when it comes to hammering out many high-profile agreements. Recall that even the notoriously stringent and long
politically unassailable Delaney clause (which mandated, by statute, a
zero tolerance policy for carcinogenic chemical residues in food that was
widely derided as unrealistic) was eventually replaced by a 1996 Food
Quality Protection Act that provided important benefits for both business and consumer health advocates.[54] Specific win-win bargains, where
they can be fashioned, will always be more attractive and satisfying than
more general trust building.

Lawmaking, especially, continues to be an arena that rewards
guarded position taking and defense of the status quo. A foundation in

federal statute law would greatly ease the strain on efforts to extract greater flexibility from the policy process. But the trick is to craft a regime that allows some actors the flexibility they seek while reassuring others that unacceptable shirking will not occur. It is no wonder that the Clinton administration EPA found itself simultaneously searching for flexibility while also defending stringency. "It is peculiar that [Project XL] and the showcase project of a pro-environmental administration is designed to help get around the very environmental laws that it is supposed to administer," observed Terry Davies of Resources for the Future. "That means something is wrong with these laws and the programs that implement them."[55] But to the extent that Project XL and other reinvention initiatives may have emanated from a desire to give environmental programs political cover against a hostile Congress, one might be inclined to view such efforts as sensible and successful.

Empowering Citizens

The cooperation and participation of environmental and community groups may be the answer to the question of reinvention's long-term political viability. If the concerns of advocates are taken seriously and protected, these groups may refrain from opposition and perhaps even offer support. For that to happen, however, citizen advocacy must be analyzed creatively and honestly.

Information, Enforcement, and Trust

How can trust be engendered? Let us define trust as confidence in the reliability of others.[56] Those "others" may be persons intimately familiar to us or, alternatively, unknown to and distant from us. In the first case developing trust may be largely a matter of repeated face-to-face interaction, leading to collective comfort, understanding, and norms of reciprocity among persons in a specific milieu (that is, a family or neighborhood).

In the second instance this cannot occur. But all is not lost, for individuals not personally acquainted (and perhaps even competitive with one another in some way) may nevertheless be able to place some confidence in a larger system or process. Individuals who may not necessarily trust one another (at least initially) could nevertheless conceivably share confidence in a procedural and informational framework for decisionmaking. Modern environmental policy in the United States, however, is conspicuously problematic in this regard. Parties to a decision (especially if it has escalated to a "controversy") may have little confidence in the reliability of a particular decisionmaking framework. Business executives, for instance, could fear they would have to make embarrassing revelations, compromise valuable trade secrets, or reveal sensitive information that could expose firms to punitive action. Even a "final" agreement, corporations fear, may not eliminate exposure to a citizen-initiated lawsuit. Private citizens wonder how to gauge the reliability of information offered by a firm or by government regulators. Advocates ask, will regulators and firms do what they promise to do? If we trust, will you (or some system in which we have confidence) verify? From everyone's point of view, is a deal a deal? It is vital that parties have confidence in one another (when possible), but they must also believe in the informational and procedural framework within which they are operating (when such confidence is not possible).

Robert Putnam makes precisely this point in discussing the institutional benefits of social capital:

> How can each [person] be confident that the other will keep his word in the face of temptation to shirk? More complex contexts, like modern government (or modern markets), bring the added complication of monitoring: How can one agent know whether another did in fact make a "good faith effort" to keep his word, in the face of multiple uncertainties and countervailing pressures? Both accurate information and reliable enforcement are essential to successful cooperation.[57]

However, one cannot accurately reduce a description of many environmental controversies to a single "business perspective" contrasted with one unified "environmentalist viewpoint." Any dissenter from a deal may energetically oppose it, perhaps through the courts, and there are certain to be dissenters to any broad recasting of environmental policy.

Moreover, simple majorities regularly suffice for establishing binding legislative and judicial decisions. For consulting citizens or engaging their participation in administrative decisions and policy implementation, however, a simple majority may not suffice. A land-use or community-level pollution control decision supported by a bare majority of residents or activists may leave too many dissatisfied participants. The losers would possibly be numerous and motivated enough to force continuation of the issue, which is very likely under conditions of heightened controversy and mistrust. Legislatures and courts, after all, make "pass-through" decisions; both laws and cases enter their respective institutions (as bills or pleadings) and then exit once a vote is taken. Neither institution has to live, day by day, with the detailed results and implications of the decisions they render. The firms, communities, and agencies that are parties to a siting or permitting dispute do not share this luxury.

Although citizens face obvious challenges in assimilating expertise sufficient to participate meaningfully in technical discussions, this hurdle can, with creativity and energy, be reasonably addressed, at least in discrete cases when deliberations are sustained and the perceived stakes are high enough to promote interest. With application and skilled assistance, citizens can often absorb technical information sufficiently to grapple with the general issues raised in many locally based debates on siting, permitting, and other pollution-related issues. When the cost and difficulty of citizen participation, including difficulties of data access, data interpretation, and preference signaling by individuals, would be prohibitively high, public interest groups may fill a vital niche.[58]

But the inadequacy of the knowledge base is the greatest hurdle for citizens and experts alike. The information problem in local environmental disputes is often (indeed, regularly) not that the expert knows things that the citizen cannot grasp. The larger problem, rather, is that much of what both would like to know is unknown (and, in the foreseeable future, likely unknowable) by anyone. Environmental justice advocates, for example, have made much of environmental policy's paltry capacity for addressing "multiple, cumulative, and synergistic" risks, although a search for "sound science" hardly describes what these advocates are up to in using this terminology.[59] More broadly, monitoring of the overall "state of the environment" is far less reliable than most citizens probably realize. In their overview of U.S. pollution control Terry Davies and Jan Mazurek find

> a dearth of information of all kinds. . . . The system lacks monitoring data to tell whether environmental conditions are getting better or worse; it lacks scientific knowledge about both the causes and the effects of threats to human and environmental health; it lacks information that would tell us which programs are working

and which are not. There is a systematic underinvestment, in some cases a disinvestment, in the information-gathering efforts necessary to run an intelligent pollution control program.[60]

Of course, even the best monitoring will not really address the cumulative risk problem at issue in many siting or permitting disputes. Knowing "what stuff is out there" will not tell one anything about how the various pollutants interact to affect long-term health. But getting greater purchase on the basic questions of loading, dissemination, and exposure might, in the long term, help inspire improved confidence among all parties that the overall system can be trusted to offer an accurate portrait of how well (or poorly) at least the primary components of protection are working (nationally or in any given locale). It is clear, for example, that the dearth of data on water quality is a serious hurdle to activating the Clean Water Act's long-dormant provisions on total maximum daily loads (TMDLs).[61] Implementation of these provisions would constitute a performance-based approach to the long-simmering challenge of nonpoint sources and therefore has found considerable support. But the program can thrive in the long run only with broad stakeholder confidence in the water quality assessments undertaken to bolster it.

Participation and Time

Arguably even more challenging for citizens than gaining the knowledge they need is whether they can reliably devote the time necessary for effective participation. Linda Greer of the Natural Resources Defense Council (NRDC) points to the Michigan Source Reduction Initiative that her organization and local activists negotiated with Dow Chemical as an instructive success story in generating monetary savings for Dow and significantly reduced pollution. But she also reminds us that while she was a paid participant, the local activists crucial to making the initiative a success were not.[62] Unlike her, they had to donate their "free time" to the project. Greer makes an important point that is easily overlooked. Jacqueline Savitz, executive director of Coast Alliance, suggests that bringing more environmental decisions down to the neighborhood level without compensating citizens for their time "confers what corporate lobbyists would call an unfunded mandate."[63] Savitz sounds a cautionary note about the prospects for effective citizen empowerment through conventional participation structures:

Well-intentioned citizens of my parents' generation are often invited to the table without any resources to cover their travel or their time, and without support for outside technical assistance. They sit beside high-paid corporate lawyers and engineers, and are expected to out-argue the lawyers and out-engineer the engineers. How could our parents be expected to provide better service to their neighbors in the absence of federal regulations than the federal government provides? Such citizen panels are more likely to serve as smoke screens than as effective advocates. Who better understands complex technical issues—your mother, or the scientists paid by the public to protect it?[64]

The compensation and expertise questions are essential to any fundamental reconsideration of the citizen's role in environmental policymaking. Both go directly to the heart of the motivational and resource constraints that have always impeded the capacity of citizens to be directly effective in complicated policy questions.

But lurking just beyond these considerations is accountability. Increased power brings with it enhanced responsibility. There is no reason to believe, despite populist political rhetoric to the contrary, that the power citizens wield as parties to environmental negotiations automatically avoids problems of self-interest and abuse of power. It is entirely understandable that the main worry among activists today is that their voices will not be heard, that the perspectives they represent are overmatched by government and business (despite repeated manifestation of citizens' power to block actions of which they disapprove). But a different concern arises about more aggressive forms of citizen empowerment. The more "solid" or institutionalized that citizen participation becomes, the more it might have to resemble, for good or ill, the bureaucratized entities (that is, government agencies and business firms) that are its partners in power. Might efforts dramatically and responsibly to enhance citizen capacity for environmental partnership create entities that require policing?

How Would Environmental Advocates Reinvent?

What ideas do environmental advocates espouse when they are pressed to envision a route beyond the current impasse? In 1996, in the wake of Clinton administration reinvention initiatives, the Pollution Prevention Alliance, a network organized by what was then known as the Environmental Defense Fund (now Environmental Defense) issued evaluation criteria for an "alternative regulatory pathway" (ARP).[65]

Like Project XL, the ARP demands "environmental protection better than would be achieved by full compliance with the standard regulatory system" and aspires to "encourage select companies to be pollution prevention and product stewardship leaders." Ideally, firms would "continuously improve their environmental performance as a standard business practice." The ARP would afford firms faithfully pursuing such an environmental orientation at least two kinds of relief: avoidance of "costly dramatic surprise changes in basic expectations, as well as inflexible requirements regarding means," and "minimized" transaction costs of traditional enforcement through the provision of "compliance assistance." The ARP, however, would insist on "consequences (e.g., per unit fee) for short-term minor noncompliance," a provision clearly at odds with the inclinations of many business-oriented supporters of compliance assistance. And the preferred ARP measurement and reporting scheme would ideally be anchored in a "materials accounting approach that tracks both inputs and outputs per unit of product," a notion anathema to many in the manufacturing community.

The ARP vision of public participation is vaguely drawn, presenting "criteria" that, while presumably comprehensive enough to satisfy the environmentalist coalition endorsing it, offer little practical guidance in designing a concrete, workable, and reproducible system. In essence, the document advises that anyone with anything important to say be included; the "right" to meaningful participation be assiduously nurtured and protected by all available means and at every relevant stage; and both the environmental performance offered by "the standard regulatory system" and any commitments made to go beyond that system to "superior environmental performance" be "fully enforceable by responsible agencies and through citizen suits."

Although perhaps effective as a strong and brief statement of environmentalist values, the ARP does not (and, apparently, was not intended to) set forth how these might be reconciled effectively with competing interests and imperatives. In trying to surmise how environmental and business values can be blended more effectively we probably do better to probe instances of attempted cooperation rather than broad statements of principle.

The Michigan Source Reduction Initiative (MSRI) pursued in Midland, Michigan, is a useful example.[66] Initiated in the fall of 1996 by the

NRDC, Dow Chemical, and a group of five community activists and environmentalists, the MSRI project (a total of seventeen smaller efforts) aimed, over the course of two years, explicitly to reduce pollution through prevention. What is striking about the effort is that it seems to have successfully reduced the pollution generated at Dow's Midland facilities, saved the company money, and effectively engaged national and local stakeholders. Moreover, skepticism apparently ran high at the outset of the project. The final report on the project describes the initial atmosphere:

> All parties entered the MSRI project skeptical that it would reach its reduction goals. Dow businesses doubted they would uncover good opportunities. Activists and environmental participants worried that Dow would not implement the opportunities the project found. Much of the skepticism on both sides derived from the fact that participants did not know of a single example of successful similar work.[67]

Yet the project exceeded its 35 percent reduction goals, reducing targeted emissions by 43 percent and targeted wastes by 37 percent. Meanwhile, "Dow estimates the project will save the company $5.4 million annually, through raw materials cost savings and reduced waste treatment costs alone, for an overall annual rate of return of 180 percent."[68] And what role did citizens play? They provided a crucial incentive for the firm by engaging manufacturing managers and engineers directly (aided by access to external technical experts). Among the four "key lessons learned" the final report indicates that "activists and environmental participants created the motivation for businesses to focus on [pollution prevention] opportunities by a date certain and provided Dow a clear rationale for implementation that went beyond dollars and cents alone."[69]

Indeed, Linda Greer, who headed the project for the NRDC, reached the somewhat surprising conclusion that even opportunities for environment-friendly cost savings would not necessarily motivate business to act. A saving of "only" $5.4 million is simply too small for a large corporation to perceive as significant, especially if considerable exploratory work and up-front investment is necessarily to squeeze it out. And if, in addition, the firm is in compliance with existing laws and regulations, the default mindset is to perceive no problem worth addressing (despite opportunities for prevention waiting to be uncovered).[70] In such a situation, committed citizens might have the legitimacy with the company's key players and familiarity with the issues needed to help prompt change. As Greer put it, "the local activists brought an urgency to the equation that we couldn't."[71]

The more episodes like MSRI one could point to, the greater would be the prospects for enhancing trust and environmental results. People might then see more win-win solutions as possible, and former adversaries as persons with whom it is possible to do business. And, indeed, the MSRI in important respects resembles the Good Neighbor Agreements that have been promoted as a way to bridge the gap between communities concerned about pollution and the local industries that generate it.[72] But the challenge of replicating, much less multiplying, the MSRI is considerable, as is generally true with pilot projects or "special" endeavors undertaken for difficult problems with unusual allocations of time, money, and creativity.[73]

The MSRI was not even reproduced elsewhere inside Dow Chemical. Indeed, Greer reports that overtures to thirty-five other companies to undertake similar projects were all declined, despite the nationally publicized success of the MSRI. This repeated difficulty in finding new partners for targeted replication of a well-publicized win-win success story understandably invites Greer to wonder just what kind of reinvention business wants.

Realistic Reform

For many years interest has been rising in "breaking out of the box" of conventional environmental policymaking, in getting beyond a pervasive adversarial mistrust in the service of a cleaner environment and other valued social objectives. Much thinking goes on about the methods that might be employed.[74] Innovation continues on many fronts. But informed skeptics in the environmental movement warn against putting all the eggs into the basket of local negotiation and alternative dispute resolution. Their suggestion that next-generation strategies, even when successful, may not always work without the safety net of conventional enforcement is one of the most important issues demanding convincing clarification.

The failure of the NRDC to find additional corporate partners for more source reduction initiatives is disheartening but illuminating, since it suggests rather concretely that a formula promising benefits for all players may not necessarily be enough to stimulate cooperation. Even if Greer and the NRDC, however, had found more companies responsive to their overtures for additional source reduction initiatives, how realistic would it be to expect citizen groups to act regularly in lieu of government policymakers?[75] As suggested earlier, any attempt along these lines appears to lead to replication of the various problems connected with the existing government bureaucracy.

Greater knowledge about the true state of the environment should help, but such understanding is no panacea. People may have conflicting values even when there is no uncertainty about empirical facts. But reliable monitoring capacity should help ease tension over time, allowing various parties at least to reassure themselves about important proximate indicators (though without dispelling all uncertainty about long-term health impacts).

The United States now faces diminishing returns from traditional civil rights advocacy, stubborn resistance to major egalitarian policy innovation, and increased concern about the distribution of environmental toxins among segments of the population. One result of these collective developments is an environmentalism pressed to bear more social freight than was thought necessary or appropriate a generation ago. A rhetoric of "environmental health" has served as an irresistible political resource in a broader social justice struggle, a way to mobilize communities and inject their interests more effectively into policy discourse. These democratizing and redistributive impulses substantially complicate the task facing next-generation environmental reformers. There exists a substantial audience attentive to environmentalism for whom the economizing that preoccupies reinvention and the constant focus on regulatory flexibility and cost minimization seem largely beside the point.

Mechanisms for participation are widely perceived as inadequate, but there is also no consensus on what adequacy looks like. As researchers at Resources for the Future have pointed out, participatory initiatives are undertaken with many aims in mind (among them, increased public understanding of an issue, increased agency understanding of the public, the generation of new policy alternatives and information, reduced conflict, and increased trust).[76] Conventional participatory mechanisms face numerous pitfalls. The two most widely used devices, public hearings and citizen advisory committees, face the continuing problem of simple nonparticipation, potentially resulting in unrepresentative processes. As one recent treatment of public participation observes, "No matter what the circumstances, many who are eligible to participate do not, and those who do participate are seldom a cross section of all who are eligible."[77] Even when the motivation problem and the "expertise gap" are successfully bridged, such mechanisms can also be prone to infighting, theatrics, and uncertain management.

But these are not inevitable, nor necessarily uncontrollable or fatal once manifested.[78] Moreover, a broader menu of alternative dispute resolution and citizen deliberation arrangements exists for pursuing objectives related to greater participation. But whatever process is selected must be taken seriously by participants and by those with whom they deal. Compensating citizens for their time (or insisting, as do some states concerned about a major burden of jury service, that employers continue to pay employees who cannot turn up at work) might help bolster a more robust participation. Doing this might also broadcast an important signal about the seriousness with which such work is to be regarded: as a major civic contribution, deserving significant material support. This might help address the trust deficit and help give any agreement reached sufficient legitimacy to withstand subsequent challenge. Environmental and business organizations alike regularly take their grievances to court, and neither will want to surrender that right. But decision processes built on firmer participatory foundations (with abundant front-end consultation or, better yet, shared responsibility for governance) might help defuse the incentive for litigation. Indeed, as noted earlier, the continued existence of some traditional modes of regulatory enforcement might be useful prods to taking nontraditional processes seriously.

We are certainly better situated to promote program-specific or firm-specific trust than to enhance the confidence of the citizenry in public or private institutions as a whole. The EPA and state environmental agencies would do well to consider the advice put forward by an Energy Department task force on radioactive waste management, discussed at length by Todd LaPorte and Daniel Metlay.[79] These include a wide range of external and internal actions to promote trust and confidence. External actions include frequent, candid, and aggressive involvement of stakeholder groups "before key decisions are made"; reaching out "consistently and respectfully" to state and community leaders and the general public; integrating institutional personnel "into the life of affected localities in a way that makes an unmistakable contribution to community affairs"; and securing "benefits for affected communities along with the resources that might be needed to detect and respond to unexpected costs arising from actions taken by the agency/firm." Internally, institutions should approach their tasks to produce the following effect: "When the public gains access to programs via improvements in external relations, they discover activities within the organization that increase institutional trustworthiness rather than decrease it."[80] The advocates of cost effectiveness and citizen empowerment ought to be able to find common ground here. Moreover, emphasize LaPorte and Metlay, public and private institutions alike must think hard about ways to nurture "institutional constancy," meaning the ability consistently to achieve outcomes agreed to in the past, something that may well necessitate "a new culture of awareness" within the institution.[81]

Finally, we must not delude ourselves that consensus (that is, unanimity in decisionmaking) is an essential foundation for trust building. Environmental issues at all levels are so conflict prone and value laden that something less will have to suffice, and even that may be inappropriate as a guide when members of the majority collude to exclude important considerations and voices. As Cary Coglianese points out, a decision everyone "can live with" is not necessarily the best basis for crafting rational and effective public policies, however intuitively appealing it remains as an ideal.[82] We will have to find pathways toward greater confidence in the systems on which all parties rely, even as underlying disagreement or dissatisfaction remain. Realistically, we have little alternative.

Notes to Chapter 5

1. Cary Coglianese, "The Limits of Consensus," review of *The Environmental Protection System* in *Transition: Toward a More Desirable Future,* vol. 41 (April 1999), pp. 1–6.

2. Laura M. Lake, "The Environmental Mandate: Activists and the Electorate," *Political Science Quarterly,* vol. 98 (Summer 1983), pp. 215–33.

3. Comments by Erik Meyers of the Environmental Law Institute at the forum "Defining a New Generation of Environmental Management," Brookings, February 24, 2000 (hereafter Management Forum).

4. The term "managerial" as used here is borrowed from Bruce A. Williams and Albert R. Matheny, *Democracy, Dialogue, and Environmental Disputes: The Contested Languages of Social Regulation* (Yale University Press, 1995).

5. Richard Harris and Sidney Milkis, *The Politics of Regulatory Change: A Tale of Two Agencies* (Oxford University Press, 1989).

6. R. Shep Melnick, *Regulation and the Courts: The Case of the Clean Air Act* (Brookings, 1983), p. 8.

7. Richard J. Lazarus and Stephanie Tai, "Integrating Environmental Justice into EPA Permitting Authority," *Ecology Law Quarterly,* vol. 26, no. 4 (1999), p. 621.

8. James Q. Wilson, "The Politics of Regulation," in Wilson, ed., *The Politics of Regulation* (Basic Books, 1980), pp. 385–86.

9. Alfred Marcus, "Environmental Protection Agency," in Wilson, *The Politics of Regulation*, pp. 267–303. On the political forces generating the unrealistic deadlines, see R. Shep Melnick, "Pollution Deadlines and the Coalition for Failure," in Michael S. Greve and Fred L. Smith Jr., eds., *Environmental Politics: Political Costs, Private Rewards* (Praeger, 1992), pp. 89–103.

10. See George C. Eads and Michael Fix, *Relief or Reform? Reagan's Regulatory Dilemma* (Washington: Urban Institute Press, 1982); and Christopher H. Foreman Jr., "Legislators, Regulators and the OMB: The Congressional Challenge to Presidential Regulatory Relief," in James A. Thurber, ed., *Divided Democracy: Cooperation and Conflict between Congress and the President* (Washington: Congressional Quarterly Press, 1991), pp. 123–43; and Jeffrey M. Berry and Kent E. Portney, "Centralizing Regulatory Control and Interest Group Access: The Quayle Council on Competitiveness," in Allan J. Cigler and Burdett A. Loomis, eds., *Interest Group Politics*, 4th ed. (Washington: Congressional Quarterly Press, 1995), pp. 319–47.

11. Alan Ehrenhalt, *The United States of Ambition: Politicians, Power and the Pursuit of Office* (Times Books/Random House, 1991), p. 196.

12. Jonathan Lash, Katherine Gillman, and David Sheridan, *A Season of Spoils: The Story of the Reagan Administration's Attack on the Environment* (Pantheon Books, 1984), p. 231.

13. Ehrenhalt, *The United States of Ambition*.

14. The EPA scandal and its impact in Congress are summarized in Christopher H. Foreman Jr., *Signals from the Hill: Congressional Oversight and the Challenge of Social Regulation* (Yale University Press, 1988), pp. 41–42. For a more elaborate account see, Lash, Gillman, and Sheridan, *A Season of Spoils*.

15. See Natural Resources Defense Council, *At the Crossroads: Environmental Threats and Opportunities in the 106th Congress* (Washington, March 2000), chap. 4. Available from the NRDC at www.nrdc.org/legislation/crossroads/ chap4.asp (September 2001).

16. Jessica Matthews, "Earth First at the Polls," *Washington Post*, November 11, 1996, p. A29.

17. Jonathan Rauch, "American Celebrates Earth Day 1970—For the 31st Time," *National Journal,* April 29, 2000, pp. 1333–34.

18. See, for example, National Academy of Public Administration, *Setting Priorities, Getting Results: A New Direction for EPA* (Washington, April 1995); and Shelley H. Metzenbaum, *Making Measurement Matter: The Challenge of Building a Performance-Focused Environmental Protection System,* case C16-

99.1530.0 (Brookings Institution Center for Public Management, October 1998).

19. Christopher H. Foreman Jr., *The Promise and Peril of Environmental Justice* (Brookings, 1998), chap. 6. See also Andrew Szasz, *EcoPopulism: Toxic Waste and the Movement for Environmental Justice* (University of Minnesota Press, 1994).

20. NAPA, *Setting Priorities, Getting Results*, p. 117.

21. William D. Ruckelshaus, "Enterprise for the Environment: Stepping Stones," Washington, Center for Strategic and International Studies (www.csis.org).

22. DeWitt John, "Good Cops, Bad Cops," in Charles Sabel, Archon Fung, and Bradley Karkkainen, eds., *Beyond Backyard Environmentalism* (Boston: Beacon Press, 2000), pp. 61–64.

23. Patrick Novtony, "Popular Epidemiology and the Struggle for Community Health in the Environmental Justice Movement," in Douglas Faber, ed., *The Struggle for Ecological Democracy: Environmental Justice Movements in the United States* (New York: Guilford Press, 1998), pp. 137–57.

24. Elizabeth M. Whelan, "Can Too Much Safety Be Hazardous? A Critical Look at the 'Precautionary Principle'" American Council on Science and Health, editorial, May 23, 2000 (www.acsh.org/press/editorials/safety052300.html [September 2001]). The precautionary principle holds that any doubt about a product's risks ought to weigh more heavily in decisionmaking than any expectations of benefit. In extreme form, the principle suggests that a product should not be used until all doubt is resolved.

25. Andrew Hurley, *Environmental Inequalities: Class, Race, and Industrial Pollution in Gary, Indiana, 1945–1980* (University of North Carolina Press, 1995).

26. Michael Brown, *Laying Waste: The Poisoning of America by Toxic Chemicals* (Washington Square Press, 1981).

27. Barry G. Rabe, *Beyond NIMBY: Hazardous Waste Siting in the United States and Canada* (Brookings, 1994); Thomas W. Church and Robert T. Nakamura, *Cleaning Up the Mess: Implementation Strategies in Superfund* (Brookings, 1993); Daniel Mazmanian and David Morell, *Beyond Superfailure: America's Toxics Policy for the 1990s* (Westview Press, 1992); and Herbert Inhaber, *Slaying the NIMBY Dragon* (Transaction Publishers, 1998).

28. Lawrence Mosher, "Reagan's Environmental Federalism: Are the States Up to the Challenge?" *National Journal*, January 30, 1982, p. 184.

29. Quoted from the ECOS website at www.sso.org/ecos/about.htm (September 2001).

30. James H. Colopy, "The Road Less Traveled: Pursuing Environmental Justice through Title VI of the Civil Rights Act of 1964," *Stanford Environmental Law Journal*, vol. 13 (1994), pp. 125–89.

31. Foreman, *The Promise and Peril of Environmental Justice*, pp. 29–30.

32. See ECOS Resolution 98-2, "Environmental Protection Agency's Interim Guidance for Investigating Environmental Permit Challenges," approved March 26, 1998, in New Orleans, Louisiana. Available at the ECOS website www.

ssoorg/ecos/policy/resolutions (July 2000). See also National Governors' Association, *Issue Brief: Federal Interpretations of Environmental Justice Claims Threaten State Programs* (Washington, October 28, 1997).

33. Christopher H. Foreman Jr., "Environmental Justice and the False Promise of Title VI," in *When the Unelected Rule: Ten Case Studies in Regulatory Abuse* (Arlington, Va., and Lewisville, Texas: Institute for Policy Innovation and the Lexington Institute, December 2000), pp. 7–8.

34. Congressional testimony by Peter F. Guerrero, U.S. General Accounting Office, *Environmental Protection: EPA's and States' Efforts to "Reinvent" Environmental Regulation*, GAO/T-RCED-98-33 (November 4, 1997), pp. 3–4.

35. John H. Cushman Jr., "E.P.A. Withdraws Plan to Empower States," *New York Times*, March 2, 1997, p. 22.

36. James P. Lester, "Federalism and State Environmental Policy," in Lester, ed., *Environmental Politics and Policy: Theories and Evidence*, 2d ed. (Duke University Press, 1995), pp. 39–60.

37. NAPA, *Setting Priorities, Getting Results*, p. 2. Quoted in Karl Hausker, *The Convergence of Ideas on Improving the Environmental Protection System* (Washington: Center for Strategic and International Studies, March 1999), p. 14.

38. Recent assessments of NEPPS sponsored by the National Academy of Public Administration include Leroy Paddock and Suellen Keiner, *Mixing Management Metaphors: The Complexities of Introducing a Performance-Based State/EPA Partnership System into an Activity-Based Management Culture* (Washington: NAPA, 2000); and Jeanne Herb, Jennifer Sullivan, Mark Stoughton, and Allen White, *The National Performance Partnership System: Making Good on Its Promise?* (Washington: NAPA, 2000).

39. Herb and others, *The National Performance Partnership System*, p. 76.

40. Paddock and Keiner, *Mixing Management Metaphors*, p. 58.

41. Ibid., p. 60.

42. Cushman, "E.P.A. Withdraws Plan."

43. Guerrero testimony, p. 5.

44. U.S. Environmental Protection Agency, *Project XL: From Pilot to Practice—A Journey to System Change*, EPA 100-H-99-007 (September 1999), p. 4.

45. Silicon Valley Toxics Coalition statement, "Coalition of Community, Environmental/Justice, and Labor Organizations Blast Clinton Administration 'Sweetheart Deal' with Intel" (wysiwyg://44/http://www.igc.org/svtc/xlaction. htm [July 2000]).

46. Cindy Skrzycki, "The Regulators: The Perils of Reinventing—Critics See a Playground for Polluters in EPA's XL Plan," *Washington Post*, January 24, 1997, p. D1.

47. EPA, *Project XL: From Pilot to Practice*, p. 4.

48. Bradford C. Mank, "The Environmental Protection Agency's Project XL and Other Regulatory Reform Initiatives: The Need for Legislative Authorization," *Ecology Law Quarterly*, vol. 25 (1998), p. 59.

49. Ibid.

50. Jeffrey P. Cohn, "Clearing the Air," *Government Executive*, vol. 29 (September 1997), pp. 45–50.

51. See Rena I. Steinzor, "Reinventing Environmental Regulation: Back to the Past by Way of the Future," *Environmental Law Reporter*, vol. 28 (July 1998), pp. 10361–72. See also Jacqueline Savitz, "Compensating Citizens," and Matt Wilson and Eric Weltman, "Government's Job," both in Sabel, Fung, and Karkkainen, *Beyond Backyard Environmentalism*, pp. 49–53, 65–69.

52. See *Federal Register*, vol. 65, February 10, 2000, p. 6698.

53. Keith Bradsher, "Clinton Allays Criticism on New Pollution Rules," *New York Times*, December 22, 1999, p. A24.

54. Christopher H. Foreman Jr., "Congress and Regulatory Reform: Achievements and Prospects," *Brookings Review*, vol. 16 (Winter 1998), pp. 10–13.

55. William H. Miller, "Washington Wreck," *Industry Week*, August 18, 1997, p. 120.

56. The trust problem discussed differs fundamentally from those often described in terms of a principal-agent relationship. In such situations a person or institution (the principal) delegates some degree of control over an activity to another (the agent) expected to function on its behalf. One might think of the House of Representatives or its majority party leadership as a principal and the various committees of the chamber as agents. Or one might view voters as principals and their elected representatives as agents. For careful empirical research that tries to discern the forces at work in these contexts, see Forrest Maltzman, *Competing Principals: Committee, Parties and the Organization of Congress* (University of Michigan Press, 1997); and William T. Bianco, *Trust: Representatives and Constituents* (University of Michigan Press, 1994). But it is implausible to conceive of relations among regulatory agencies, business firms, and citizen activists in this way, for these are parties to an ongoing relationship of negotiation rather than delegation.

57. Robert D. Putnam, *Making Democracy Work: Civic Traditions in Modern Italy* (Princeton University Press, 1993), p. 164.

58. See Sheldon Kamieniecki, David Sahie, and Julie Silvers, "Forming Partnerships in Environmental Policy: The Business of Emissions Trading in Clean Air Management," *American Behavioral Scientist*, vol. 43 (September 1999), pp. 107–23.

59. Foreman, *The Promise and Peril of Environmental Justice*, esp. pp. 28–29.

60. J. Clarence Davies and Jan Mazurek, *Pollution Control in the United States: Evaluating the System* (Washington: Resources for the Future, 1998), p. 269.

61. General Accounting Office, *Water Quality: Key EPA and State Decisions Limited by Inconsistent and Incomplete Data*, GAO/RCED-00-54 (March 2000). On the TMDL initiative more generally, see Jim Boyd, "Unleashing the Clean Water Act: The Promise and Challenge of the TMDL Approach to Water Quality," *Resources*, no. 139 (Spring 2000), pp. 7–10.

62. Comments by Linda Greer of the Natural Resources Defense Council, Management Forum.

63. Savitz, "Compensating Citizens," p. 67.

64. Ibid., p. 68.

65. Quotations in the following paragraph are taken from the document entitled "Alternative Regulatory Pathway: Evaluation Criteria," dated October 1996 and prepared by the Pollution Prevention Alliance. Available at alt-path.com/arp.htm.

66. This discussion draws on Natural Resources Defense Council, *Preventing Industrial Pollution at Its Source: The Final Report of the Michigan Source Reduction Initiative* (Washington, September 1999).

67. Ibid, p. viii.

68. Ibid, p. 3.

69. Ibid., p. ix.

70. See Linda Greer's comments in the interview "Environmentalists and Dow: Chemical Reduction" (www.nrdc.org/cities/manufacturing/ilgdow.asp [September 2001]).

71. Ibid.

72. Sanford Lewis and Diane Henkels, "Good Neighbor Agreements: A Tool for Environmental and Social Justice," *Social Justice,* vol. 23 (www.cpn.org/sections/topics/environment/stories-studies/lewis_henkel.html [September 2001]).

73. On the challenge of replicating and multiplying creative initiatives, a good brief treatment is Alan Ehrenhalt, "To Innovate, You Have to Know How to Multiply," in Ehrenhalt, ed., *Democracy in the Mirror: Politics, Reform, and Reality in Grassroots America* (Washington: Congressional Quarterly Press, 1999), pp. 98–101.

74. See also DeWitt John, *Civic Environmentalism: Alternatives to Regulation in States and Communities* (Washington: Congressional Quarterly Press, 1994); Lawrence Susskind, Paul F. Levy, and Jennifer Thomas-Larmer, *Negotiating Environmental Agreements: How to Avoid Escalating Confrontation, Needless Costs, and Unnecessary Litigation* (Island Press, 2000); and Ken Sexton, Alfred A. Marcus, K. William Easter, and Timothy D. Burkhardt, eds., *Better Environmental Decisions: Strategies for Governments, Businesses, and Communities* (Island Press, 1999).

75. I am indebted to Cary Coglianese for making this point in a private communication.

76. Thomas C. Beierle, "Public Participation in Environmental Decisions: An Evaluation Framework Using Social Goals," Discussion Paper 99-06 (Washington: Resources for the Future, November 1998); and Rebecca J. Long and Thomas C. Beierle, "The Federal Advisory Committee Act and Public Participation in Environmental Policy," Discussion Paper 99-17 (Washington: Resources for the Future, January 1999).

77. John Clayton Thomas, *Public Participation in Public Decisions: New Skills and Strategies for Public Managers* (Jossey-Bass, 1995), p. 25.

78. For a more positive assessment of participation in the Great Lakes region, see Thomas C. Beierle and David M. Konsky, "Values, Conflict, and Trust in Participatory Environmental Planning," *Journal of Policy Analysis and Management,* vol. 19 (Fall 2000), pp. 587–602.

79. These recommendations and the problem of building and rebuilding "trust and confidence" are discussed in Todd R. La Porte and Daniel S. Metlay, "Hazards and Institutional Trustworthiness: Facing a Deficit of Trust," *Public Administration Review*, vol. 56 (July–August 1996), pp. 341–47. Note that for LaPorte and Metlay, *trust* is "the belief that those with whom you interact will take your interests into account, even in situations where you are not in a position to recognize, evaluate, and/or thwart a potentially negative course of action by 'those trusted.'" *Confidence*, on the other hand, "exists when the party trusted is able to empathize with (know of) your interests, is competent to act on that knowledge, and will go to considerable lengths to keep its word." (p. 342.) The combination of trust and confidence yields trustworthiness.

80. Ibid., p. 344.

81. Ibid., p. 345.

82. Cary Coglianese, "Is Consensus an Appropriate Basis for Regulatory Policy?" in Eric Orts and Kurt Deketelaere, eds., *Environmental Contracts: Comparative Approaches to Regulatory Innovation in the United States and Europe* (Kluwer Law International, 2000), pp. 93–113.

CHAPTER SIX

Conclusion:
The Next Generation

DONALD F. KETTL

In framing the next stages of environmental policy, the U.S. Environmental Protection Agency (EPA) faces a huge, largely uncharted challenge. The EPA is the nation's flagship organization to promote a safer, cleaner environment. Yet the EPA does almost nothing on its own. Rather, it does almost everything in partnership with other players. The Department of Justice represents the EPA in court. Private contractors do most of the work in the Superfund program, dedicated to cleaning up toxic waste sites. Local governments and private companies manage landfills, and local governments handle storm water and sewage treatment. State governments oversee most of the permit process. Moreover, the Environmental Council of the States (ECOS) estimates that more than 70 percent of the EPA programs that *can* be delegated to the states *have* been delegated already—and that the states carry out more than 70 percent of the day-to-day management of the nation's environmental protection policies. The states carry out 97 percent of all of the environmental inspections and 75 percent of the enforcement actions.[1]

The EPA thus rests in the profound paradox of devolution: it does relatively little on its own, but it is responsible for getting the environmental job done. Its task, therefore, is to strengthen the strategies and tactics required not only to build the partnerships that produce environmental results but also to devise new approaches to resolve problems that stymied the first generation of environmental policy. The paradox of devolution does not only define the EPA's role. It also defines the challenges the agency must conquer.[2] The EPA's job is to work with Congress to craft broad policy. Its regulations set the basic ground rules. It imposes penalties. But the actual business of managing environmental policy happens increasingly in the states and local governments. How the EPA sets the tone in Washington shapes environmental performance—and vice versa: environmental performance depends on how the EPA manages devolution. The EPA does little itself, but national environmental policy depends on what it does do.

All this requires a fundamental shift not only in the EPA's policies and strategies but also in its partners. However, as Resources for the Future's Terry Davies points out, "The inertia of the system is tremendous."[3] Getting it to move is difficult enough. Charting the course in which to move can be even harder.

Puzzles for the Next Generation

What are the central issues that the next generation of environmental policy must resolve? In policy, there will be heavy pressure to prevent backsliding on the progress made in the first generation—and to develop better strategies for problems, like nonpoint source pollution, that the first generation did not attack well. In economic terms, there will be heavy pressure to do so without increasing government's costs for collecting information and managing regulations or without increasing industry's costs for compliance. And in political terms, there will be heavy pressure from state and local governments to strengthen devolution. Companies want help to compete in the unforgiving global marketplace; and environmental interest groups want to keep the environment clean. As Bowdoin College's DeWitt John argues, "The central question is this: is the system improving the conditions of the environment?" That question leads to two puzzles: "First, is the system creating net benefits? And, secondly, is it maximizing those benefits?"[4] To that we can add a third question: can the political system deal with these questions—or will these inescapable questions require a reconfiguration of the political and administrative forces?

In many ways, of course, these puzzles echo the benefit-cost analysis battles that surrounded environmental policy in the 1980s. Conservatives have long argued that environmentalists have single-mindedly focused on making every corner of the environment cleaner, regardless of whether that constituted the best use of scarce resources and of whether alternative strategies could produce the same results at lower costs. The next-generation debate grew from efforts to balance these concerns. Budget realities made clear that neither the EPA nor its state partners would receive large infusions of new money. Political realities made clear that industry groups would resist any effort to shift costs to the private sector and that environmental groups would fight any attempt to roll back environmental standards. Maintaining the environmental gains while attacking unresolved issues required new and creative tactics to squeeze more environmental performance from a tight budget.

Language, Evidence, and Information

Complicating the debate, however, is the problem of finding a way to talk about the next steps in environmental policy. The intense conflict over federal policy, especially during the Reagan administration, polarized the debate. Conservatives worried that liberal environmentalists wanted tough regulations at any price, regardless of results; environmentalists worried that conservatives wanted to reduce the government's role and sacrifice a generation's worth of environmental gains. That spilled over onto the devolution debate. In an echo of the civil rights–era federalism battles of the 1960s, some environmentalists worried that more reliance on the states would weaken government's oversight of environmental performance. They were concerned that the states had very different capacities and therefore that devolution would produce widely varying results. Devolution, of course, is about introducing variation: matching national goals to local conditions. But debates about the pace and the strategy of environmental policy inevitably became enmeshed in the political tug-of-war that shaped debate at the end of the twentieth century. They framed the issues that shaped the debate around the regulatory flexibility Barry G. Rabe discusses in chapter 2.

In the mid-1990s, the Center for Strategic and International Studies, the Keystone Center, and the National Academy of Public Administration (NAPA) convened a stakeholder project involving more than eighty participants. Their goal was to explore the problems in environmental policy and to devise solutions that could find broad consensus. Their two-year effort, chaired by former EPA administrator William D. Ruckelshaus and culminating in a 1997 report, recommended a three-part strategy driven by performance and partnership: transforming the EPA's regulatory system to focus more intensely on results; increasing the use of incentives to encourage all players to move to a cleaner environment; and promoting a higher level of shared responsibility in the private sector for environmental results.[5]

For private companies, the attraction was increasing their flexibility to meet the varying environmental standards in the United States and other countries, especially the European Union. They have sought, through strategies like ISO 14000, to construct a corporatewide strategy focused on high levels of performance instead of compliance with the regulations of individual companies, as Graham K. Wilson's chapter points out. The compliance-based focus, they discovered, led their managers to move along different tracks, which made it difficult to set and manage corporate policy and resources. For governments, the attraction was substituting partnerships for the confrontation that characterized the relationship between regulators and the regulated during the first generation of policy. For environmentalists, the attraction was focusing squarely on results instead of process and litigation. For everyone, the hope was that moving beyond compliance would produce higher levels of environmental performance at lower cost.

The E4E project (an Enterprise for the Environment initiative to improve the quality and usefulness of environmental information) produced surprising consensus on results, just as earlier work had produced strong consensus on the need for a next generation of environmental policy.[6] It quickly proved that it was one thing to produce consensus in favor of a more flexible, performance-based system. It was another to prescribe, in the detail required to manage environmental policy, just how this ought to work in practice. For some players, environmental performance meant focusing on a minimum threshold of environmental quality and providing flexibility in meeting it. For others, it meant creating stronger incentives for more stringent standards. The focus on performance thus spurred a debate not only on how to ensure the most flexibility in the system but also on how high to set the policy bar.[7]

The concepts were new, bolstered by regional experiments and experience from abroad.[8] The evidence supporting the approach was anecdotal, from case studies that were strong but certainly not definitive. The Chemical Manufacturers Association, for example, launched its "responsible care" program. American Chemistry Council members committed themselves "to support a continuing effort to improve the industry's responsible management of chemicals." The program required companies to work constantly to improve their health, safety, and environmental performance; to respond to public concerns; to help one another to improve performance; and to report progress to the public.[9] Other research identified the path some corporations were taking toward "environmental excellence."[10]

Still, the calls for partnerships for environmental performance were as much hortatory as analytical. They represented a consensus on the need to move beyond the first generation of environmental policy, a general roadmap of the direction in which to move, and a sense that efforts to reduce conflict ought to guide the next steps. If the consensus was broad, the lack of a strong evidentiary base limited the persuasiveness of the case to those already committed to the new course. Some analytical fuzziness, especially on what constituted "environmental performance," made it possible to build consensus without specifying a precise policy course. The recommendations from NAPA in 2000 helped sharpen that course. And NAPA also commissioned a large collection of research papers, whose findings provided a far stronger analytical base to support the next-generation strategy.[11]

This five-year process underlined a somewhat surprising finding. Although there was broad consensus on the need to chart a fresh course and a sense of the direction in which to move, the lack of precision handicapped the reform effort. Within and outside the EPA, reformers struggled to develop a clear course of action and to maintain political support in a political environment that proved always tumultuous. But beyond the analytical, theoretical, and research problems lay a profoundly pragmatic reality. The next generation of environmental policy was, at its core, a strategy to shift the government's strategy from ensuring regulatory compliance to building environmental partnerships, and from relying on process to focusing on performance. It was a system designed to be driven by information instead of litigation.

That transformation does not only require a shift in strategy. It also requires a shift in resources and the development of new management capacity. Does the system produce improved environmental conditions? Determining the answer requires good information, but most of the information has been anecdotal, not systematic, partly because the system has a heavy bias in favor of funding traditional environmental management, including regulation and inspection, and against next-generation approaches, including information gathering. And partly because the information tends to flow through traditional media-defined channels of water, air, and soil. The information tends to be poorly linked across the media, making it difficult to provide good data on how programs affect industries or individual communities. As one Environmental Policy Forum participant put it, "We just don't know what we need to know. . . . When we do have data, it is not well linked across programs." [12] And as Shelley H. Metzenbaum added, "Over much of the last decade, many people have called for performance-focused, information-driven environmental protection systems. It is a great phrase. But realistically, few people understand what it really means or at least how to do it."[13] The steps described in chapter 3 by Metzenbaum provide a guide for building a performance-driven information system.

Information and Performance

But what should the information be used for? As DeWitt John contended, "What you need is not just information about environmental conditions but communication and decisions about what that data says. And that is not a technical matter. It is a small 'p' political matter, not a partisan matter but a matter of public understanding."[14] Such communication requires information that is clear, comparable, relatively free from distortion, and readily accessible. In short, the performance process is about communication, not measurement.

Metzenbaum argues persuasively that this communication happens in three ways. First, performance management helps identifies goals, and goals motivate. They provide a target at which managers can aim. Second, performance management can help motivate employees by building enthusiasm for the agency's mission and by strengthening the linkage between managers' activities and the results they produce. Third, performance management can help inform managers and others in the policy network about what works and what does not. That way, Metzenbaum argues, "We can do more of what works and less of what doesn't." In fact, she contends, "One of the challenges in an effective performance management system is to get the motivational value of performance measurement to be compatible and non-conflicting with the informational value."[15]

NAPA's exhaustive study on twenty-first-century management for the EPA concluded, "To make the nation's environmental management system work effectively in the information age, the nation needs authoritative information about environmental conditions, and about whether agency efforts have helped improve those conditions." However, NAPA found, neither the EPA nor state environmental agencies have adequate information to assess the connections between their policies and environmental results. In fact, "no agency systematically gathers information about the impacts of regulation and other programs on environmental conditions."[16] It is, quite simply, impossible to improve environmental quality without devising a system to gauge quality and measure performance.

However, as David Goldston, legislative director for Rep. Sherwood Boehlert (R-N.Y.), concluded, "It's very difficult to figure out how you define better environmental performance in a way that would actually prevent this from being abused and which really accomplishes its goals—when you're not really sure of what kinds of projects you're going to be having." For example, if the government measures "performance" in terms of emissions, then the focus is on individual facilities. That discourages areawide and cross-media projects. If the government measures "performance" across media, however, it becomes more difficult to assess the specific risks that individual activities contribute. Some analysts resort to "the sort of 'I know it when I see it' kind of definition." But, Goldston points out, if everyone had enough trust to write a law like that, the system would not provoke the endless public debates that have surrounded it for decades. The Natural Resources Defense Council's Linda Greer agreed, saying, "In the absence of crisp definitions of better performance, some of the stuff that we've spent a lot of time on in our experience has really not been worth our time or EPA's time or the states' time. And the whole idea will get a bad rap unless we try to straighten it out." [17]

Greer argues persuasively, "You can't have accountability without more information." But "the problem with information," Goldston points out, "is that information is both the least and most intrusive kind of regulation you can have. It's the least because it doesn't tell you to do anything other than release the information. It's the most because information is the key to almost every industry." Companies worry about exposing secrets to competitors and about exposing themselves to greater legal liability than the law requires.[18]

Information is both everything and nothing. It has the risk of overwhelming everybody in the process. It has the potential for driving everything. It has the potential for being harmless and for just providing some basis for people to talk about. It has the potential for driving the fundamental core of the regulatory regime. Collecting it, digesting it, and using it costs money, and managers—in the public and private sectors—are leery about investing scarce resources in a process that does not build on the first generation's norms and that exposes everyone to greater risk. Taking that risk is even more difficult when elected officials, especially legislators, often show little interest in using performance information to shape policy decision.[19]

Information about performance is central to environmental reform. However, public and private administrators alike have few incentives for building effective performance management systems, especially if policymakers show little inclination to rely on the data for setting policy. That puts a fundamental paradox at the core of the reform.

Trust

If performance information is the foundation of the next generation of environmental policy, collecting it runs up against tough problems. The process is expensive. It is hard to agree on what constitutes "environmental performance" and how to measure it. Policymakers often show little taste for using the information that is collected.

Perhaps even more fundamental, however, is the problem of trust. As Robert E. Roberts, executive director of the Environmental Council of the States, explained, "Regulators don't trust regulatees, and regulatees don't trust regulators. States sometimes don't trust the feds. The feds often don't trust the states—or at least, so it looks from our position. Pick a player and there is somebody else in this that really thinks that that player, if not closely watched, will do an extremely bad thing." In fact, "this is a public policy field which is almost built on an absence of trust."[20]

Some players in the environmental policy arena suggest that the key to building trust is beginning with agreement on the baseline—where the process starts—and the cost effectiveness of alternatives to move beyond that baseline. Doing so, however, is difficult in an arena as litigious as environmental policy. Few nations stage so many environmental battles in the courts. For example, as Graham K. Wilson describes in chapter 4, for environmental policy in the Netherlands, government, and industry collaborate in framing a compact that sets policy goals and how they will be enforced. The differences in political structure and culture would frustrate efforts to import that process into the United States. As one observer noted, the "compact-based system of the Netherlands is not going to happen here. It is at odds with our political culture. It is at odds with our political institutions. It is at odds with the structure of our interest groups." Moreover, none of the interests in the Netherlands "would politicize it [environmental policy] because they would view that as suicidal, and that is so different here." Even less aggressive strategies, like ISO 14000, have moved more slowly in the United States than in other nations, in large part because American companies have feared that the program would put them at greater legal jeopardy. But as one observer warned advocates about efforts to introduce more collaborative environmental strategies, "I think that you have a much harder road to hoe than your counterparts in other countries."[21]

Almost everyone agrees that more collaboration would strengthen performance in American environmental policy. Supporters point to strategies that have worked well in other nations; critics point to features of the American political system that would slow or stall collaborative strategies. Information is the foundation for the twenty-first century. Trust is the key to useful information. And trust has long proved elusive in environmental policy. The most successful reforms, as Rabe and Metzenbaum point out in chapters 2 and 3, have built on recapturing that trust.

Managing Environmental Policy

Since its creation in 1970, the EPA has been organized by media—principally by air, water, solid waste, and toxic substances. Congress has passed functionally based environmental legislation, from the Clean Air Act to the Resource Conservation and Recovery Act. The EPA's offices have followed the functional pattern of legislation, which in turn grew out of the air, water, solids, and toxics problems that spurred Earth Day in 1970 and the environmental policy that followed for a generation. The functional approach has made great sense. It has focused attention squarely on the nation's toughest environmental problems, and it has allowed the EPA to build substantial expertise in fighting these problems. It is hard to imagine alternatives that would have provided a stronger running start.

As the EPA neared the end of its first generation, however, new problems strained the agency's organizational strategy. Fewer problems remained within media-defined boundaries. Much of the pollution in the Great Lakes came from airborne acid rain and runoff from agricultural production; the water pollution, in short, flowed from air and soil problems. Next-generation issues like nonpoint source pollution often caused similar boundary problems. At the state and local levels, officials often cared less about air, water, or soil pollution than about cleaning particular neighborhoods or regions. Federal officials tended to think in functional terms; local officials tended to think in area terms. More of the first-generation problems evolved into issues that paid less attention to the media-based structure of congressional legislation or the EPA's structure. Most of the next-generation problems grew out of a place-based focus. As the Environmental Council of the States describes the problem,

> Under the current organization, the media offices frequently adopt individual priorities or unique approaches to agency-wide priorities. This collection of goals forces organizations that do business with the EPA to learn several sets of operating rules and problem definitions and to adopt a piecemeal approach which fits the specific goals of each office. There are many instances of this, but one example is the EPA's Environmental Justice (EJ) effort. The issue is being addressed by at least three different offices—the Office of Environmental Justice (OEJ), the Office of Civil Rights (OCR) and the Office of Solid Waste and Emergency Response (OSWER)—each defining the issue differently, with different approaches and priorities, but with little to no collaboration. OEJ is completing a guidance document on Environmental Justice that was drafted by EPA staff without input from the States. Last year, OCR made the same mistake initially on the Title VI Guidance, but then included States in developing the next version following substantial opposition from a number of groups. To repeat that mistake does not give States confidence in the process. . . . A coordinated collaboration would yield the best use of resources and the greatest impact on the issue.[22]

The EPA thus faces a tough dilemma. Organized by function, it must solve placed-based problems, which are becoming more and more common. The EPA officials have experimented with various reorganizations, including organizing by both place and function and organizing different programs in different ways. The rich tradition of public administration literature, however, warns that managers can organize by function, place, people, or process—but that managers need to choose one. Attempting to mix organizational styles leads to confusion about roles, conflicts about responsibilities, and problems in performance.[23] Thus, not only does the EPA face new challenges in confronting a next generation of policy problems, it faces an irresolvable trade-off in determining how best to manage them.

The best solution might well be organizing by function at the headquarters level, so that the EPA can assemble teams of leading technical experts in the problems it faces. It is much easier to build expertise in toxic chemicals or pesticides if the organization can focus resources on each problem in turn. It is also much cheaper to assemble the experts in one team instead of having to recreate a team for each part of the country. On the front lines, the best solution might well be organizing by place. What matters most at the community level is how disparate pollution problems come together to create quality-of-life problems and how disparate pollution fighting strategies can improve that quality of life. The EPA's challenge is to discover how to merge these two strategies into a well-functioning system: to be regimented enough at headquarters to build clear policy around cutting-edge science and to be flexible enough at the local level to adapt policy to local needs. It is a matter of building one policy to drive all decisions without resorting to a "one-size-fits-all" strategy of implementation.

This problem, frankly, is one of the toughest in public management. There is no reorganization that will solve it. Any reorganization that tries multiple paths risks confusion and inefficiency. Any reorganization that tries a place-based approach risks sacrificing functional expertise—and vice versa. Indeed, the EPA's experiments during the 1990s to find new ways to balance these conflicting demands only underlined the basic argument. The most promising alternative is to redefine the role of the EPA's regional offices as the place where the functionally based regulations and expertise of headquarters is translated into the place-based needs of individual states and communities. As DeWitt John put it, "If the thrust of the enterprise is to move away from regimentation to more flexibility, and especially to a more place-based flexibility, the key place that political leadership, that political function must take place is in the regional office of EPA."[24]

The effort to rebuild the EPA's next-generation strategies around the regional offices, however, has struggled through a series of problems. The EPA's headquarters staff has been bogged down in ongoing policy battles about the focus and direction of its policies, including struggles in the 1990s about whether to slash its enforcement powers. Indeed,

Washington policymakers have generally under-recognized the importance of regions. From the state level, the regional offices have served as the lightning rods for the inevitable intergovernmental conflicts over how much flexibility to allow state and local governments. The regional offices thus have been squarely in the crossfire of conflicting expectations and have received relatively little political support from inside the EPA. As a result, John explained, "You can't get agreement about what is acceptable. And you can't get a decision out of the regional office level. You just get lots of different people saying different things and confusion, delay—and that delay is a no."[25]

Solving the next-generation environmental policy issues requires making regional offices the center of environmental policy and equipping them to make the critical transformation between strategies. If the problems were daunting and the solutions fuzzy, the EPA's experience during the 1990s at least suggested this was the right direction in which to move.

Environmental Governance

At the core of the political battle is the problem of how—indeed, whether—to balance the *cost* of environmental regulations with the *benefits* they produce. As Rabe's chapter demonstrates, the current regulatory system is not based on an adequate understanding of the level of emissions that facilities produce. For some emissions, such as volatile organic compounds, the system tends to underestimate—and undercontrol—pollution. For others, such as carbon monoxide, the system tends to set permit limits well above the actual emissions levels. The current system thus is fundamentally flawed: it does not match regulatory strategies well with the pollution problems they are trying to cure. We do not have good information about what we are doing, how much the system costs, and what benefits it produces.

Performance-based strategies, such as the Charles River experiment that Metzenbaum describes, offer promise for producing better understanding of these critical linkages. However, experience also shows how hard it is for policymakers to embrace the performance process. Despite the evidence from powerful case studies and the broader rhetoric supporting performance strategies, the environmental system tends to push back toward a command-and-control approach supported by fines and litigation. That approach brought many of the gains of the first generation, but it is poorly suited to solve the problems of the next. Furthermore, a concern for environmental justice, discussed by Christopher H. Foreman Jr. in chapter 5, adds complexity to an already difficult collection of problems.

The EPA and state regulators alike face the challenge of bridging the gap—policy and administrative—between the two generations. They must rise to new challenges without abandoning the strategies that proved successful in conquering the old ones. The experiments, successful and not, described in this book show that regulators can indeed construct new tools that can rise to these challenges. However, the authors in this book also make a persuasive case that expecting regulators to negotiate these problems on their own is probably asking too much. In the end, rising to the challenges of the next generation requires enhanced legal and statutory frameworks.[26] In part, an adequate response must strengthen the foundation on which information-based, performance-driven reforms build. In part, an adequate response means providing leadership for what are, in the end, difficult—and inescapable—policy, administrative, and political problems.

Notes to Chapter 6

1. See Environmental Council of the States (ECOS) memorandum to Scott Sutherland of the Bush-Cheney transition team, January 11, 2001.

2. For a useful catalog of devolution strategies, see the website of the Environmental Council of the States at www.sso.org/ecos/states/state-delegation-chart.htm.

3. Comments at the forum "Defining a New Generation of Environmental Policy," Brookings, January 8, 2001 (hereafter Environmental Policy Forum).

4. Ibid.

5. See www.csis.org/e4e/e4e.html (February 14, 2001) and the final report, Center for Strategic and International Studies, *The Environmental Protection System in Transition: Toward a More Desirable Future*, 1997.

6. See chapter 2 in this volume.

7. This argument framed much of the debate at the forum "Defining a New Generation of Environmental Management," Brookings, February 24, 2000 (hereafter Management Forum).

8. For example, see the materials developed for the Enterprise for the Environment project (www.csis.org/e4e/ipppage.html [February 14, 2001]).

9. See www.cmahq.com/rc.nsf/open?OpenForm (February 14, 2001).

10. Terry F. Yosie and Timothy D. Herbst, "The Journey towards Corporate Environmental Excellence: Integrating Business Methods With Environmental Management" (Washington: Enterprise for the Environment, 1997). See www.csis.org/e4e/yosierpt.html (February 14, 2001).

11. The report is National Academy of Public Administration (NAPA), *environment.gov: Transforming Environmental Protection for the 21st Century* (Washington, 2000).

12. Environmental Policy Forum.

13. Ibid.

14. Ibid.

15. Ibid.

16. NAPA, *environment.gov*, pp. 170, 173.

17. Quotations in this paragraph are from the Management Forum.

18. Ibid.

19. See, for example, William T. Gormley Jr., "Environmental Performance Measures in a Federal System," Learning from Innovations in Environmental Protection, Research Paper 13 (Washington: National Academy of Public Administration, 2000).

20. Management Forum.

21. Environmental Policy Forum.

22. See ECOS memorandum, January 11, 2001, pp. 5–6.

23. See Luther Gulick, "Notes on the Theory of Organization," in Luther Gulick and L. Urwick, eds., *Papers on the Science of Administration* (New York: Institute of Public Administration, 1937), pp. 3–45.

24. Environmental Policy Forum.

25. Ibid.

26. For a broader discussion and a detailed set of recommendations, see NAPA, *environment.gov*.

Index

Index

Aaron, David, 141

Accountability: Clean Charles 2005 Initiative, 101–04; definitions, 93; funding incentives and, 99; informational, 107; media attention and, 88; need for, 99–100; performance focused, 100–04; policy mandates for, 93; problems with, 94–99; process focused, 94–95; public approval, 102. *See also* Compliance strategies

Activity-focused management: accountability and, 94–95; command-and-control regulation, 122–23, 188; ISO *14000,* 129–31; persistence of, 65, 106; weaknesses of, 59–62. *See also* Performance management; Regulation, command-and-control

Agencies, regulatory. *See* EPA (Environmental Protection Agency); Intergovernmental collaboration; Policy innovation

Air quality, 17, 31, 48–49, 104–05

Alternative regulatory pathway (ARP), 165

American Chemistry Council, 180–81

Anderson, Steven, 28, 31, 41–42, 43

Ayres, Jeffrey M., 139

Bavaria, 129

Behn, Robert D., 97

Boehlert, Sherwood, 183

Boston. *See* Clean Charles 2005 Initiative

Boston University, 75

Bovine spongiform encephalopathy (BSE), 119, 126

Brander, Kevin, 83–84

Brehm, John, 24

Britain, 118–19, 124, 125–26

Brookline, Mass., 67

Budgeting and funding, 42–43, 82, 91–92, 99

Burford, Robert, 150

Business associations: competition among, 135–36; cooperative agreements and, 128–29; international comparison, 124–25, 132; international regulation and, 141; regulatory flexibility and, 133